American Literature

& the culture wars

GREGORY S. *Jay*

CORNELL UNIVERSITY PRESS *Ithaca & London*

AMERICAN
Literature &
t h e CULTURE

Cloth printing
10 9 8 7 6 5 4 3 2 1
Paperback printing
10 9 8 7 6 5 4 3 2 1

Library of Congress
Cataloging in Publication Data
Jay, Gregory S.
    American literature and the culture
wars / Gregory S. Jay.
        p. cm.
    Includes bibliographical references
(p.   ) index.
    ISBN 0-8014-3393-2 (cloth : alk.
paper).—ISBN 0-8014-8422-7 (pbk. :
alk. paper).
    1. American literature—History and
criticism—Theory, etc. 2. American
literature—Study and teaching—
United States. 3. Pluralism (Social
sciences)—United States. 4. Literature
and society—United States. 5. Multiculturalism—United States. 6. Culture
conflict—United States. 7. Canon
(Literature) I. Title.
PS25.J37   1997   97-3948
810.9—dc21

In memory of my father, LESTER JAY

c o n t e n t s

acknowledgments

So many people have contributed to the ideas and proposals in this book that I despair of knowing how to acknowledge them all. Since one of my goals is to synthesize and explain the rich new scholarship in American literary studies, I am indebted to everyone who has participated in this movement and apologize in advance to those I overlooked or was not able to cite.

During his tenure as editor of *College English*, Jim Raymond urged contributors to fashion a better dialogue between the concerns of teachers and those of literary and cultural theorists. He challenged me to try writing something for its audience. Scarcely did I anticipate that he and his successor, Louise Smith, would be so hospitable to my efforts or exert such an influence on the direction of my work. Judith Fetterley and Lil Brannon asked me to join the faculty of a summer program sponsored by the National Council of Teachers of

English, where I delivered the remarks that eventually became the foundation for Chapter 2. The presentations and conversations at that week-long institute continue to resonate for me to this day. Jane Gallop invited me to present a talk at a conference on pedagogy she organized; this was the hardest writing assignment I can remember and resulted in the first version of Chapter 3, a turning point in the book's development. Marguerite Helmers and Ron Rindo brought me to UW-Oshkosh as a consultant during the revision of the English department curriculum, an experience that gave me material and momentum for Chapter 4.

I believe it was Dale Bauer who first suggested that the essays I was writing should be made into a book, and I thank her for spurring me to the task. Donald Pease encouraged me during a troubled time in the manuscript's history and offered a number of helpful comments. Bill Cain responded to the draft version with convincing arguments for substantial cuts and major reorganization, thus prompting me to improve its overall coherence. As I got down to the wire, Patrice Petro took time from an extraordinarily busy schedule to read the manuscript with great care, demonstrating once more the combination of friendship and intellectual community that I so value in her.

No one has been a better friend and critical reader during the past six years than Gerald Graff, who also was generous enough to share his office for six months. The experience of arguing, organizing, and writing with Graff proved a constant source of inspiration, even when I thought I would go mad after yet one more call or E-mail questioning a point or sentence I believed we had agreed on. He remains an example to me of clarity, dedication, good humor, and intellectual honesty. I consider myself tremendously fortunate to have had his help.

Paul Jay continues to handle with finesse the job of being both a big brother and an intellectual soul mate. It would be ridiculous to try summarizing here all I owe to our mutual adventures. Only he will be able to appreciate just how profoundly my work and life benefit from our multifaceted collaborations. Suffice it to say that I look forward to many more.

Over the years my thinking about American literature and the culture wars has benefited from conversations and exchanges with many smart students and generous colleagues. Of special help to me were the graduate students in my UW-Milwaukee seminars on literary criticism, nineteenth-century American fiction, contemporary multiculturalism, and the place of ethics in critical theory. Among so many helpful colleagues in Milwaukee and beyond, I thank in particular John Alberti, Randy Bass, David Bergman, Michael Bérubé, Kimberly Blaeser, Herb Blau, Mitch Breitwieser, Sidney Bremer, Pamela Caughie, Jay Fliegelman, Frances Foster, Michael Geyer, Todd Gitlin, Kristie Hamilton, Gordon Hutner, Cheryl Johnson, Paul Lauter, Hank Lazer, Steven Mailloux, Andy Martin, Ken McCutcheon, Ellen Messer-Davidow, David L. Miller, Cary Nelson, Christopher Newfield, Thomas Piontek, Marjorie Pryse, R. Rhadakrishnan, Valerie Ross, Tom Schaub, David Shumway, Ron Strickland, Bonnie TuSmith, and John Wilson.

Work on this book was materially aided by generous support from two department chairs, Jane Nardin and Jim Sappenfield, and two college deans, William Halloran and Marshall Goodman. The Center for Twentieth Century Studies awarded me a fellowship that provided much-needed time for research and writing, and the assistance of a marvelous staff. Kathleen Woodward, director of the Center, once more receives my gratitude not only for her resources but also for her enthusiastic commitment to interdisciplinary scholarship. The Center also sponsored and housed the 1995 National Endowment for the Humanities Institute for secondary school teachers that I directed on the topic "Rethinking American Studies: Connecting the Differences." I am very grateful to the twenty-five participating teachers in the institute who taught me so much, and to the faculty who worked in collaboration with me, especially seminar leaders Joyce Kirk, Rolando Romero, and Mike Wilson. In the course of acknowledging the major support of the NEH, I thank chairman Sheldon Hackney for taking the time to read my work and to direct me to sources that helped my argument along.

This is the second time that Bernhard Kendler has shepherded a volume of mine to press. I greatly appreciate his supporting my projects and providing the candid criticism that makes his advice so valuable. My thanks go to all the staff at Cornell, particularly to Terry McKiernan and Lou Robinson, and to my freelance editor, Amanda Heller, who did a terrific job.

• • •

With the exception of the introduction, each chapter of this book builds on and substantially revises a previous essay or article. I am grateful to the publishers for their permission to reprint material from the following:

"Knowledge, Power, and the Struggle for Representation." *College English* 56.1 (1994): 9–29.

"Not Born on the Fourth of July: Cultural Differences and American Literary Studies." Approximately 22 pages from *After Political Correctness: The Humanities and Society in the 1990s*. Ed. Christopher Newfield and Ron Strickland. Boulder, Colo.: Westview Press, 1995. 152–73. Copyright 1995 by Westview Press. Reprinted by permission of Westview Press.

"Taking Multiculturalism Personally: Ethnos and Ethos in the Classroom." *American Literary History* 6.4 (1994): 613–32. The original conference paper appears in *Pedagogy: The Question of Impersonation*. Ed. Jane Gallop. Bloomington: Indiana University Press, 1995. 117–28.

"The Discipline of the Syllabus." In *Reconceptualizing American Literary/Cultural Studies*. Ed. William E. Cain. New York: Garland. 1996. 101–16.

"The End of 'American' Literature: Toward a Multicultural Practice." *College English* 53.3 (1991): 264–81.

GREGORY S. JAY

Milwaukee, Wisconsin

American Literature

& the culture wars

i n t r o d u c t i o n **Making Ends Meet**

uring the past two decades, a main feature of our nation's "culture wars" has been the increasingly fierce quarrel over the teaching of American literature. Debates about terms such as "cultural literacy," the "canon," "political correctness," and "multiculturalism" have spilled over from the campuses onto the pages of popular magazines and even been featured on the nightly news. Judging from the uproar, one might think that we were seeing nothing less than the end of American literature — or at least the end of any consensus about how to define and teach it. This sense of an ending, however, is equally matched by a feeling of opening horizons, as dozens of forgotten or overlooked books and authors come into view. Even the classic texts of the tradition have been reopened by new methods of interpretation, so that *The Scarlet Letter* and Emily Dickinson and *The Waste Land* suddenly take on unexpected and often disturbing meanings. As the twentieth century comes to an end, much that we have taken for granted about our nation's literature is being challenged. Yet the prospect for the twenty-first century looks bright, for this challenge offers us a vitally enriched tradition and a more diverse set of tools for understanding it.

This book intends to explain and advance this challenge. In doing so, I will be questioning both the scope and the purpose of American literary studies. What ends do we pursue in the study and teaching of an "American" literature? Has the idea of a canon of great books reached the end of its usefulness? Where does American literature end and Mexican or Caribbean or Canadian or postcolonial literature begin? Is multiculturalism the end of civilization as we know it or the start of an overdue regeneration of our politics and pedagogy? How has the political economy of making ends meet in an era of downsizing and privatization affected academic freedom and the course of academic study? What happens in the classroom when we try to put an end to the conventional ways in which we have conceived and taught our subject? Playing off the pun in the title of this introduction, then, I want to explore this set of questions about the "ends" of American literary studies. This exploration includes rethinking our ends both in the nominal sense of "pragmatic intention" (goal, aim, objective, design, scheme) and in the verbal sense of "reaching a conclusion" (limit, terminate, cease, halt, expire). By focusing attention on these many ends and the controversial issues they involve, I hope in part to explain how this once arcane academic discipline ended up at the center of the culture wars. While asking some skeptical questions about these new directions, I argue forcefully in favor of opening the borders of the field of American literary and cultural study. My intention is both to reach the unpersuaded and to contest some of the assumptions and tactics of those who are already committed to reform.

Arguments opposing recent new directions in the approach to American culture have largely dominated public discussion, from the outcry over museum exhibitions on the American West and the bombing of Hiroshima to congressional hearings on the History Standards project and on reauthorization for the National Endowment for the Humanities and the National Endowment for the Arts. In the trade press, virtually all the headline-grabbing volumes have taken antagonistic positions toward the reform of cultural study, including Dinesh D'Souza's *Illiberal Education*, Allan Bloom's *Closing of the American Mind*, Richard Bernstein's *Dictatorship of Virtue*, Arthur Schlesinger, Jr.'s, *Disuniting of America*, and Christina Hoff Sommers's *Who Stole Feminism?* to name just a few. Even Michael Lind's call for a renewed "liberal nationalism" in *The Next American Nation* succumbs to antiacademic rhetoric, as well as echoing the neoconservative line that "multiculturalism is not the wave of the future, but an aftershock of the black-power radicalism of the sixties" (13). Likewise Todd Gitlin, a real tenured radical who helped found Students for a Democratic Society in the 1960s, writes *Twilight of Common Dreams* to lament the "breakdown of the idea of a common Left" and the rise of identity politics, which he blames on black separatists and their imitators who have unjustly demonized white male liberals.

In general, the American public has received a relentlessly negative picture of what the professors are up to, cast in the exaggerated and sensational language of scandal and cynicism that now constitutes the required tone of American journalism. Among the national trade press books only Gerald Graff's *Beyond the Culture Wars* and Lawrence Levine's *Opening of the American Mind* stake out positions explicitly sympathetic to contemporary innovations in the study of literature and history. John K. Wilson's *Myth of Political Correctness* and Michael Bérubé's *Public Access* do a skillful job rebutting what they see as the exaggerations and biases in conservative attacks on higher education, but they are not mainly concerned with positively arguing how recent scholarship has improved the quality of our campuses and classrooms.

The case for a new curriculum, nonetheless, has been building since the 1970s in a steadily proliferating bibliography, though few readers off campus have had much opportunity to hear a fair or substantial report of it. At the risk of offending by omission or appearing unduly pedantic, I think it important here to mention a few landmarks, at least in the development of my own thinking about how to transform American literary studies. Taken together they indicate how the discipline is evolving in dialogue with what Cornel West cogently describes as the "new cultural politics of difference." Two highly influential volumes that helped initiate the widening of horizons are *This Bridge Called My Back: Writings by Radical Women of*

Color, edited by Cherríe Moraga and Gloria Anzaldúa, and *All the Women Are White, All the Blacks Are Men, But Some of Us Are Brave: Black Women's Studies*, edited by Gloria Hull, Patricia Scott, and Barbara Smith. These were foundational texts in opening the canon, in linking the study of race and gender, and in connecting the social change movements of the 1960s to the campus reforms of the subsequent decades. In *Three American Literatures*, published by the Modern Language Association and edited by Houston Baker, scholars of Chicano, Native American, and Asian American literature presented one of the first professionally legitimated volumes arguing for a dramatic reconception of the nation's literary boundaries. These new contours were reinforced by the many pathbreaking essays contributed to the *Columbia History of the American Novel*, edited by Emory Elliott. The process of recovering buried treasure from our literary history is the scholarly job central to the remaking of the canon, as evidenced by work such as Judith Fetterley's *Provisions: A Reader from Nineteenth-Century American Women*. Recent provocative books that continue this rethinking of what and how to teach include Henry Louis Gates, Jr.'s, *Loose Canons* and bell hook's *Teaching to Transgress*. Many professors now write thoughtfully about their experiments with an altered American literature curriculum, as in *The Canon in the Classroom*, edited by John Alberti. Crossing the lines between the public and the academic are authors such as Toni Morrison and Adrienne Rich. In her novels and prose (notably *Playing in the Dark*), Morrison extends the range of voices speaking the story of America and its literature and insists on challenging the ideology of "whiteness." The essays and poems of Adrienne Rich have likewise been among the most powerful inspirations to the movement for connecting women's liberation, multicultural literacy, and democratic pedagogy.

The professors still have a way to go, however, in laying out a coherent, persuasive public case for academic reform in their various disciplines and classrooms (see Bérubé and Nelson). Since the canon debate has been particularly passionate and widespread in the field of American letters, and since the study of American culture inevitably spills over into the arenas of society and politics, it makes sense to use the controversies in this particular discipline as a point of focus for clarifying what is actually happening on campus. The teaching of

American literature has, after all, always been part of larger efforts to transmit social, political, moral, and even religious ideals to new generations of students. Pedagogy in this discipline stumbles quickly into questions such as Crèvecoeur's "What is an American?" The question of what makes a book "American" often gets combined with the question of what makes a book "great," especially when we must choose which books to read or study. Eventually we have to ask, "What is the aim of teaching 'American' literature?" Is it the appreciation of artistry or the socialization of the reader? The achievement of cultural literacy or training in critical thinking? Can it be all these things without contradicting itself (or hopelessly confusing the student)?

Intentionally or not, the selection of books and methods for teaching holds a mirror up to our nature and offers a vision of our future. When a teacher assigns Harriet Jacobs instead of Herman Melville or Elizabeth Bishop instead of T. S. Eliot or Arturo Islas instead of Saul Bellow (and such dilemmas are unavoidable, if only because the semester is finite), these choices are value judgments that may alter the interpretation of American cultural history offered to students. To those many commentators who glibly quote the maxim that academic politics is so nasty because so little is at stake, I would counter that (at least in American cultural studies) the arguments are so fervent because the stakes are so large. We are arguing over nothing less than our understanding of who we have been as a people and where we are going as a society. Insofar as some academics have supported their profession with traditional defenses of aesthetic education or protestations that their work has no political dimension, they are naive. Here the conservatives have the better case, for they begin with the commonsensical observation that pedagogy is always to some degree an instrument for the transmission of values and the shaping of a society. The conservative attack itself becomes deceptive, however, when it fails to make clear whether its goal is to purge pedagogy of any politics (which cannot be done) or to make pedagogy into the instrument of only one political perspective (which should not be done).

As the citations in this book demonstrate, I am well aware that many have preceded me in making parts of the argument I am advancing. In *Canons and Contexts*, for example, Paul Lauter offers what may be the best collection to date articulating the history of debate over the character of American letters and the rationale for new methods of study. Not content with theory, Lauter also serves as general editor of the groundbreaking *Heath Anthology of American Literature*, now widely adopted by reformers in the discipline. In fact, I take the position represented by *Canons and Contexts* and the *Heath Anthology* as my starting point, and hope to show where we can go from there. Whereas Lauter and others labored mightily to open the canon, revisionists now face many thorny questions about what to do in the wake of the end of consensus and the advent of multiculturalism. Controversies over "identity politics," for example, or about whether multiculturalism is a panacea or a ploy mark the next stages of development into which reformers are heading. Likewise, just as the opening of the canon resulted from the progressive social movements of the 1960s, the current moment of reappraisal borrows much of its machinery from critical theory — that body of literary and cultural analysis associated with the methods of European structuralism and deconstruction which arrived with such fanfare in the United States during the 1970s and 1980s (see Derrida, "Ends of Man," and Lauter, "Afterword"). Although denunciations from the cultural right often lump the canon-busters, feminists, and multiculturalists together with the semioticians and deconstructors, in practice these various movements are radically distinct and often in disagreement. One thing requiring explanation today, then, is how to mediate the competing claims and divergent concerns of these various reform movements. In the end, how can American literary and cultural study accommodate these often contradictory agendas? Can it do so and still maintain both its disciplinary integrity and its reformist zeal? If there is to be compromise, which agendas should be stressed and which deferred? Will these decisions be made by focusing chiefly on the internal arrangements of academic business or with one eye also on higher education's embattled place in American cultural politics?

My frequent use of the plural pronoun ("we" and "our") in this book raises the question of whom I imagine myself addressing. Traditionally a book is written or marketed with a definite idea of its central audience. It is perhaps a result of today's debates over multiculturalism and (in Schlesinger's phrase) the "disuniting of America" that the notion of a central audience appears out of date. If there is any broad consensus in American literary studies as we head into the twenty-first century, it is that we have reached the end of the era of consensus (see Bercovitch, "America as Canon"; Carafiol; Pease). My book is written with the knowledge that there is a diverse audience out there, and that the dividing lines intersect in unpredictable ways. Some of these divisions are matters of race and ethnicity, some of generation, some of politics and social position, some of sex and gender, some of the gap between the academy and the larger educated public. Teachers, students, and readers of American literature are my primary audience. But I assume that this audience holds a range of positions on the fundamental issues under debate today, and I endeavor to respect that variety of opinion even as I try to persuade people to my points of view. I also imagine my readers to include some beyond this main audience, including people in other academic fields as well as people in other walks of life. With that broader audience in mind, I have tried to write a more accessible prose and occasionally to restate my points in different ways (at the risk of appearing to repeat myself).

It would be simplistic, I think, to approach the question of audience by dividing readers into two hypothetical camps, those "for" change and those "against." When we get down to details about what changes people have in mind, we find a bewildering array of alliances and resistances. Some are for changing the canon but may also be against deconstructionist theory. Some are against the "politicization" of teaching but may also favor a more historical approach to literature. Some advocate feminist criticism but may also be partisans of rigorous aesthetic standards. There simply isn't one "side" that could form a "central audience." Such a division would not work even if one wanted to put it right down the street between the ivory tower and the real world, since on both sides of that line we find the same disunities. On a range of issues this book stakes out independent territory, sometimes agreeing with the reformers and sometimes disagreeing, depending on the particular issue at hand. Although I am on the whole more an advocate than a critic of change, the reasons for my advocacy and the specifics of the changes I envision may often put me at odds with my allies or in strange conjunction with my antagonists (as, for example, when I argue that multiculturalism should be understood as an ethical matter).

Part of my purpose, then, remains to reach people who are skeptical about changes in the American literary canon or about "political correctness" on campus. I hope to convince them that there has been much misrepresentation in attacks on today's professors, and that the case for progressive reform in the curriculum of American studies is a solid one. I believe that some who share my views may benefit from exploring with me how we might persuade our colleagues and the public (and most evidence indicates that we have not done this well yet). Thus, this is not a handbook for the already converted. Readers who begin in sympathy with my arguments will, however, find a good amount of practical advice on how to go about reforming our practice as well as our rhetoric. I also hope to persuade some of the champions of change to reexamine the theories, terms, and strategies on which proponents of the new American studies have relied. To quote the title of one of the better anthologies on the culture wars, the time has arrived to explore the possibilities "after political correctness" (Newfield and Strickland).

Many on and off campus share my sense that the polemical divide between left and right can be an unhelpful one. In his prizewinning book *Beyond the Culture Wars*, Gerald Graff argues that by "teaching the conflicts" we can begin to move beyond taking sides and toward engaging in a responsible dialogue about our differences. (Graff and I have co-written an essay since then that offers a sympathetic criticism of the left's program of "critical pedagogy.") With Graff I believe that we should avoid simply writing handbooks for the initiated or denunciations of our enemies and rather should try to write even for our resisting readers. Graff's project helped inspire the National Conversation on American Pluralism and Identity, an initiative designed by Sheldon Hackney, chairman of the National Endowment for the Humanities. The NEH is sponsoring a variety of events in communities, churches, schools, museums, and public forums to encourage a dialogue that might take us all beyond the war of words. As part of that initiative, in 1995 I directed Rethinking American Studies, a four-week summer institute for secondary school teachers, where I tried out a number of the ideas presented in this book. As a group, we reached the conviction that our core ethic must be to bring diverse voices to the table and to facilitate a challenging exchange of stories. Those are goals I have sought to meet in these pages. Whether I have executed this plan adroitly is a different matter from whether I should adopt such a plan, which I believe I should.

The book might have been more unified in tone had I restricted it to a more narrow intended audience, but that would have harmed both the book and the debate it seeks to join. At times there is a different kind of oscillation in this book from that between defense and persuasion, and this is the movement back and forth between theoretical argument and practical advice. Although it may at times be disconcerting, this variation stems from my effort to harness intellectual debates to everyday questions of pedagogy. I believe that most readers will share my sense that such an effort is vitally important, and that questions about teaching have rightly gained a more prominent place today throughout the disciplines of higher education (even among the theorists). There may be something of an unavoidable trade-off here, since neither the theory nor the pedagogy can be as detailed as both might be if they ignored each other. But given that there are already many books that concentrate on one at the expense of the other, the choice to offer a unique combination of both seems to me the right one.

If my imagined audience forms any kind of coherent community, it is that of readers who believe that what we study matters, whether we do it in the classroom or in book clubs or alone at the beach on vacation. More specifically, my audience is made up of all those who have the sense that the sometimes inscrutable debate about what constitutes the "American" in American literature (or American history or American studies) is far more than an academic matter, since it goes to the heart of who we imagine ourselves to be as a society and a nation.

• • •

The sequence of chapters in this volume proceeds from a general overview of the culture wars today, through the specific ways in which it is being fought out in American literary studies, and finally to some ideas about how to teach those conflicts. I work to establish both the historical and theoretical contexts for today's dilemmas, taking readers through contributions from critical theory as well as arguments over American identity conducted by writers from colonial times to the present. At the heart of this narrative is what I call the "struggle for representation." In Chapter 1, which takes that topic as its title, I show how the struggle for representation in literary theory belongs to a larger clash over the meaning and justice of representation which is taking place in the spheres of contemporary culture and politics. I clarify how contemporary theories of representation and identity make any blanket advocacy or denunciation of identity politics (i.e., the notion that a person's politics is determined by one factor of identity, such as race or class or gender) misleading at best. The encounter between 1960s-type social movement reformers and 1980s-type critical theory reformers is thus staged as a way to move forward toward articulating the promises and problems of multiculturalism.

The culture wars in American studies can be explained if we see them as not only a clash inside the academy between movement reformers and critical theorists but also a confrontation between these (uneasily united) academic innovators and the rising tide of religious and political conservatism in post-1960s America. But this is at best only a partial way of historicizing the current polemics. The debates now raging over representation and cultural identity are at least as old as the republic; recalling that longer history could help us attain a calming distance on our own conflicts and a correcting perspective on some of the competing claims. In Chapter 2, "Not Born on the Fourth of July," I provide a historical context for the present quarrels over literature and politics introduced in Chapter 1 by mapping the vexed legacy of Jefferson's Declaration of Independence. In examining how the working class, enslaved Africans, abolitionists, and early women's rights activists turned Jefferson's words to their own ends, I want to remind us that American identity has always been a contested issue. The culture wars and debates in answer to the question "What is an American?" have been with us from the start in a way that belies some of the nostalgic calls for a return to unity and consensus. Although I am in disappointed disagreement with many self-described left liberals who have joined the (neo)conservative side in the culture wars, I do concur with Gitlin's suggestion that the troubled legacy of Enlightenment political liberalism deserves a hearing before we throw it into the dustbin of history. European theory in some of its guises has joined forces with American social movement radicalism to critique not simply the shortcomings of American democracy but the very principles of its ideology. In Europe this critique has been most famously countered by the work of Jürgen Habermas, whose arguments have influenced or been paralleled by a host of American thinkers who still take the critique of liberalism seriously (whether it comes from movement radicals or poststructuralist professors). The case of the Declaration of Independence presents us with a challenge, for in it we find a tactical use of Enlightenment principles, an affirmation made strategically in the face of devastating injustice. This history makes it possible to rethink the purposes and effects of teaching documents such as the Declaration, novels such as Ellison's *Invisible Man*, and speeches such as King's "I Have a Dream." If these texts are themselves contradictory, tactical, and subject to diverse historical appropriations (as I try to show), what do we think we are transmitting when we teach them? What "cultural work" do we imagine we are doing in interpreting them? What ethos do we mean to espouse by our pedagogy?

As should be clear, this book grows at least as much out of my teaching experience as out of my research and writing. It appears more important than ever to insist on the inseparability of teaching and scholarship, especially in light of the often ignorant assertions about how indifferent or uninvolved research scholars are when it comes to teaching. My writing and my teaching are in constant dialogue, for each provides a check and a balance to the other. For the humanities critic, the classroom is more often than not a laboratory, a place of experimentation whose hard-earned results eventually (with any luck) find their way into publication. For me, the experiment with multiculturalism and pedagogy ended in questions about ethics, a result that surprised me at first. After all, much academic talk was (and still is) about "politics"; it assumes the priority of the political over the ethical. The central theme of poststructuralist criticism, it seemed, was "power," and its critique of liberalism pointedly borrowed from Nietzsche in interpreting morality as a disguise for the will-to-power. My experience teaching multiculturalism led me to question the adequacy of this critique. Many of the writers I studied, and many of the students I worked with, asserted ideas about *agency* that once more had us discussing the ethics of the choices we make about our identities and their effects. The notion that there *were* meaningful choices, and that each of us was responsible for and to those choices, ran against the tide of determinism in theories about the "social construction" of the "human subject," though at the same time these theories gave us a better understanding of the history of our choices and the contexts that conditioned them. Categories of race or gender or class, because of their very historical constructedness, are not sure indexes to a person's character or way of life, even if these factors can never be ignored in calculating our identities. But this "antiessentialist" argument raises ethical questions, as it seems to undercut the identity, and thus the power, of people who have long been discriminated against precisely because of the category with which they have been identified. To say that categories such as race are fictions does not seem an adequate response to the force of those categories in real life, and such attitudes appear ethically dubious coming from people who have known very little of that discrimination firsthand.

When I looked around, I saw that the European theorists, too, had taken an "ethical turn," something of a surprise considering the Nietzschean roots ("beyond good and evil") of much poststructuralist cultural analysis. In Chapter 3, "Taking Multiculturalism Personally," I pursue this ethical turn and reflect on the impasses of identity politics in the multiculturalism debate. I begin by reviewing the disparate definitions and practices of multiculturalism, which is now many things to many people. As in Chapter 5, my argument is in part autobiographical, as I look into the mirror of my own conflicted identities and the role they have played in my work as a teacher and an interpreter of literature. I wonder about multiculturalism as an ethos, and what the relationship can or should be between one's ethos in life (as a citizen or parent, for example) and one's ethos as a teacher. I wonder what standing ethos (from the Greek for "character") and ethics can have in the era of the deconstructed subject and the end of humanism. In arguing that my version of multiculturalism constitutes the challenge of an ethical practice, I try to combine the theoretical arguments of the philosophers with the literary and historical lessons of the writers to whom I have put myself to school over the last several decades. Perhaps most important, I ask again about ethical relations in the classroom — about the ethics of authority and responsibility, especially when consensus about cultural values and historical truths may be at an end.

The final two chapters continue this discussion of the cultural significance of teaching in the humanities, with specific attention to the past, present, and future of American literary studies. In Chapter 4, "The Discipline of the Syllabus," I explain in part why the culture wars so often take the form of the mocking or championing of course titles. The function of the syllabus in constructing the discipline needs to be understood, and the history of the American canon reviewed, in this light. Everyone's pedagogical situation differs, however, so I realize that the nostrums I offer may be only partially relevant in the case of each reader, and only indirectly so for readers who are not themselves faced with the practical question of what to assign at the beginning of the semester. This is not to say that the discussion does not speak to those outside the profession; on the contrary, in rehearsing something of the history of the American syllabus, I hope to persuade the general reader that today's controversies over what and how to teach are best understood when we know more about that history. Historical knowledge can prevent us from overreacting to today's changes and provide us with the information we need to evaluate these changes. Not all the focus here is on the past, however. I go on to examine recent attempts to use theories of a text's "cultural work" or its capacity to represent a group as new criteria for constructing the syllabus. These solutions have many virtues, but their consequences and flaws need to be clarified.

So, now what do we do? Although each of these chapters offers some guidelines or ideas for pedagogy, I felt the need to address the topic most directly in the conclusion, though even here I had to make some excursions into theory and history. Chapter 5, "The End of 'American' Literature," shows how the struggle for representation in the canon debates can yield an expanded geography for the discipline and better approaches to teaching it. One direct result of the encounter between movement reformers and critical theorists was to push the latter to explain how their often abstruse speculations translate into classroom and curriculum practice. What began as high academic discourse at research universities developed into a resource for rethinking virtually every aspect of the everyday labors of educators.

Deconstructing *Moby Dick* in the pages of a journal was quite different from deconstructing its role in one's classroom or on one's syllabus. Similarly, movement reformers who used literature to show the arbitrary social construction of race, class, and gender stereotypes found that the logic of their argument led them inevitably to question the legitimacy of these categories for cultural identity. What may have begun as a gesture to affirm the experience of a marginalized group could end up as a critique that undermined efforts to establish clearly the identities of such groups, so that movement reformers did indeed begin to sound a lot like the French-inspired deconstructors of representational identities. Not incidentally, Chapter 5 (like Chapter 3) also includes personal reflections on my experiences as a teacher, as I trace how reenergized concern with issues of race and geography and gender suddenly puts the pedagogue's authority at risk.

Teaching texts from previously marginalized groups cannot be advanced simply on the basis of establishing or celebrating the separate identity of the group, especially when modes of literary or cultural analysis emphasize how such identities are as much the product of representation as they are its object. This goes for the identity "American" as well. The "end" of American literary pedagogy, I contend, does not bring us to the abolition of "American literature" as a subject, as some readers might mistakenly but perhaps understandably infer from Chapter 5's title. Rather, the end I aim for is a comparative curriculum of connecting the differences, one in which the competing visions and rival representations can enter into dialogue with one another. While it is important that different cultural groups find their voices, it is equally important that they listen to one another, and even learn how to tell one another's stories instead of only repeating their own. The curriculum I propose differs from the standard "celebration of diversity" or "cultural pluralist" models, which too often set texts side by side without engaging them in conversation or without asking how they might be made accountable to each other. These models often overlook the real historical tensions and differences in power between competing answers to the question, "What is an American?" The conflicts between the texts of American literary history need to be brought into the open and explored, not papered over either by a soothing narrative of national harmony or by an equally misguided story of separate traditions.

I wrote this book over a seven-year period, having presented an early version of Chapter 5 at a conference in 1989 and revising parts of each chapter through the winter of 1996. Quite self-consciously, I saw my arguments as interventions designed to change the way we in American literary studies go about doing our business, and as forays into explaining to a skeptical public what we do. Some of them have an undisguised polemical character and are meant to provoke a response. Some readers may find the tone of the book too aggressive or opinionated, particularly given its academic origins and context. This is a risk I am willing to take, partly out of a desire to blur the lines between university press and trade press publication, and partly because the rhetoric of the culture wars makes such a style inevitable to some degree, though I recognize its limitations. I remember the somewhat guilty pleasure I felt in coming up with the title "The End of 'American' Literature," which I modeled after David Noble's title *The End of American History*. (Since that time and as the fin de siècle approaches, there has been an embarrassing number of "The End of . . ." books.) The appearance of the first version of that chapter as an essay in the March 1991 issue of *College English* changed my career to a degree I had not anticipated. Although I had written two previous books and edited others, nothing I had done earned me the notoriety of this piece. Obviously I was on to something. The culture wars were heating up, and my essay became something of a vehicle for partisans on many sides. In retrospect I do not attribute this response to my originality, for others were making some of the same points. There was something about my rhetoric, and my manner of combining theory with pedagogical controversy, that made the piece an effective though disputed instrument. Many of my colleagues remarked on my attention to questions of pedagogy, which were then rarely on the agenda of the dominant academic discourse on theory. For better or worse, I became drawn into more such controversies, and soon produced a series of essays that took off from the first, elaborating and qualifying and occasionally contradicting its arguments.

Those essays became the basis of this book. To fashion a coherent volume and to answer criticisms of my previous versions, I have revised each chapter to some degree, making substantial subtractions and additions along the way. The polemics have not disappeared, though they have been moderated at times, partly out of the desire to persuade the not already converted. In the case of "The End of 'American' Literature," however, I felt the necessity to revise most extensively. I had received a good amount of commentary about the essay (some of it published in a *College English* forum to which I responded), and felt there were extensive modifications and improvements worth making. I was tempted to let it stand as originally published, but it seemed wrong to reprint it without revisiting some of its weaker moments. Many new examples also came to mind, and there was fresh scholarship to account for as well. I am not the person to judge whether the changes I have made will convince my detractors, infuriate my supporters, or just increase the army of the indifferent.

As I put the final touches on this volume, the nation remains enrolled in something like a nonstop national seminar on the topic of "What is an American?" Each election, each media event (such as the O. J. Simpson murder trial), and each public catastrophe (such as the Oklahoma City bombing) becomes instantly assigned to the syllabus, a fresh text for interpreters of our cultural identity. Public issues such as immigration, welfare, support for the United Nations, or international trade are added rapidly to the curriculum. In these and other public cases, debate quickly turns to questions that also resound in the narrower precincts of academe: Who and what properly belong to the category of the "American"? How are we to preserve and protect the supposedly "exceptional" or special essence that is the meaning of America? I hope my discussions contribute to a growing skepticism about the usefulness and morality of this search for America's one essential meaning. Of course, our historical moment is not the first time, and will not be the last, when the question of "un-American" activities takes center stage. It would be utopian to think that one could finally put an end to this unfortunate quarrel. Nevertheless, we remain obligated, I believe, to raising the level of the debate a few notches, and this is where educators can play a role, whether in their capacity as teachers or as "public intellectuals." Much of the quarrel has taken place in an uninformed darkness, where the obscurity created by ideological stereotypes and historical inaccuracies makes the discovery of common ground impossible. So this book is in part about setting the record straight, though I do not anticipate the achievement of a new consensus anytime soon. The end I have in mind, rather, is one in which we struggle not only to represent ourselves but to do justice to the stories of others. These other stories are also America's, and America is also their story.

o n e **The Struggle for Representation**

eeking touchstones for my exploration of the culture wars, I settled on two quotations, one from the African American novelist Paule Marshall, the other from the Palestinian American literary critic Edward Said. Marshall, in telling the tale of her genesis as a writer, pinpoints that moment in the struggle for representation when empowerment comes from discovering one's own cultural identity. In the Harlem of the late 1930s, the young Paule listened keenly to the power of words coming from "the poets in the kitchen," as her mother and other West Indian women spun stories out of ancestral experience. "While not abandoning Thackeray, Fielding, Dickens and the others" she found at the Brooklyn Public Library, Marshall "started asking the reference librarian, who was white, for books by Negro writers":

No grade school literature teacher of mine had ever mentioned [Paul Laurence] Dunbar or James Weldon Johnson or Langston Hughes. I didn't know that Zora Neale Hurston existed and was busy writing and being published during those years. Nor was I made aware of people like Frederick Douglass and Harriet Tubman — their spirit and example — or the great 19th-century abolitionist and feminist Sojourner Truth. There wasn't even Negro History Week when I attended P. S. 35 on Decatur Street!

What I needed, what all the kids — West Indian and native black American alike — with whom I grew up needed, was an equivalent of the Jewish shul, someplace where we could go after school — the schools that were shortchanging us — and read works by those like ourselves and learn about our history. It was around that time also that I began harboring the dangerous thought of someday trying to write myself. (11)

Like many others from marginalized groups, Marshall expresses her frustration at being shortchanged in school, which leads her to desire separate institutions of learning to make up for her community's imposed lack of self-knowledge. Her mention of the Jewish shul reminds us that America's racial and ethnic groups have a long history of using separate cultural institutions to preserve their community's identity. In the language of identity politics, she wants to "read works by those like ourselves and learn about our history" in order to "write myself." She wants representation, both in the mirror of history and in the yet-to-be written pages of her fiction. Echoing a theme that runs throughout African American literature, Marshall stages the achievement of literacy as the underground railroad to freedom, though here she turns the theme on its head, since she seeks literacy in her own people's culture rather than in the master's tongue.

If Marshall's passage may be taken as representative of one pole in the struggle for representation, Edward Said's essay "The Politics of Knowledge" occupies a place somewhere near the opposite end of the spectrum. Although Said has been a passionate critic of Western "Orientalism" and its oppressive caricatures of the "Other," his more recent writings express considerable skepticism about the uses of identity politics. He begins his essay with an anecdote telling how, at an academic conference, a black woman who was an eminent professor of history attacked him for Eurocentrism, pointing out that his paper discussed only white males and did not address the experiences of black women. Said ruefully notes that this skilled questioner turned his own previous theoretical polemics against him. What ensues is an ambivalent attempt by Said to think beyond identity politics, which leads him to this conclusion about the culture wars:

> Although I risk over-simplification, it is probably correct to say that it does not finally matter *who* wrote what, but rather *how* a work is written and *how* it is read. The idea that because Plato and Aristotle are male and the products of a slave society they should be disqualified from receiving contemporary attention is as limited an idea as suggesting that *only* their work, because it was addressed to and about elites, should be read today. Marginality and homelessness are not, in my opinion, to be gloried in; they are to be brought to an end, so that more, and not fewer, people can enjoy the benefits of what has for centuries been denied the victims of race, class, or gender. (31)

To end the injustices that narrow categorizations impose, Said advocates what he calls "worldliness" (and what David Hollinger calls "cosmopolitanism"). Worldliness "is the opposite of separatism, and also the reverse of exclusivism," offering a global practice of *comparative* literature which links works to one another across cultural boundaries. Said asserts that this linkage depends on our seeing such works as having universal aesthetic virtues of style, pleasure, and illumination: "Otherwise they will be regarded only as informative ethnographic specimens, suitable for the limited attention of experts and area specialists" (28).

Whether it be in literary study or global politics, Said cautions against "the supremely stubborn thesis that everyone is principally and irreducibly a member of some race or category" that cannot ever be assimilated to or accepted by others. Originating in the mind of Western imperialist adventurers, this way of thinking produced "such invented essences as the Oriental or Englishness, as Frenchness, Africanness, or American exceptionalism" ("Politics" 21–22). Ironically, the identity politics of the oppressors became the identity politics of the oppressed, as nationalism was taken up as a primary (and necessary) weapon against imperialism. Said sees this turn as an understandable reaction to imperialism, yet as in danger of repeating some of the delusions that fostered that imperialism. "Victimhood, alas, does not guarantee or necessarily enable an enhanced sense of humanity," he argues, with pointed reference to Israel's treatment of the Palestinians (30). As for texts and traditions previously maligned or excluded, "the restoration of such works and interpretations of their place in the global setting . . . can only be accomplished by an appreciation not of some tiny, defensively constituted corner of the world, but of the large, many windowed house of human culture as a whole" (28).

Recalling Paule Marshall's experience, however, one can still insist that separate attention to silenced or previously ignored voices — through affirmative actions in the library, school, department, syllabus, and critical study — is a prerequisite to any "worldliness" in which the formerly excluded can attain representation *in their own terms.* That kitchen of Marshall's childhood was not a tiny corner but a whole world of wonder and knowledge. Said's utopian call for "worldliness" is admirable, but he too quickly passes over the intricate ways in which "*how* a work is written and *how* it is read" are colored by "*who* wrote" it. The tension and dialogue between Marshall's appreciation of the need for separatism and Said's compelling call for a border-crossing worldliness underlie much of the controversy in the culture wars. In this chapter that tension, and the spectrum between the two positions, will be explored as it shows up in the specific contests over representation in politics and higher education. In brief, I think that both arguments are right, and that no formulas for excellence or reform can afford to ignore the virtues of each.

• • •

Efforts to clarify the culture wars or to negotiate peace between the combatants quickly run into a fundamental obstacle: we disagree about the core meaning of the terms in dispute, such as "race," "ethnicity," "nation," and "culture" itself. We cannot come to terms because it is the terms themselves that are being contested. Students of language will point out that any term (whether a simple noun such as "chair" or a complex concept such as "justice") becomes an ambiguous representation once subjected to historical and theoretical scrutiny. Indeed, postmodernism may be the condition of living permanently with deconstructed terms whose unreliability does not relieve us of the necessity of depending on them. The struggle for representation involves, as I will show, very large issues touching on politics, economics, and ideology, but these all have tangled roots in struggles over language. In trying to understand how the culture wars started and why people feel so strongly about them, we can start by examining some of the key words being contested. This is not a trivial literary or pedantic exercise. The power of words is very real and comes partly from the history of their use. Analogies can be seen that connect the struggle over words with struggles over representation in the arenas of education, the media, the arts, and government. More self-consciousness about the language that we employ can only help, as will a sensitivity to how words shape cultural identities. Questions of identity are, after all, in large measure a matter of naming (as in "What is an American?").

"Race," for example, was for centuries used to denote a group of people who shared a common set of experiences, behaviors, and values, and thus was not easily distinguishable from "ethnicity" or "nation" or "social group." "Race" preceded "nation" in the modern political sense, though it was quickly taken up as a term to justify the creation of national borders in the era after the Renaissance.[1] This political use of "race" rigidified the borders of the concept itself, as did the "racialization" of race by biological and scientific racism from the eighteenth to the twentieth centuries. But most modern nations have been made up of people from a variety of ethnicities or races, and most modern societies display features contributed by a diverse group of cultures. Separatist movements usually arise in reaction to intercultural contacts, and worldliness usually depends on the vibrant cultural life of separate groups. Hybridity and border-crossing are more often the rule than the exception, especially in the literatures of the U.S. (see TuSmith 1–32).

1. Walt Whitman frequently wrote of "race" in terms of class, as when in "The Eighteenth Presidency!" he calls for a "Counteraction of a New Race of Young Men" to reform the nation's politics (1312).

In arguing for a "postethnic perspective" that goes "beyond multiculturalism," David Hollinger writes, "Race does not serve us at all well . . . when we want to talk about culture" (36). Hollinger's position that "racism is real, races are not" (39) seems to give less rather than more attention to the history and effects of racial practices (and in this regard "postethnic" has the same drawbacks as "postfeminist"). In rightly repudiating a crude biological belief in "race" as the determiner of culture, Hollinger appears to forget that "race" and "culture" were indeed roughly synonymous terms until at least the mid-nineteenth century, when "race" began to lose its general meaning of "a people" and gained its modern conflation with skin color and other physical characteristics. He sees error in the equation of race with culture for a number of reasons: race has no scientific standing as a category for discerning differences in human behavior; race is a political category without a predetermined cultural content; a culture may be participated in by people from a variety of races; the concept of race cannot be foundational for a culture since it is a product of culture itself. Many analysts find more merit in "ethnicity," since the term makes smaller, more historically verifiable claims that do seem to point toward relatively homogeneous cultural groupings around traditional elements such as language, customs, food, art, and religion. It makes sense, some think, to talk of Polish or Vietnamese or Brazilian culture, but not of black or white or brown or red or yellow cultures (and Hollinger for one has his doubts about categories such as African American and Asian American, since these cover over the ethnic differences within such large rubrics). Yet since race remains a powerful political category, even Hollinger admits that advocating its abandonment would probably do further harm to those who have been traditionally victimized by discrimination. This may be why he does not call his book *Postracial America*, though that choice might have more directly confronted the issues at stake (compare Cornel West's choice of title in *Race Matters*).

Posing the question "Why keep talking about race?" David Roediger contends that "the central political implication arising from the insight that race is socially constructed is the specific need to attack *whiteness* as a destructive ideology rather than to attack the concept of race abstractly" (3). Since race is traditionally construed as something that only "people of color" have, getting rid of race will not necessarily undo the presumption of white supremacy. Egalitarian and humanitarian calls to go beyond race tend to evade the problem of whiteness, leaving the invention and privileges of whiteness unquestioned. Talking about race in terms of whiteness, argues Roediger, leads to "questions of why people think they are white and of whether they might quit thinking so" (12). Putting white back into the color scheme of race helps us see that the social construction of race includes, and may even be founded upon, the construction of whiteness. Ideologies of whiteness have played an outspoken role in the legal, political, social, economic, and artistic arenas of American life. The equation of race with culture may not stand up to rigid theoretical scrutiny; indeed, in America we need to remind people continually that American culture — from music and religion through food, the visual arts, and literature — borrows heavily from the cultures of Africa and Latin America and Asia as well as from myriad European ethnic groups. It would be ludicrous to call American culture in general a white culture. The ideology of whiteness has nonetheless played a pivotal role in determining how these cultural resources are made available or valued, by and for whom they are practiced, and on what terms they are admitted to the national repertoire.

Despite many attempts to pin down the terms of discussion, the identification of race with ethnicity, culture, and nation continues to be a feature of discourse on the culture wars, and such identifications occur among people who are otherwise in deep disagreement with one another. In the case of debates about "multiculturalism," for instance, one often finds that the term is used when "multiracialism" would be more exact. Ronald Takaki's book *A Different Mirror: A History of Multicultural America* is an incisively informative account of how racial and ethnic and religious groups have struggled for land, wealth, and power in the United States. *A Different Mirror* is not, however, a history of "multicultural America," since it contains almost no comparative analyses of cultural forms such as literature, music, art, religion, cinema, or sexual behavior. Here the use of "cultural" as a synonym for "racial" is a bit deceptive, and illustrates why some critics prefer speaking of an "antiracist" movement instead of a "multicultural" one. But by insisting that racial differences provide no legitimate grounds for bigotry and prejudice, antiracism runs the risk of demonstrating that racial categories are themselves meaningless, a result not always welcomed by people in minority communities for whom race is an important avenue for cultural identity and community pride. "Multiculturalism" has the advantage (or, for some, the disadvantage) of affirming or celebrating particular cultural groups rather than simply being against racism.

The shifty meaning of the words "race, "culture," and "nation" shows up dramatically when we consider the emergence of what are called "panethnicities." Panethnicities include the categories European American, Native American, African American, Asian American, and Hispanic or Latino American. Within each one of these categories we find people of every imaginable skin color, of diverse local ethnicities, and from various language groups and nation-states. Since in the United States race has long been centered on whiteness and its other, and since the black/white difference has been the dominant factor in defining race, this new constellation of multiracial panethnicities bewilders analysts and ordinary citizens. The panethnicities come closer to representing cultural groups than races, at least if race is simply reduced to skin color. Yet while Hispanics are grouped together out of the presumption of a shared language and religious heritage, Native Americans have hundreds of indigenous languages and spiritual traditions, and Asian Americans are similarly divided among Christians and Confucians, Buddhists and Taoists, speaking many tongues from many nations with distinct cultural features of their own.

It seems that just as the novel use of "race" to distinguish basic biological features rather than cultural ones became predominate in black/white discourse, panethnicities emerged to restore the importance of culture at the expense of biology. Even blacks became African Americans, renewing the debate over whether black and white Americans belonged to different cultures or just to different races. The contemporary preference for cultural groupings gives strength to the argument against using "race" at all to distinguish between people, though this scientifically sound position once more tends to let racism slip out of the picture or off the hook. Multiculturalism, then, emerges as a sign of the partial triumph of thinking in terms of panethnicities instead of races, given that race discourse was always centered on a black/white model that then also applied to white supremacy over red, brown, and yellow.

Although this turn to the multicultural model pleases many people of Asian or Latin American or indigenous descent, liberating their experience from subordination to the white/black story, African Americans respond ambivalently. They criticize multiculturalism because it pushes aside the preeminence of blackness in thinking about ethno-racial difference, a move they interpret as a refusal to confront racism. Meanwhile, activists within the panethnicities find power in the new way of categorizing themselves, even though the identity politics of these groupings is often more salient than the cultural commonalities supposedly underpinning them. The tendency to celebrate the culture of each panethnic group is still part of a reaction to the old construction of whiteness, which included explicit claims of the superiority of European or Christian or Western ways of life. In the United States, the addition of the national term "American" to most panethnic categories indicates an essential political dimension. These rubrics represent movements that, although claiming allegiance to prior traditions, assert the right to reshape the American scene at least partly in their own image. Often they embrace an America that is reluctant to receive them. The panethnic modifier signals a conscious effort to answer the question "What is an American?" with an unorthodox reply.

It would be a waste of time, and missing the point, to denigrate panethnic social constructions by pointing out their incoherence or inner diversity or political motivation. The people involved in these communities are quite well aware of their sociohistorical rather than natural or divine origins. They know the differences between Nuyoricans and Chicanos, or Zuni and Hopi, or Korean and Vietnamese. Otherwise they would not have to labor so hard to establish and sustain panethnic coalitions. We would do better to reflect on how these panethnic configurations work, at this moment in U.S. and global development, as strategies in the struggle for representation. Panethnic categories are effective means for extending democracy and self-determination. They provide the cultural resources that communities require in order to analyze and express their experiences and to strengthen the recognition of those experiences by others. They give individuals a renewed sense of self and better means to determine their course of life and its meaning. By redistributing how a nation values the groups within it, the construction of panethnicities reallocates social power in ways that redress social injustice and enhance democracy. Panethnic groups become political forces at the ballot box as well, challenging dominant power structures in material as well as cultural arenas. The fact that the exact outlines of these panethnic groups change is no reason not to support them as cultural movements of great value. However imperfect, they are necessary and rich vehicles for the self-fulfillment of individuals and their communities.

"American," after all, originated as a panethnic term to unite Northern European whites who had moved to the United States. The endorsement of the panethnic strategy lay behind the acceptance of the notion of the "melting pot." Hence the confusion of whites who feel that they are "simply Americans" rather than members of an ethno-racial movement: "American" is such a successful panethnic construction that its members have naturalized its contours and ceased to see it as a historical configuration that has changed in the past and will change in the future. There was always an unrecognized tension between the civic or political essence of the "American" (as one who believed in the Constitution and the Bill of Rights) and the racial or cultural essence of the "American" (as one who embodied the supremacy of European, Christian, and white ways of life). Multiculturalism grows out of this recurrent tension between the two definitions of the American: the multicultural movement bases its critique of inequality on the civic and political principles of the nation, yet it also articulates a variety of American ways of life that do not conform to the Anglo-Saxon norm.

Rather than propose to end the struggle for representation by proclaiming the correct terms for the future, I would argue that we still need a better understanding of the history and effects of these terms before we move beyond them. This is where the study of literature and culture comes in, for these are arenas in which people seek identities and explore the possibilities of representation. "Representation" is itself a key word requiring scrutiny, as the remainder of this chapter will show. Since at least the mid-1960s, representation has been subjected to all manner of elaborate theoretical investigation. Psychoanalysts, structuralists, poststructuralists, deconstructionists, feminists, reader-response critics, minority and postcolonial thinkers, and gay and lesbian activists all have contributed to exploding the notion that representation works innocently or transparently. Building on the intellectual legacy of semiotics (the study of how sign systems are constructed and organized), contemporary interpreters of culture and society now regularly argue more over *how* things are represented than over *what* things "really" are. As we heard from Marshall McLuhan, the medium is often the message, and as Jean Baudrillard never tires of reminding us, we seem to live in a world of pure simulations with no corresponding substance or reality beneath them. We traffic in representations and consume images. Today, the first target of a revolutionary uprising is usually the local television station, and the first objects of repressive dictatorships are newspapers, fax machines, universities, and other means of reproducing representations.

The culture wars are in part about the relationship of academic knowledge to political power. This relationship can also be understood, in some decisive ways, in terms of a struggle for representation. This struggle is multifaceted, plural, complex: it includes struggles over the theory of representation as well as over the actual cultural and political distribution of representation. The questions we face might be put this way: Who represents what to whom, for what reasons, through what institutions, to what effect, to whose benefit, and at what costs? What are the ethics of representation? What kinds of knowledge and power do authorized forms of representation produce? What kinds of people do such representations produce? Who owns or controls the means of representation? And what new ways of representation might better achieve the goals of justice and democracy in the overlapping worlds of education and politics?

Some have argued that the liberal tradition, with its commitment to expanding "recognition" for different classes of individuals, provides a good approach to the crisis of representation. The philosopher Charles Taylor, in a rich and powerful work, argues that we need to theorize the "politics of recognition" more carefully, especially as regards the debates over multiculturalism in education and government. Although I do not have space here to do justice to Taylor's analysis, I want to suggest that the term "representation" rather than "recognition" provides a more comprehensive framework within which to explore the issues of knowledge, cultural identity, and politics. Classic liberal theory begins with the individual as its primary unit, whereas current conflicts over representation stem from the claim that *groups* also have a right to representation. Moreover, the language of recognition tends to reinforce rather than investigate the privileged position of those who do the recognizing, while also tilting the emphasis toward personal relationships and away from political economy. (For a critique of the liberal multiculturalism of thinkers such as Taylor, see Giroux, "Post-Colonial Ruptures"; for a position that often parallels Taylor's, see Hollinger.) "Recognition" belongs more narrowly to the philosophical discourse of the law and of rights, whereas "representation" tends to bridge the gap between politics and culture, since it is a term often used in analyzing films, paintings, poems, and novels as well as political systems. "Representation" also raises questions about the relationship between *agency* and *media* which are crucial to understanding our postmodern dilemmas.

Whereas the first wave of theorizing about representation is often characterized as textual, considering representation from literary or philosophical or conceptual standpoints, the second wave is characterized as materialist and political. But these oppositions are simplistic. Louis Althusser's discussions of "ideological state apparatuses" (including schools) and Michel Foucault's work on "discourse" and "disciplines" combined the analysis of representation as idea or art with a focus on the material, institutional, and bodily means by which representations come into being and achieve their effects. Given the bibliography devoted to these and other recent theorists, I will not go over this ground again. The point is to ignore attempts to set up the question of cultural analysis as a choice between the artistic and the economic, or the textual and the material, as if the old chestnut about "base and superstructure" still held sway. In the reflections that follow, I underscore this contemporary sense of representation as a complex set of cultural practices, in which "practice" indicates activity that is at once conceptual and physical. "Representation" refers both to systems of knowledge made out of signs and to material or economic arrangements for the (re)production of knowledge. Representations may be said to be "powerful" in both senses. On the one hand, they derive their force from the conceptual and affective rhetoric of their sign systems — from their formal use of words, plots, symbols, colors, images, allusions, and ideas. On the other hand, their power emanates from the material institutions that house and produce them — schools, churches, culture industries, law courts, private foundations, and government agencies. The struggle for representation goes on in both the semiotic and the material arenas and is shaped by how we understand the relationship between them.

The sense of grievance felt by many academics in the wake of the political correctness debate expresses itself frequently in the language of (mis)representation. To cite one instance, the original statement of principles of Teachers for a Democratic Culture objects to "a campaign of harassment and misrepresentation" aimed at proponents of new forms of knowledge and new practices in education. Some critics were quick to point out the apparent irony here, that a profession so lately charmed by the poststructuralist assertion that *all* representation is misrepresentation should now insist on the importance of accurate accounts of its work. This irony, however, rested on the common misunderstanding of poststructuralism and deconstruction as theories that deny the possibility of meaning (for an evenhanded discussion of politics and deconstruction, see Paul Jay, "Bridging the Gap"). Although such theoretical movements did indeed ask about how representations get constructed, and about the inherent flaws in their reproductions, poststructuralism and deconstruction began with the assumption that (like race) representation matters — which is to say that it is both materially important and, in important ways, material. Representation is a matter of actual practices and economic arrangements which can give the most fantastic ideas the power of life and death. It is only because language and other sign systems work so powerfully and have such great consequences that we need carefully to analyze their claims and their technologies.

• • •

By the early 1990s, the (mis)representation of "theory" as an academic fad that had abandoned truth for nihilistic free play had won wide public acceptance. Yet, contradictorily, the uproar over political correctness, multiculturalism, feminism, and deconstruction demonstrates that many among the press and the public also believe that academics have been all too effective in representing their ideas and taking control of the institutions of representation. It is clear that the backlash against the academy stems not from a belief that academics are playing a game of trivial pursuit, but from the conviction that academics are producing *a body of different truths* that threaten certain traditional value systems and institutions. What the political correctness debate and related phenomena display, symptomatically, is precisely the connection between representation in the field of knowledge and representation in the fields of society and politics, though up until now academics have been woefully inept at representing the character and value of their work to a larger audience. (For discussions of this ineptness, see my "First Round of the Culture Wars," and Bérubé.)

The accusation that academics have abandoned truth, standards, and merit thinly disguises the reality: as part of a global reassessment, American culture is undergoing a fundamental debate over how to define these very terms (along with, not coincidentally, race and gender and class and nation). That debate stems not only from changes in the study of history or art or literature, but also from massive changes in the student body. That body is increasingly made up of women, people of color, and persons from underprivileged social and economic backgrounds. "In 1960," observes Lawrence Levine, "only some 6 percent of college students were from minority groups; by 1988 the number had risen to almost 20 percent. In 1960 women earned only 35 percent of the bachelor's degrees and 10 percent of the Ph.D.'s conferred; in 1990 they earned 54 percent of the B.A.'s and 37 percent of the Ph.D.'s. By 1985 27 percent of the faculty in institutions of higher education were women, and more than 10 percent were non-White" (xvii). These numbers have grown somewhat in the 1990s, though not nearly as much as they should (especially the numbers and salaries of women faculty).[2] Levine's

---

2. Women make up only about 12 percent of full professors nationwide, and have made their greatest inroads at community colleges, where pay is lowest. Women hold 38 percent of all faculty positions in those colleges. At the top Ivy League schools, women are indeed showing up in increasing numbers at the assistant professor level (averaging between 20 and 42 percent), but female appointments at the full professor level on these campuses

former home campus, the University of California at Berkeley, became the first major state university with a majority of "minority" students. Their representation in the national student body has forced us to question many of the traditional concepts and practices of our disciplines. "The academic curriculum," observes Gerald Graff, "has become a prominent arena of cultural conflict because it is a microcosm, as it should be, of the clash of cultures and values in America as a whole. As the democratization of culture has brought heretofore excluded groups into the education citadel, with them have come the social conflicts that their exclusion once kept safely distant" (*Beyond the Culture Wars* 8).[3]

Seen in the context of America's changing demographics, the struggle over representation emerges as a *historical event* and as a challenge to develop more just representation in culture, politics, and knowledge. As W. J. T. Mitchell argues, however, professors should not reduce the current struggle to a "paradigm shift" that merely allows business as usual to go on under another guise by turning the politics of representation into yet another academic specialty. Although it would be a mistake to conflate the history of the academy with the history of the world, struggles for representation on campus still can be placed on a larger cultural map, where the boundaries between nations, regions, identities, cultures, institutions, and subjectivities are being everywhere contested or overrun. All around we can see what Mitchell terms "instances of reconfiguration and relocation of cultural and critical energy, reversals of center and margin, production and consumption, dominant and emergent forces" (13). Patterns of relocation and reversal, of hierarchies overturned and borders transgressed, are characteristic of the postcolonial era's new relationships between the First, Second, and Third Worlds. Indeed, they suggest how outmoded such a naming by numbers may be.

---

still average between 7 and 13 percent. Pay inequities between men and women at the same academic rank are still rampant. (See "Rare in the Ivy League.")

3. See also Amy Gutmann's helpful discussion of the "democratic virtue" of debating our "inevitable disagreements" over education (11).

Local arguments over cultural diversity, the canon, affirmative action, admissions, financial aid, and theories of cultural studies turn out to be instances of change that have a global context. In fact, they mark the advent of the era of "relentless globalization" itself, as Michael Geyer argues. In the United States, this globalization tends to destabilize the system of higher education as it loses its monopolies on knowledge production, socialization, and the construction of ideology. Universities must increasingly compete with private corporations and foundations, with the media, and with various activist groups that have made claims to representation in these arenas. "Scholarship" goes on at the Heritage Foundation; "education" comes through MTV, advertising, the talk shows, and Hollywood cinema; "ideology" and "subject positions" are produced by social movement organizations through their mass mailings, cable shows, Internet and Web resources, and other public avenues.

This globalization works across the national boundaries of the United States as well, as our economic, educational, media, and political institutions compete in the world marketplaces created by late capitalism and postcolonialism. "While a grid of global transactions has relentlessly synthesized global time, it has not homogenized societies as the turn-of-the century theorists had expected," observes Geyer. "We experience the world whole before we know how to think it — or narrate and, in all its meanings, represent it" (528). The global struggle over representation, then, participates in — even as it fails to recognize — a global struggle over the ownership of property and the constitution of new subjects (workers, consumers, voters, stockholders, bureaucrats). "The history of twentieth-century globalization is the history of the large-scale privatization of the global commons by incorporated, legal subjects rather than the constitution of a universal public sphere" (Geyer 530). According to David Rieff, the "newly globalized consumer economy" is "multiculturalism's silent partner": "Capitalism is the bull in the china shop of human history," wrecking hierarchies, overturning binary oppositions, crossing borders, and transvaluing values faster than any poststructuralist, feminist, deconstructionist, or Afrocentrist could imagine (68). When it comes to multiculturalism, says Rieff, the business leaders are way ahead of the academics: they have already moved production (of knowledge as well as of commodities) across American and Eurocentric boundaries. It is folly, he concludes, for academics to posit multiculturalism as some subversive doctrine that may be used to threaten The System: multiculturalism is simply the shadow cast by global capitalism in its endless search for cheap resources and profitable markets.

Rieff (and to some extent Geyer) never questions the equation of consumer capitalism with repression, inauthenticity, and dispossession, even as we witness the stampede of the former communist populations toward the market economy. Are the peoples of these regions simply the dupes of capitalism, as the critical theorists once said that the masses were the dupes of religion or of the entertainment industry? Or must there be a more complicated (and, yes, post-Marxist) account of the relationship of freedom and liberty to the ownership of property, access to the media, and control of the flow of information? It is not at all clear that the globalization of consumer economics has meant only a reduction in freedom or happiness: such a one-sided critique is the luxury of people who already have Visa cards, cable TV, and fax machines.

I do not want to lose those of my readers who are strongly in sympathy with Geyer's and Rieff's arguments. Every day we read more articles about the increasing gap between the rich and the poor, both in the United States and abroad. In *Cultures of United States Imperialism*, Amy Kaplan and Donald Pease assemble a formidable collection of essays examining the usually unacknowledged role of empire building and imperial conquest in American history. All too often the question "What is an American?" was answered by imperial adventures, territorial conquest, colonial administration, and cold war ideology. The discipline of American studies avoided this history through domestic narratives about the "frontier" or the "virgin land" or American "exceptionalism," though America was no exception when it came to the expansion of nationalism into imperial power. Nonetheless, I want to point out that the ritual anticapitalism of the academic left in the humanities is problematic, and not only because of the professoriate's privileged class position.

The economic focus of the globalization argument tends once more to emphasize orthodox class analysis, and so again to marginalize race, ethnicity, nationalism, religion, gender, and other issues. Something is suspicious when feminism and multiculturalism are criticized for their failure to acknowledge that economic class, in the last analysis, determines all. Too often this argument becomes a device for sweeping race or ethnicity or gender aside and silencing those who speak on their behalf. How else to understand the alacrity with which many self-identified leftists joined the culture war *against* feminism, Afrocentrism, literary theory, and multiculturalism? The culture wars skewed the old left-right split, as white men who championed class struggle sided with white men who struggled to keep women and minorities out of the class. With the term "class," we again stumble across a problem of terminology and classification (witness recent discourse on the "underclass" and the "overclass," as in Lind). Here and elsewhere, then, my references to class and class struggle assume a tension within these phrases, a tension between economistic analyses that ignore race and gender on the one hand, and culturalist analyses that underestimate how the social construction of race and gender gets informed by political economy on the other. Once more I suggest that we refuse to choose sides in a false dichotomy, as if class analysis could proceed without feminism's critique of gender roles or without the benefit of analyzing the role of race in the history of colonial imperialism or of the welfare state.

It also needs to be pointed out that some of these exposés appear to conflate multiculturalism with multinational capitalism, when in fact much of multiculturalism is about local *resistance* to globalization and universalization, whether this be the resistance of a former colony to the World Bank or the resistance of the African American studies department to university budget cutters.[4] There may be some brands of watered-down multiculturalism of the "We are the world" variety, diminishing the differences between cultures and interpreting globalization as the spread of American-dominated monoculture. Often these brands confusedly include polemics that warn about the dangers of "Balkanization" and "tribalism," not recognizing that the assertion of national or local identities may represent important ways of resisting the homogenizing powers of globalizing "free market" universalism. In trying to negotiate between the competing claims of separatism and universalism or identity politics and cosmopolitanism,

4. On multiculturalism in a global context, see Gordon and Newfield 297–388; Chicago Cultural Studies Group, "Critical Multiculturalism."

multiculturalism performs the valuable task of insisting on the role of the local at a time when so much pressure exists toward globalization. But multiculturalism also perceives the local as contingent on the global, that is, as a dynamic identity that is always in the process of borrowing from or adding to or transforming the resources and ideas of other cultures. To use the lingo of cyberspace, multiculturalism might be said to view cultural relations as an interactive network of many centers, each receiving and distributing according to its interests, beliefs, and skills. Of course, such a networking again raises important issues of access to representation, of ownership of the network, and of interpreting what comes across the grid.

The debates about difference in the classroom have been one locus where these tensions in the understanding of multiculturalism and class have been most unavoidable, if misunderstood (see bell hooks's chapter "Confronting Class in the Classroom" 177–89). The realities of class struggle in the United States today show up in the classroom, and the classroom is one of the places we use to try to forge new ways of classifying current economic and cultural formations. One need only think of the debates over affirmative action and sexual harassment, and then remember their connection to the new scholarship in minority and women's history, and then recall the expression of this history in formerly overlooked poems and novels, and then connect these to developments in legal studies around issues of gender and race, and then circle back to social-change activism by women and people of color in various communities to appreciate how the struggle for representation joins so many otherwise distinct parts of our lives.

Yet despite these connections linking campus issues to the real world, the divisions separating social groups remain stark, as does the line separating academic change and social change. As much as some of us on campus would like to celebrate the increasing representation of women and minorities on our syllabi or (in lesser numbers) among our students and colleagues, we cannot forget that integrating a curriculum is not a substitute for ending injustice elsewhere. Hazel Carby notes that although "in white suburban libraries, bookstores, and supermarkets an ever-increasing number of narratives of black lives are easily available . . . those same readers are part of the white suburban constituency that refuses to support the building of affordable housing in its affluent suburbs, aggressively opposes the bussing of children from the inner city into its neighborhood schools, and would fight to the death to prevent its children from being bussed into the urban blight that is the norm for black children." Consumer capitalism markets the writings of a Terry McMillan or an Amy Tan because they sell, not because they can be directly linked to ending racism. One has to guard against the danger of aestheticizing social inequality or of turning the Other into a commodity: "For white suburbia, as well as for white middle-class students in universities, these texts are becoming a way of gaining knowledge of the 'other,' a knowledge that appears to satisfy and replace the desire to challenge the existing frameworks of segregation" (197). This is a harsh criticism which itself does not do justice to the complex phenomenon of multiculturalism, but Carby's warning is well worth remembering because the mistake she targets could be so dangerous.

The globalization of consumer capitalism and the opening up of the curriculum have brought increased possibilities of representation to previously subjugated peoples; but this makes it more important than ever to examine the kind, quality, and justice of this new world order of representations. The theoretical observation made popular by poststructuralism — that all representations contain certain *systematic* flaws — should lead to the question of who benefits or loses in such systems. Once one recognizes that the flaws of representation are to some degree *motivated*, individually or structurally, that they serve the interests of particular people, classes, or institutions, then the link between representation and political power, or between representation and race or ethnicity or gender, becomes a compelling issue. In the academic world, this has meant turning the critique of representation back upon academic work itself, examining everything from literature anthologies and scientific experiments to anthropological texts and the curricula of medical schools. More rarely, this critique includes examining the class hierarchy of the campus itself: of service workers (mostly minority), academic and clerical staff (mostly women), adjunct instructors, and teaching assistants laboring in relative invisibility. Is this class hierarchy reflected on in class during discussions of class?

I will return later to the academic side of the struggle for representation, but first I want to point again to its place in the larger social and political debate over the *justice* of representation (see Young). "Representation," after all, is a key term in democratic politics. The documents, institutions, theory, and practice of government in the United States depend on organizing representation fairly and effectively. Just as humanities theorists have come to doubt the traditional claims for representation made in the fields of art and scholarship, so contemporary political critics have challenged the claims made for democratic representation. They point to the failure of government to "represent the people" and to particular ways that certain groups are excluded from social or political representation. The traditional politics of parties or even classes is being replaced by a politics of representation in which everyone belongs to, joins, or is assigned a "special interest group." Symptomatic of these developments, "identity politics" claims to rectify the injustices of misrepresentation by pointing out the systematic ways in which individuals are (mis)treated *as members of groups* rather than as isolated persons. In response, groups persist in championing these identities with some pride, casting off the negative interpretations given to them by the dominant group and claiming the right to represent their reality truthfully, whether through the institutions of art and education or in the jury box or legislative chamber. Thus, Jeffrey Escoffier, in "The Limits of Multiculturalism," writes of "representation in two senses of the word: the obvious one of *political* representation, referring to the role of a delegate or spokesperson for a particular community, and the second one of *cultural* representation, connoting the symbolic content of various cultural forms and the ways that particular social groups are portrayed in fiction, movies, or television" (61). And, I would add, in academic studies, department structures, university budgets, curriculum, and syllabi.

Escoffier asserts that "the classical schemas of political representation in the United States have collapsed." This assertion depends on the observation that supposedly "universal" ideas or representations in the realm of culture have in practice privileged certain groups and marginalized others, as has also occurred in the realm of politics, where political representatives fail to represent many of their constituents. In the wake of the classical schemas, "multiculturalism is a loose ideological framework that offers a new model of representation," predicating claims to representation on the basis of cultural groups and traditions rather than individual rights (62). But how firm are the definitions of these groups, and when can we say that someone belongs to one? "A politics based on identity," observes Barbara Epstein, "encounters not only the problem of the fragility of particular categories of identity, but the fact that everyone occupies various categories at once. One may be female but white, or black but male; virtually everyone is vulnerable to some charge of privilege" (25). It "is not clear," concludes Escoffier, "how to represent complex identities *politically*" (66; see also Taylor). The same holds, I think, for academic knowledge: it is not clear how the widely challenged classical schemas of representation can be replaced by a more just representative system if there is no agreement about the "unit" or basic element grounding the claim to representation (that unit in the classical schema, at least theoretically, was the Enlightenment individual).

We remain historically in the midst of a struggle for representation where the righting of past injustices has an ethical claim to priority. The case against the classical schemas is very strong, though that case often borrows its terms and arguments from the classics (for an extended example, see my discussion in Chapter 2 of the Declaration of Independence). Uncertainty about how best to amend or replace the former schemas, however, should not preclude the effort, especially in light of so much evidence of injustice and misrepresentation. Nor should the flaws of the classical tradition lead to simplistic calls to "trash" Western civilization or to ignore the dialectical virtues of the Enlightenment, which after all contained much of the rhetoric of liberty, equality, justice, and the pursuit of happiness now enlisted in the cause of the marginalized (for a good discussion of this point, see Gitlin 210–19).

• • •

To many academics, public critics, and activists, the crisis of representation actually originates in the long-standing practices that prevented the presence on campus (and elsewhere) of women, Jews, blacks, persons of color, the poor, avowed homosexuals, and other underrepresented populations. When former dean Donald Kagan of Yale and others look back nostalgically at the campuses of yesteryear, portraying them as places of quiet harmony and consensus, they usually fail to acknowledge that this complacency was the conscious product of exclusion and that it came about by rigorously enforcing a policy of homogeneity. There was little conflict on campus because the possibility of different lives and viewpoints was a priori minimized. The only affirmative action programs were for athletes, high school class presidents, the relatives of important contributors, and the children of alumni. Few people seemed worried then about "bias" in admissions (for more on these issues, see Gutmann's chapter "Distributing Higher Education").

"Critics of the current politicization of the universities err grievously, I fear," writes Alan Kors, "in their idealization of the presixties past of American undergraduate life, remembering the 10 percent who kept some flame alive, and forgetting the boarding-school callousness of the rest" (62–63). In the course of objecting to what he perceives as a return to the principle of in loco parentis by intrusive social-engineering liberals on today's campuses, Kors, a conservative historian, member of the National Association of Scholars, and Bush appointee to the National Council on the Humanities, strongly repudiates the nostalgic myths about the past of the American academy:

> I attended, in the early sixties, the Princeton of mandatory chapel, parietal hours, and young men sworn never to act in a manner unbecoming to a gentleman. I was not impressed by the manifest cruelty, moral vacuity, and self-absorption of its products, or by the utter irrelevance of the university *in loco parentis* to the actual ethical tenor of human lives there. Teaching as a conservative throughout the late sixties and early seventies, and living among undergraduates as a resident faculty member in an educational college house, I indeed found my students off-the-wall politically and self-indulgent intellectually, although I do believe the extremes often obscured the more representative reality of actual undergraduate lives. Nonetheless, however rebellious their politics and however experimental their lifestyles, they were far kinder, more mutually sensitive and compassionate, and far more ethical in their personal interactions than the "parented" gentlemen with whom I had attended the old Princeton. The university had abandoned its parental role, but men and women were less manipulative of each other, the races and ethnic groups more tolerant of

and more caring toward each other, and individuals more profoundly likely to treat each other as ends and not means. (62)

Similarly, Gerald Graff's chapter "The Age of the Gentleman's C" argues that, prior to World War II and well into the 1960s, a tradition of anti-intellectualism and cultivated ignorance dominated the elite institutions of higher education. Graff's historical account shows that, contrary to popular belief, educational requirements today are generally far tougher than in the past, that faculty and students take intellectual issues more seriously, and that the entrance of women and minorities into a previously uncompetitive system has accelerated the raising of standards (*Beyond the Culture Wars* 86–124; see also Levine).

In a calculated effort to rebut misrepresentations of today's academy by the critics of political correctness, the statement of principles of Teachers for a Democratic Culture opens with a counterrepresentation that, in retrospect, may itself be party to a bit of mythmaking (since I helped draft this paragraph, I feel more than authorized to criticize it):

> Colleges and universities in the United States have lately begun to serve the majority of Americans better than ever before. Whereas a few short years ago, institutions of higher education were exclusive citadels often closed to women, minorities, and the disadvantaged, today efforts are being made to give a far richer diversity of Americans access to a college education. Reforms in the content of the curriculum have also begun to make our classrooms more representative of our nation's diverse peoples and beliefs and to provide a more truthful account of our history and cultural heritage. Much remains to be done, but we can be proud of the progress of democratization in higher education.

A deconstructive critic of rhetoric might note that this passage borrows heavily from the dominant language of American liberalism, precisely the tradition that many in the academic reform movements have targeted as the source of the problem (Newfield 308). Much damage has been done in the name of truth, progress, and democracy. Yet, implicitly, the claim for the positive value of the crisis of representation is made here in the name of truth, progress, and democracy, despite the fact that these words have been used to exclude many people and groups from representation on campus and in scholarship. This paradox suggests the need for a more self-conscious and sophisticated inquiry into the double bind of Enlightenment rhetoric.

The effort to represent the academy to the public in a more favorable light must inevitably draw on the resources of that rhetoric, but in the process may be in danger of misrepresenting itself. This inevitable comeback of Enlightenment ideals may be less the product of the dominance of a false ideology than a testimony to the lasting effectiveness of these utopian concepts. Moreover, a failure to analyze the relationship between political ideals and historical institutions may lead to a number of mistakes: the bad effects of institutions might be attributed to ideas instead of material arrangements of resources and power, and thus symbolic resolutions offered where concrete changes are needed; or, conversely, institutional shuffling may be proposed where a fundamental deconstruction of conceptual foundations is needed.

While reformers on campus have become expert at exposing the flaws of the traditional concepts of the Enlightenment, they may in the process have thrown the baby out with the bathwater, misrepresenting the difficulties and misuses of these ideas as if they were the essences of these ideas. For example, a great achievement of critical theory over the past three decades has been to emphasize *structure* in the understanding of language, art, society, and politics. This focus on the power of structure clashes with the Enlightenment's philosophy of individualism. There has been a consequent lessening of attention to individuals or singular elements or unique events. Explanations for human behavior now look to impersonal structural forces, such as social systems, psychological formations, artistic conventions, institutional rules, linguistic laws, or economic arrangements. Yet carried to extremes, this structuralism turns into determinism, and so fails to explain the differences between individual people, texts, cultures, or political philosophies. Just as taking someone as an individual can do an injustice to his or her group identity, so seeing someone only in terms of that identity can do an injustice to that individual as a person. The tasks of the future, then, include representing and institutionalizing truth, democracy, justice, and liberty *differently*, and in ways that better accommodate the claims of individual, social, and cultural diversity. I would second Christopher Newfield's proposal that we strengthen our theoretical and practical commitment to egalitarian and participatory democracy both on and off campus, since this is one means by which representational power can be reallocated and knowledge altered.

What has been happening on and off campus since the 1960s is an effort — sputtering, haphazard, sometimes overzealous, always underfinanced, imbued with passion, hobbled by cynicism, inspired by theory, clumsy in practice — to pursue these tasks and redefine them. By focusing on the problem of representation, the connections between academic knowledge and political power, or between intellectual institutions and social privilege, suddenly appear clearer and more understandable. The exclusion of certain groups from representation on campus and in academic work reinforced their banishment to the periphery of political and cultural significance. It denied them access to, and thus control and ownership of, the means of self-representation, whether through the instruments of the culture industry or those of government and business. This denial of the means of self-empowerment to certain groups corresponded to their misrepresentation in the products and institutions of the dominant culture, whose individuals and practices could flourish without any responsibility to the underrepresented.

Thus, what was required on campus (and off) was a new response, as well as a new sense of responsibility, including the ability to respond with something other than tolerance, condescension, or intimidation when groups arose to demand the inclusion of their self-representation in the workings of the culture as a whole. One result of this demand was the development of controversial and not always perfect remedies of representation. These new practices were designed specifically to address inequities in the access to and control of representation and to correct injustices or falsehoods in the content of representation. Such remedies included area studies programs for women and minority groups, affirmative action in admissions and hiring, regulations regarding oppressive behavior and speech, challenges to the canon, protests against the influence of military contracting on university research, restructuring of tenure and promotion procedures, refusals to host discriminatory employers such as ROTC, and provisions for representing students, staff, and faculty in substantive ways in the governance of campus affairs. As Newfield notes, though, the "liberal managerial democracy" which administers most campuses sometimes demands conformity as the price of inclusion: admission to the "common culture" may come at the cost of abandoning those differences of perspective, value, or interest that threaten the status quo.

The success, often paltry or evanescent, of the remedies I have mentioned helped occasion the struggle over representation known as the political correctness debate. In that quarrel, as Ellen Messer-Davidow argues in "Manufacturing the Attack on Liberalized Higher Education," academics often missed the point, allowing the issue of accurate or inaccurate representation to obscure equally important issues, such as the practical matter of who represented what to whom, at what cost, to whose benefit, and through what network of overlapping institutions, technologies, think tanks, government agencies, and academic conventions. If Marx taught us that political analysis must consider the ownership of the means of production, late communism and late capitalism both teach us that contemporary social power is largely regulated through the material as well as the ideological control of the means of representation. The crisis of representation brought on by the PC dispute stemmed in part from the exploitation or seizure of the public representational apparatus — such as the media, think tanks, and government agencies — by the forces of reaction, even as academics (to their credit) were busy refashioning the local structures of representation on campus. In other words, real changes in the access to and control of the representational apparatus on campus brought on a fierce assault by those off-campus who saw their interests threatened.

As Messer-Davidow tells the story in her essay "The Right Moves," the right responded to reform on campus by carefully constructing an alternate set of representative institutions (the Moral Majority, the Christian Coalition, the Heritage Foundation, the American Enterprise Institute, the Olin Foundation, and so on) which eventually enabled the conservative takeover of major government and private positions during the Reagan-Bush era. This new institutional network then served as a springboard for placing its own representatives on campus in the form of the National Association of

Scholars, a group launched and paid for by operatives of the Republican Party and the groups just named (see Diamond). Even after Clinton's election, NAS officials commanded front-of-the-line privileges to attend the confirmation hearings of NEH chairman Sheldon Hackney and apparently provided Republican senators with much of the script for their questioning. Trained by well-financed experts in the fields of public opinion and media, the messengers of the right soon saw their stories reprinted in most of the major magazines and newspapers and occupying prominent places on the best-seller list. What Michael Bérubé, in his justly famous account, called "the media's big lie" was in fact a product manufactured by new sectors of the right-wing knowledge industry.

The right's triumph in the arena of public representation was in high contrast to the poor public relations skills of academics. Expert at media such as the sophomore lecture, the graduate seminar, the job interview, the grant application, the critical article, the devastating footnote, the self-righteous polemic, the deceptive memo, the dazzling theoretical digression, or the arcane treatise, many scholars found themselves incompetent when pulled into the arenas of the op-ed page, the *Times* best-seller, the PBS *News Hour*, or the sound bite worlds of NBC and *Newsweek*. More fundamentally, most critics and scholars have little or no access to these venues, having long ago abandoned (or been abandoned by) the "public sphere." Academic regulations that ignore or even penalize publication in such venues when it comes time to decide tenure or merit raises do not help the situation either. The academic crisis of representation in the public sphere stemmed from a lack of training and experience, a predictable result of elitism and specialization, and the factory speed-up that has left most academics with little or no time for anything outside of already exploding professional obligations. Like Chaplin on the assembly line in *Modern Times*, none of us can hope to keep up. In this respect, academics are coming more to resemble every other category of postindustrial worker.

In brief, the types of expression at which professors have become expert do not serve them well when they enter the domains of modern public representation. Indeed, most professors produce representational products for which there is little audience. We in the academy rarely produce artifacts such as the television program, the interview, the trade-press book, the opinion piece, or the journalistic review, for which there is some substantial market. Indeed, we have to translate our knowledge and skills when we do enter into these public practices, an act of translation for which we are not trained, for which we are not rewarded, and which may endanger our careers. To learn these practices effectively also means engaging in other, often mundane but powerful technologies of representation: writing press releases, getting on the Rolodex, giving interviews, assembling databases and mailing lists, lobbying legislators, networking private and public officials, writing for magazines, or sending out letters to the editor.

Translation, however, also means transformation. Making the effort to bring academic work into a larger public sphere will require rethinking the terms, scope, and audience of that work. The tradition of academic contempt for mainstream culture and popular venues does not help the academic cause. More important, the larger, more diverse audiences of the public media do not share many of the intellectual premises taken for granted on campus. Writing for these audiences could have a healthy effect on academic rhetoric, moving it away from the self-righteous polemic that often infuses political discourse in the United States. I myself believe that some of the assault on "political correctness" hits a real target when it uncovers instances of arrogant dogmatism, unethical propagandizing, and the unthinking repetition of stale concepts and clichés. The left does not have a patent on these errors, but neither is it immune to them. No one benefits if professors allow misrepresentations of their work to become an excuse for abandoning the responsibility to be self-critical.

But what can be accomplished by joining a "public sphere" that does not include much of the public, that has not itself been reformed, that is part of the struggle for representation rather than a neutral space for reporting on it? Many people, and not just academics, have consciously chosen to repudiate the public sphere, especially as the claims to authority, diversity, democracy, and truth made by agents of that sphere are often at odds with the facts. Accounts still regularly appear documenting the lack of racial, gender, and ethnic diversity on the editorial boards, in the newsrooms, among owners and publishers, and of course on the TV screen. Although Jürgen Habermas's work has done much to rehabilitate the notion of the public sphere and the importance of community, his failure to consider adequately how the operations of the public sphere exclude unwanted voices cautions us against too readily returning to traditional models of public representation (see Mitchell 12). On the contrary, the lessons of everyday life as well as of academic theory point toward the need to think of the public sphere not in terms of the Greek agora or some idealized space of conceptual dialogue, but rather as a material network of representational technologies (a suggestion made all the more realistic now that the Internet is upon us). Questions should always be asked about ownership of and access to the network, about its economic and ideological costs, about how the devices of the network shape and alter the messages it sends, about who the constituents of the network are, about the contradictions between different agencies of the network, about unequal training in the means of using or receiving the productions of the network. This debate has gained renewed prominence with the growth of the "information superhighway" and the World Wide Web, which threaten (again) to divide us along class lines, along divisions between the technological haves and have-nots.

Most of the "public sphere" in the United States is privately owned. One of the largest exceptions to this rule is the network of state-funded institutions of education, including colleges and universities. It is no surprise that the PC debate came as the culmination to a sustained effort to defund the state institutions of education and to privatize them wherever possible. The destruction of the public sphere was a principal goal of the New Right under Reagan and Bush, who regularly appointed government officials to agencies whose missions they emphatically rejected and which they undermined at every turn. (William Bennett and Lynne Cheney, both former chairmen of the NEH, led a high-profile but unsuccessful campaign to abolish the agency after the 1994 Republican congressional victories seemed to promise a final solution for the culture wars.) In order to bring the representational apparatus of the educational system under tighter ideological control, privatization proponents work to discredit the public image of schools, colleges, and universities. Their campaigns aim to stall efforts to maintain or increase education funding by state legislatures and municipalities already bankrupted by having to pay for programs that the Republican administrations refused to fund (and that, because of the budget deficit they created at the federal level, even Democrats will be hard-pressed to address). Representing the systems of education as recurrent failures, the agents of privatization work to make these institutions increasingly dependent on private moneys, whether through a voucher system at the elementary and secondary level or through the use of grant and foundation money at the research university. When offered millions by the Olin Foundation to support a program in the capitalist groundings of American law, few of the nation's most prestigious institutions said no, strapped as they were by budget reductions and spiraling costs. The necessity of making ends meet leaves schools and colleges vulnerable to the ideological pressures of private donors. Although the public sphere of the past had its problems, a restructured, democratized, and revitalized public sphere could be a vital defense against the subordination of the public good to unregulated private interests.

The issue of what serves the public good brings us back once again to campus debates over curriculum, programs, admissions, and speech codes. Identity politics involves the assertion by specific groups that former prescriptions of the public good have been bad for them. From various authorities, past and present, we have heard that integration was no good, homosexuality was no good, working women were no good, popular culture was no good, the eight-hour day was no good, the vote for women was no good, too many Jews in prominent places was no good, too many of the wrong kinds of immigrants was no good . . . The list goes on. A democratic theory of education, argues Amy Gutmann, proceeds not so much by taking sides as by educating citizens in how to conduct arguments in a setting where persuasion, rather than force or dogma, is in principle (if not always in fact) the rule. The citizen's ability to represent his or her interests can be enhanced by education, which may be said to have a duty to help citizens obtain and exercise the authority for decision making that democracy places in their hands. "As long as we differ not just in our opinions," she writes, "but in our moral convictions about the good life, the state's educational role cannot be defined as realizing *the* good life, objectively defined, for each of its citizens" (28). Yet, there are categorical imperatives of nonrepression, nondiscrimination, equal opportunity, access to representation, toleration, nonviolence, which are essential virtues in a democratic state. These virtues can and should be goals of the educational system. Colleges and universities in particular can educate citizens in "the moral demands of democratic life. While not a substitute for character training, learning how to think carefully and critically about political problems, to articulate one's views and defend them before people with whom one disagrees" is a vital and proper purpose of higher education and is central to its mission in a democratic society (Gutmann 173).

The widespread contempt for politics in America today stems partly from the observation that past definitions of the public good have frequently been the hypocritical mask for a naked exercise of power on behalf of the interests of some privileged group. This degenerate definition of politics as pure will-to-power informs most reports that condemn the "politicization of education," for these reports implicitly assume that politics is by nature a bad thing. It is not. Politics is a name for all the ways by which people make decisions about their lives within a community, including decisions about education. Only those who wish to dominate that community benefit when others give up on politics. If we understand politics as the vital process by which a society debates and pursues the good, then we will be more comfortable with the inherent role that politics has in education. Efforts to rid education of politics rest on corrupt notions of politics and impoverished visions of education.

When critics say that education has become too politicized, then, this may be an indication that important debates over crucial human issues are once more finding their proper place on campus (see the excellent chapter "When Is Something 'Political'?" in Graff, *Beyond the Culture Wars*, and his "Teach the Conflicts"). The towers of academe need to be regularly shaken by genuine controversy, not strangled by the vines of utilitarianism and ideology. What more proper place to contest ideas of morality, justice, selfhood, community, truth, and the public good than the college campus? If issues of race and gender and class divide society, then should not these be given a full airing and exploration in the curriculum? The production of a false consensus, whether through the repression of discourse or the imposition of an ideology, is bad education and bad politics. There will be times when real differences collide; these collisions should be part of the processes of education and politics, not excuses for ending the discussion or imposing one side's view of the truth. In a democracy, education will include lessons in the intellectual, social, moral, and political dimensions of living with people whose beliefs differ sharply from one's own. What happens when one person or group asserts its vision of the good, only to find that another person or group sees that very thing as the embodiment of evil? The modest increase in the access to representation of women and minorities produced strong challenges to past definitions of the public good. In fact, it challenged the very definitions of the "public" and of the "good." These challenges continue the tradition of democratic politics, which rejects a fixed definition of the good and commits itself to an endless process of public argument about the best ways to understand and realize the changing values of society. Moreover, these challenges include a healthy insistence on historical knowledge, on testing the rhetoric of a society against the record of its practices. In such testing, political ideas cease to be timeless commemorative fixtures and become rather the ideals whose checkered history can provide a lesson for the future.

Calls for open debate and a free exchange of views, however, can be naive and potentially oppressive if they fail to address the unequal starting points and positions of the antagonists. What good does it do to stage a debate if only one side gets a place on the platform or if others show up hobbled by material deprivation and social intimidation? Taking steps to alter the balance of power and resources among potential agents of representation will help offset the legacy of past discriminatory practices. One way to achieve this end is by making curricular and institutional investments in the representation of the marginalized. These may include separate courses and majors as well as area study programs in African American, American Indian, gay and lesbian, and other fields of investigation.[5] These investments can

---

5. I am aware of the ongoing debate over the terms "American Indian" and "Native American" among people in the communities to which these terms are meant to refer. Exchanges on the Native American Literature Internet discussion group in 1994, for example, revealed strong arguments for and against both terms. I use both in the course of this book, with some preference for "American Indian." Although it might be more accurate to

help produce the knowledge that enables us to adjudicate the disputes we are now having. How, for example, can we judge the value of a long-overlooked literary work or distant civilization if it has never received the kind of sustained academic scrutiny and interpretive thoughtfulness accorded to Shakespeare or Periclean Greece? How can mainstream departments be trusted to represent the previously excluded when that exclusion is often essential to the very construction of their discipline and its objects of study? Teaching the conflicts is fundamental, but we should also take steps to address the starkly unequal power and resources of the conflicting parties.

• • •

The struggle on campus over the quality, character, and distribution of representation participates, I have argued, in larger national and global changes (for more on this dimension, see Chapter 2). Across the country and around the world, the insurgent demands of specific groups for greater power to represent themselves have upset the unity of established states. The tide of nationalism breaking in the wake of European, Soviet, and American colonialism has refigured the map, leading us to question what states represent what

refer only to tribal names, this leaves us without a term for the shared cultural features and historical experiences of indigenous peoples. "Native American," with its parallelism to "African American" and "Asian American," works well to designate the hybrid character of writing by, for example, Navajo or Ojibway authors who use English and borrow from the forms of its literary genres to write about the contacts between whites and indigeneous people. But "American Indian" probably does the work just as well, and without the unwanted connotations of "native." My informants tell me that "Indian" is the preferred term within and between members of actual tribal communities today, very few of whom use "Native American" except when talking to whites. "Indian" better recalls the historical experience of the tribes and more strongly suggests the non-American culture and history of the indigenous (even if its use perhaps requires a certain ironic appropriation of Columbus's misnomer). "African American" and "black" present related though perhaps less presently contentious problems. In using "African American," I want to suggest that we consider "American" in the larger context of the Americas, thus referring to the African diaspora in South as well as North America and the Caribbean. So goes the struggle for representation.

peoples or what peoples wish to be represented by what states. The very assumption that the nation is coterminous and identical with a "people" is both the foundation and the folly of resurgent nationalism, which, like identity politics in the United States, inevitably produces more, rather than less, difference when it tries to represent itself as having a singular and homogeneous identity. The same paradox will affect area studies programs and departments, as efforts to found a curriculum or syllabus on the identities of nations, peoples, races, or other categories (what *do* they teach in an "English" department?) lead us to see the diversity within these groups. But this is an argument for, not against, such programs, since only by working through and rigorously debating the basic facts and theories of a discipline can past stereotypes be laid to rest and new affiliations be formed.

In the political arena the struggle for representation has many dimensions. American citizens from every group voice a sense that they are not represented by their government, though many of these voices (especially the white ones) are monotonously represented on the nightly news (to no apparent effect, it seems, except perhaps to commodify their disenfranchisement or further the quixotic will-to-power of a Ross Perot). Americans live in a putatively representational democracy wherein who, or what, gets represented in government appears more and more determined by wealth, institutional power, and structures of access — all of which narrow the number of operative agents to a tiny few compared to the population as a whole. The decline of political parties, once one of the only effective (if often corrupt) means by which poor and working-class citizens could participate and get representation in the political process, has left average citizens baffled by the prospect of effectively exercising their representational agency.

The proliferation of political action committees, think tanks, foundations, and various national and grassroots organizations signals both the vacuum left by the crisis of political representation and the confusion that ensues as alternative structures of representation vie for influence and power. Recent elections show that turning the TV dial is at least as important as punching the ballot card in today's democracy, as political parties are more marginalized than ever by the ability of mass media to determine and represent people's interests.

Social movement groups display increasingly effective skills at using the media, and in many elections these groups now run their own ad campaigns or ballot initiatives to push their agendas. The disuniting of America may be most accurately measured here, perhaps, since this competition of groups in the marketplace of voters bypasses the requirement for alliance once imposed by political parties. (This may not be too different from the splintering of the ivory tower by the interest group politics of departments and specializations.) When groups must work together for a party or larger cause, they are motivated to find common ground and make compromises. When groups compete in the media, they are motivated to express their interests in stark, hyperbolic terms that demonize other points of view. The interest group working alone tends to represent only itself, although this often takes the form of misrepresenting others. "Negative campaigning" in this light looks much like identity politics.

Whether we analyze the problem of representation in the public sphere or in the sphere of education, we find a similar failure: groups appear less and less willing to engage one another in real dialogue because they do not see themselves as belonging to a greater whole. So much energy has been spent dismantling former ideals of unity and community — exposing their flaws, treacheries, and injustices — that we are left with little time or passion for imagining positive alternatives that could connect us. Even as we acknowledge the need to address the injustices of past misrepresentations, we also need new practices of representation that will portray horizons of consensus. These practices will have to aim toward methods of representation — in politics, the arts, the humanities, and science — that include the fullest possible range of human experience, regardless of previous prejudices about what constitutes the facts and who has the right to determine the truth.

If the current tendency is toward social formations of disarray, the future needs to include more efforts toward building alliances out of the knowledge and empathy that real dialogue makes possible. This dialogue does not have to begin by silencing some voices so that all may hear some predetermined or traditional tune of universal humanity. As I argue throughout this book, the way toward greater connection is through our differences, by engaging and not evading them. Engaging our differences means becoming responsible for them, knowing their history and realizing their effects. Such engagement is quite distinct from simply celebrating or demonizing our differences, since that too often becomes a way of ignoring the validity of other people's experiences. A new democratic ethic of representation still includes separate efforts to address real historical and material inequities. These efforts are prerequisite to establishing a "common ground"; but without an effort to form coalitions across our differences, those separate efforts are not likely to be funded or to make much headway. A democratic approach to representation would take into account the different contingent relationships of specific social groups and individuals to the network of representation. The denial of representation in the case of women, people of color, gays and lesbians, or the poor requires local and variable remedies, some of which will be in conflict.

Having already dwelled on its limitations, I am obviously not calling for an across-the-board application of identity politics to the struggle for representation. But I am suggesting that a variety of affirmative actions can address past inequities by redistributing access to and control over representation. The kind of "worldliness" Said advocates will require the kind of sensitivity to diverse representations that Marshall advocates. Let me add that the attempt to democratize and redistribute representation does not involve asserting that only the marginalized speak the, or even their, truth. Rather, the important thing in democratic discourse is that the interested parties be brought together to negotiate their differences face to face. The inclusion of the Other in the room decisively changes the dynamic, the ethic, and the direction of discussion. The inclusion of a black woman on the Senate Judiciary Committee might have altered the way Anita Hill was treated and how Clarence Thomas responded (see Lubiano). The inclusion of minority students in the classroom changes what the professor and the other students feel free to think and say, and that is more often to the good than to the bad in a society plagued by bigotry. The inclusion on the syllabus of Harriet Jacobs next to Henry Thoreau, or of William Apess alongside James Fenimore Cooper, or of Anzia Yezierska with F. Scott Fitzgerald changes the context in which we interpret each writer and the ways that we understand them. The subaltern cannot speak if she is never let into the room.

From the Judiciary Committee to the Curriculum Committee, the appearance of the Other disturbs dominant institutions and practices of representation. But human subjects occupy more than one social or cultural or even ethno-racial position, and so they have many kinds of Otherness *inside them*. Categorical oppositions, you-versus-me or us-versus-them, do not account for the Otherness within. That Otherness, too, that internal diversity of the human subject, calls for representation, a job done particularly well by literature and the humanities. Taking account of that internal diversity can be understood as an ethical as well as a political imperative, for it could help mitigate some of the violence perpetrated in the name of identity politics, whether on behalf of the privileged group or the outsiders. We need to recognize the Otherness within ourselves as much as the Otherness that may separate us from different people. This shared sense of Otherness might then become a way of making our schools as well as our politics responsible to a wide set of subjectivities. Rather than going "beyond multiculturalism" (have we even gotten there yet?), this ability to respond to Others offers the way toward a meaningful diversity instead of into one more masquerade of consensus.

Art, literature, historical inquiry, philosophy, and cultural theory all help further this process of becoming accountable to Otherness, susceptible to the differences within and between ourselves. They give accounts of this experience and help us practice handling its effects. These speculative dialogues and aesthetic experiences, however, should accompany, not replace, the necessary job of analyzing the differences that material and institutional arrangements have on social opportunity and cultural representation. Aesthetic study does not preclude interpreting the political economy of culture (or vice versa). In theory and in practice we could pursue a different accountability of representation, beginning with our accountability to history and one another. All who work within the representational apparatuses (from the boardroom to the newsroom to the schoolroom) need to come to terms with this accountability, for it is essential to the democratic and ethical ideals that make justice workable.

In this practice of accountability, I think, lies one way of bringing together the separatism of Marshall and the worldliness of Said which I discussed at the outset of this chapter. In terms of pedagogy, the attacks on separatist courses and programs (such as the much-maligned Afrocentrism) have distorted the picture, since the vast majority of innovative offerings tend more toward the side of world-liness, putting traditions and canons and cultures into comparative dialogue with one another. A commitment to representing specific cultural groups in the curriculum is not a commitment to a mindless celebration of its history or values. Often the point of such affirmative action is simply to get people or ideas or cultural objects together across the divide that separates them, moving them together into the room, onto the syllabus, into a public space of conversation, comparison, and accountability. While each seeks the skill and power to represent its own interests, each must also render its representations accountable to the others. Each should consider how the production of its own self-representation affects others, sometimes to the point of distorting or destroying the others' power to represent their own different interests. This self-examination about how we represent things cannot be limited to questioning the effects of oppressive words or practices. It should also consider the effects of too quickly jumping to accusations of racism, sexism, homophobia, harassment, or some other judgment that puts all the responsibility on the shoulders of someone else, turning difficult political and personal issues into simplistic moral dramas of good and evil. Institutionalizing our crises of representation as a permanent feature of pedagogy or political life may not seem at first an ideal solution, but in the long run it may be a very useful device for addressing the public good.

While reformers assert that today's institutions of higher education remain dominated by traditional groups and ideologies that perpetuate misrepresentation, critics of academe claim that standards of excellence have been lowered by a misguided politicization of the campus. Given that there are some four thousand institutions of higher education in the United States, it is difficult to issue a summary judgment of victory or defeat in the culture wars. Pick your issue (the canon, admissions, versions of history, women in science); the results are mixed and depend on which institution you examine. My own experience as an English professor on a variety of campuses leads me to the conclusion that although significant improvements have been made, the degree of change in the ivory tower has been overestimated by its enemies and underestimated by its proponents. Changes appear more extensive in my own discipline (American literature and culture) than in many others. That said, women, people of color, and gays and lesbians have achieved more respect and prominence in many institutions of higher education than in Congress, the military, the churches, the major corporations, or most unions. Colleges and universities today serve a much more representative spectrum of the American public than they did a generation ago (though economic constraints on access put this inclusiveness in jeopardy). Similarly, feminism, critical theory, multiculturalism, deconstruction, and numerous innovations in the humanities and social sciences have become established though not wholly accepted practices. In the face of continued resistance, they have devised powerful means for changing the representation of social reality and thus for affecting the organization, interpretation, and governance of everyday life. Most important, perhaps, the quality of what is taught in the classroom has improved enormously. Students today regularly study artistically accomplished and historically significant literary works that were unknown and out of print a decade ago, and they emerge from courses in history, philosophy, and art with a much broader knowledge of events and works in those areas than did their peers twenty years earlier.[6] From the evidence, I can only conclude that it is precisely because higher education has done so much (though not enough) to redistribute access to representation that colleges and universities have come under such vitriolic attack. Judged by an absolute standard, these successes may seem paltry. But in the actual world of everyday struggle, they deserve our affirmation and support.

6. Lawrence Levine similarly claims to be "convinced by everything I know and have seen [that] the American academic world is doing a more thorough and cosmopolitan job of educating a greater diversity of students in a broader and sounder array of courses covering the past and present of the worlds they inhabit than ever before in its history. . . . The major consequence of the new heterogeneity on campuses . . . has not been repression but the very opposite — a flowering of ideas and scholarly innovation unmatched in our history" (17, 21). Levine provides a devastating review of the history of higher education in America to rebut recent charges that things are going downhill, when in fact improvement is visible across the map.

t w o **Not Born on the Fourth of July**

round the nation and across the globe, one question surfaces repeatedly: Is the elemental unit of political theory and culture to be the individual or the group? A series of corollary questions follows: How do we respond to the fact that the creation of any national identity always involves the exclusion of certain citizens, whether through the subtle omission of their beliefs from dominant institutions or through the violence of outright genocide? Is democratic freedom possible if the individual is treated according to how society values the group to which it assigns that individual? Can a person resist such discrimination individually, or only through changing the way the group is represented? To turn from questions of theory to conditions of history: Can the nation-state be a viable political or cultural entity now that the technology of industrial production, transportation, and communication makes global mobility so pervasive? Can the power of multinational corporations be resisted without strong nation-states predicated on affirmation of common cultural values and social goals? Are categories such as race or ethnicity any longer viable as fundamental components of cultural identity now that the natural and humanistic sciences have discredited them and people increasingly marry and reproduce across such lines? Or have our crises been precisely the product of wrongly thinking that we could transcend such categories in appeals to universal principles (whether those of Marxism or Western humanism)?

In Chapter 1 my approach to some of these questions focused on the competing claims of the particular or separate, on the one hand, and the universal or ideal, on the other. In the struggle for representation, a certain irony appears in the fact that any attempt to represent the particular leads to something general or universalizing: in giving a name to the European American or African American or Asian American experience, we recover a particular knowledge only at the cost of generalizing contradictory details into a reductive unity. Similarly, rejections of the universalizing or idealizing rhetoric of liberal Western humanism are often made not only in the name of the particularly marginalized but also in the name of general values: truth, justice, fairness, freedom, equality. In the present chapter I continue this line of inquiry in two ways. First, I explore further the relation of the United States' particular problems with culture and identity to events occurring internationally, thus seeing events on our college campuses as part of a larger story. In trying to frame the current cultural discord in this country, then, I think it useful to remember that the struggles for representation here are not unique. Yet they do have a very specific and unusual history which ought to be revisited if we are to avoid treating the present crisis as a kind of biblical Fall from a previous Eden of communal harmony. So, in the second part of this chapter I turn again from this global perspective to the local history of Enlightenment idealism in the rhetoric of American culture. My examples are the uses of the Declaration of Independence by labor activists, black abolitionist writers, and white women's rights activists in the antebellum era, with a final look at the revival of this rhetoric by Ralph Ellison and Martin Luther King, Jr.

I offer this journey back because I believe that the divisions in American culture today can best be understood historically, and understood first of all as a symptom of the nation's recurrent historical amnesia. As a nation we do not like to remember the past. Freedom from the past, after all, has been our national myth, and that innocence has often been a key to our achievements. We tell ourselves that we received our unique identity in a moment of revolutionary forgetting, when we declared ourselves independent of the Old World. We think a new world can be made because we have shed the old one and renamed ourselves. At some time or other every American has been Jay Gatsby. Unfortunately, we have gone on fabricating stories about ourselves through repeated acts of amnesia, forgetting our own divisive history in the process of creating our common future. How else could a nation descended from immigrants, expropriated peoples, and imported slaves wake up one morning to a debate over the meaning of multiculturalism?

The Enlightenment rhetoric of universality employed in the Declaration and in the Constitution portrays a relatively harmonious society ("We the People"), but that peace obscures the interdependence of rights and powers. The resistance of men and slave owners to the women's rights and abolitionist reformers, like the resistance in the United States today to affirmative action, Indian treaty rights, or gays and lesbians in the military, stems from a realistic understanding that the application of universal principles results in particular change. Since the original postulation of an abstract universal human subject (that "We" of the Founding Fathers) had actually been predicated on an unequal distribution of social power among particular cultural groups, the response of those left out must necessarily be double-edged: on the one hand, they must claim membership in the very universal category of humanity from which they have been excluded, and entitlement to the rights that go with it; on the other hand, they must insist on affirming the value of the particular group to which they feel tied and whose fate has largely determined their destiny as individuals. Somewhat paradoxically, we understand universal rights by recognizing the historical, concrete, and contingent lives led by individuals in real social classes. The contradictions inherent in classic liberal political theory, then, still inform today's struggles for representation, shaping the debate between the advocates of identity politics and their opponents (whether liberal humanists upholding Enlightenment individualism or poststructuralists opposed to essentialism).

In the heat of these disputes, it is vital to remember that no group can be formed without postulating some quality, experience, or factor *universal* to members of the group; likewise, any universality that does not have a basis in, and a respect for, the particular qualities and experiences of human lives as actually lived is worthless and may well be an unintended ally when dominant groups force their will on a society. Ultimately, cultural identity is not something inherent to an individual but a meaning that persons attach to themselves or others as a result of social determinations and subjective choices. Cultural identity, in sum, is an ethos, a way of life. It follows that an ethics of social change requires altering the systematic, material, and impersonal forces that condition and account for the lives of individuals. At the same time, it also requires respecting the freedom of individuals to determine the character of their lives and to create meaningful accounts of them. This general ethos of accountability, in turn, has particular relevance when we consider how to teach American literature and toward what ends (as I hope to show in Chapter 3). In literature, ethos appears in the accounts or stories we give of our lives, whether in the role of writer telling the tale or of reader making the story his or her own. Empathy, identification, or "feeling what it would be like to be in someone else's shoes" is a classic ethic of accountability in the literary experience. The rich contribution of multiculturalism has been to expand vastly the borders of this storytelling and this accountability, and so to provide stronger foundations for us as ethical subjects as well as citizens. In the particulars of the texts we find the differences out of which justifiable universals can be made, universals that are responsible to more than one small group of people or narrow set of experiences.

• • •

The scenario has become familiar. After a long history of apparent uniformity and consensus, a nation suddenly collapses. Political institutions and ideologies that had once been its supposed foundations are blown down like a house of cards. Beneath the appearance of a monolithic history and singular future there abruptly bursts forth the reality of irreconcilable differences. Citizens increasingly see themselves primarily as members of particular regional, racial, ethnic, religious, economic, or sexual groups rather than as individuals with a common society, culture, or system of beliefs. A shrinking economic pie and a ferocious struggle for limited resources polarizes citizens into competing interest groups. Where once the identification of the individual person with the universal national spirit was seen as an equalizing force that promised the eventual participation of all in directing the country's fate, this universalism is now roundly condemned as a ruse that obscures the subordination of disempowered groups exploited by an entrenched elite. The political culture descends into exchanges of condemnation, recrimination, and even gunfire; the fracturing of any sense of commonality leads to an appalling cynicism and lack of compassion. Argument centers on proving who has been the most victimized and who the most reprehensible. The classic question of politics — What is the common good? — is replaced by the question: What's in it for me and my friends?

Readers will recognize that this scenario, with many qualifications, fits the recent history of the United States, but they will also see here the stories of the Soviet Union, Yugoslavia, and a host of other nations as the twentieth century gives way to a postcolonial (PC), postmodern, multicultural future.[1] Since global patterns link the cultural crises around the world, the forces causing dissensus in the United States ought partly to be interpreted from an international perspective. The struggle for representation knows no borders. Many nations are trying to find a way to balance the claims of individuality, ethnic or racial solidarity, democracy, economic development, women's liberation, and nationalism. The principles of self-determination and freedom abstractly embodied in theories of democracy clash with the desires of particular groups to create social systems predicated on their own traditional beliefs. The globalization of the labor force and the mobility of international capitalism create economic competition that often exploits the resources of patriotic nationalism and of ethno-racial, religious, and gender bigotry.

1. For an overview, see Hollinger, *Postethnic America: Beyond Multiculturalism.*

Those resources may also be mined by popular culture when it offers fables that symbolically address contemporary political or cultural issues. Films such as the 1996 blockbuster *Independence Day*, for example, marketed for months before its premiere over the July Fourth holiday, continue to play to the American anxiety about national catastrophe and "aliens," even as the good-guy forces assembled to combat the new "them" now reflect the commodified image of multiculturalism. The film's intention to celebrate an alliance of blacks and Jews with whites in a common cause exists uneasily alongside trite but vicious ethnic and sexual stereotypes (most egregiously in the case of the Jewish homosexual who dies while calling out for mama). Like other post-Vietnam films, *Independence Day* puts at its story's center the remasculization and reempowerment of the white male as hero (see Jeffords). Near the climax of the film, as the formerly emasculated American president prepares to lead a global bombing mission against aliens from outer space, he delivers a stirring oration that curiously combines universal humanism with American imperialism: "Mankind. The word has new meaning for all of us now. We are reminded not of our petty differences but of our common interests. Perhaps it's fate that today is the Fourth of July, and we will once again be fighting for our freedom. . . . From this day on, the Fourth of July will no longer be remembered as an American holiday, but as the day that the world declared in one voice that we will not go quietly into the night. . . . Today, we celebrate our Independence Day" (148).

With the Americans in the lead, the whole earth prepares to be reborn on the Fourth of July. It is as if scapegoating the extraterrestrials will vanquish the legacy of imperialism on earth and make the Third World grateful once more for the superior power of the West. The American president carries the symbolic name of "Whitmore": meaning more wit, more savvy and intelligence, and more white. Like Walt Whitman, Whitmore is a figure who thinks he can represent everyone. Any doubt about the racism of the film is resolved when, to illustrate victory, the camera pans an African savannah where traditionally dressed tribesmen wave spears in jubilation at the sight of the downed alien craft. The actuality of the postcolonial condition, much of which is to be found in the quite modern cities of the Third World, goes unrepresented, or is erased by a visual narrative that returns the happy primitives to their place in the world. Globalization takes the form of the extension of Western greatness rather than a process of collaboration between equal partners.

In real life postcolonialism often leaves former dependent states in splintered ruins, while the once imperial powers themselves suffer internal breakdowns complicated by an influx of postcolonial refugees (as, for example, in Great Britain and France). At the level of political ideology, any recourse to the rhetoric or policies of universalism, humanism, and common culture is often denounced from the start, a victim of its own record of hypocrisy and bad faith. Yet the economic interdependence of the globe's regions continues to increase, defying the tide of tribalism as multinational corporations transgress political borders. Likewise, the technology of communication, from the PC (personal computer) and fax machine to the "information highway" of the World Wide Web, does not respect the lines drawn by factions on a map. The exchange of images and consumer goods bridges peoples to create commonalities in the practices of their everyday lives. *Independence Day* now has its own "international" Web site. My PC can connect me to the world, though of course my ownership of one says something particular about my privileged place in the universe.

Back in the United States, what so many insurgent groups have in common — from African American and Native Americans to women, the working class, recent Asian immigrants, and gays and lesbians — is their insistence that we all have an ethical and political responsibility to remember our history differently. That is why the debates over political correctness (PC) and educational curricula are so important and so symptomatic. The history of oppression in America is tied to the oppressive way history has been represented and taught, in the mass media and popular culture as well as in the schools. Revisionists, moreover, go beyond debating ideas to focus attention on the material institutions that produce cultural identities, and so the agitation of political activists has surprisingly joined forces with the skepticism of poststructuralist academics eager to deconstruct the ideologies of Representational Man.

Surprisingly, the result has often been classroom experiences in which a recognition of differences creates more, rather than less, common ground. Students work past outmoded myths and stereotypes to discover realities which are truer, if less comforting, and these may form a better workshop for citizenship than anodyne offerings that blandly and uncritically celebrate the American dream. A Latina activist in one of my classes experienced something of an epiphany reading the literature of Jewish immigration: in it she found stories of borders, of menial labor, of struggles to maintain cultural traditions — in short, concerns that echoed those she brought to her reading, but that differed from them in many specific ways. She connected the Latino and Jewish stories without reducing them to a single narrative, keeping their differences in mind even as she saw a solidarity (rather than a sameness) between them. Some of her sense of being uniquely victimized, she said, began to wane in this empathetic perception of another's plight, though her outrage at injustice also found another target. Part of her anger (and this is all too typical in the classroom today) was directed at her own past education, which had included so little about the Jewish and Chinese and Chicano histories she now so avidly absorbed. In such moments we can glimpse the future of a "common culture."

If politics is in some degree essentially about the distribution of power, and if knowledge about the powerless tends to be biased or simply left out, then redressing the imbalance will be seen by some as a "political" rather than an "academic" matter. But teachers cannot help the fact that they inherit schools, textbooks, and ideas that reflect the biases of the past. Surely it is the responsibility of teachers to correct those biases as best they can. These educational biases are in part caused by the way political power has been distributed in the United States. Through discriminatory application of categories such as race, ethnicity, class, sexual orientation, and gender, people whose perceived identity did not conform to the politically correct line in the past have been excluded from power. This political motive behind traditional educational biases means that those who seek to tell the story differently will inevitably be accused of "politicizing" the curriculum when in fact they are simply trying to point out the effect that politics has already had on what we study and what we value.

We should not have been surprised, then, when the exaggerated story of political correctness gained such rapid and powerful ascendancy in the public sphere. The same biases that dominated higher education also shaped the personnel and policies of broadcasters, magazines, think tanks, and government officials. Even Marxists and other left intellectuals joined the ranks criticizing feminists, multiculturalists, and literary theorists, for these newer academic movements challenged the cultural politics of the Old Left as well. Thus, from all sides we heard about how an alien conspiracy of tenured radicals, leftover 1960s activists, feminists, and minority scholars has succeeded in taking over U.S. colleges, imposing upon them a uniform ideological program of lowbrow totalitarianism that rejects Western civilization in favor of Afrocentrism, deconstructive nihilism, Hollywood films, Harlequin romances, and MTV. We are routinely told that the agents of political correctness have brought politics into the ivory tower, indoctrinating their students and tolerating no opinions that do not match their own. This ludicrous exaggeration of the power of groups that are still very much on the margins reflects the degree of fear on the part of the establishment that these groups and their concerns may actually now be winning some influence.

Such attempts to blame progressive intellectuals for imposing a standard of political correctness on our campuses perversely misrepresent the truth of history, which is that educational institutions have always been partly in the service of dominant social and political institutions. After all, most colleges are owned and run by churches, corporate boards, or local and state governments. Where were today's born-again champions of democracy, freedom of thought, and evaluation by merit during all the years when women were denied admission to many of the nation's top colleges and universities? Where were they during all the years when Jews, blacks, and others were similarly discriminated against? Why were the *Atlantic*, *Time*, *Newsweek*, the *New York Times*, and the rest of the media relatively silent during the decades when curriculum and teaching practices amounted to a "thought police" on behalf of white Anglo-Saxon males? Who cried out *then* about "political correctness" on campus?

Although I do not mean to suggest that literary study should become a branch of political science, we ought not complacently imagine that culture and politics have no ties that bind. Contrary to some accusations, it was not the irrelevance of work done by activist academics and critical theorists that precipitated the crisis at the universities. Rather, it was the increasingly irrelevant character of higher education that prompted the move toward multiculturalism. The virulent campaign of the anti-PC crowd testifies to exactly how relevant the reforms are, how precisely they have hit the target, and how far the powers that be will go in protecting their privileges. Just take a look at the success with which Republican presidents and their congressional allies reversed the gains made by women and minorities since the 1960s and you can imagine what some conservatives have in mind for education. Defunding and "privatization" have already gone far in destroying the autonomy of schools. As for free speech, it was the justices of the Supreme Court of the United States who ruled that doctors at clinics receiving federal funds could not even mention abortion to their patients. *They* are the real thought police, and they remind us of the Court that decided, in the *Dred Scott* case, that blacks had no rights that a white man need respect. Fortunately the Supreme Court does not yet have jurisdiction over our course syllabi; if they do extend their political control from the womb to the classroom, there are many opinions we in the universities will be forbidden to express.

But insofar as the crises on campus over political correctness and identity politics are symptomatic of disunity among Americans, we should look to the economy as one of the explanations for the breakdown of commonality. As I cautioned earlier, by no means do I wish to sweep gender or race or ethnicity aside to focus on economics as the "real" issue. The rigidity of the sides in the disputes over PC and identity politics might be eased, however, if the antagonists focused more on how notions of cultural assimilation and the "melting pot" lose their ideological credibility when times are tough. Moreover, we now have a wealth of scholarship and commentary that links economic issues to those of ethnicity, race, and gender, so that we are presumably less likely to discuss shifts in the job sector, for example, without also considering women's increased role in the wage labor market or the continuing effects of African American underemployment. Since the 1960s the United States has experienced a steady decline in the number of entry-level manufacturing jobs that require few skills and offer good wages and a chance for some upward mobility. To this diminution of the manufacturing base one should add the cutbacks in government jobs programs begun under Ronald Reagan and continued by the Congress and subsequent administrations.

Both these phenomena have specific impacts on different ethno-racial groups and on women. These kinds of manufacturing jobs, for example, were a vital channel for the assimilation of every immigrant group, including the large numbers of blacks who moved north into industrialized cities after the 1890s. Now the growing underclass has become more difficult to assimilate into the economy, whatever the social or ethnic group of the individual. As a result, racism, anti-Semitism, xenophobia, violence against women, and overt acts of bigotry are on the rise nationwide. The depravity of our politics feeds at the trough of material despair, even as systematic ideologies of bigotry promote harmful economic policies and prevent solidarity among the afflicted.

The economic crisis has compounded a cultural crisis of scape-goating, separatism, selfishness, cynicism, and rank exploitation of anxieties and fears. Social and immigrant groups that cannot look forward to assimilation turn more readily to insisting on the preser-vation of what cultural identity they do have, since no route toward a common identity or common culture appears open. In an era of im-posed scarcity, competition for jobs, housing, college admissions, and other necessities takes the shape of group conflicts as individuals band together to strengthen their hand in the struggle for a piece of the shrinking pie. The rhetoric of scarcity makes it more difficult to redistribute wealth to right past injustices, such as the denial of equal opportunity to women and minorities, even as the rich get richer.

Individuals belonging to social groups that have been the regular victims of bigotry and discrimination fight even harder to get some small increase for themselves, and step up the ferocity of their de-nunciation of the group that has benefited from their exploitation. Whites often respond to this challenge to their dominance in the same way in which they respond to the overall decline of economic opportunities: they look for a scapegoat and portray themselves as the true victims, fortifying the walls of prejudice and selfishness rather than building bridges of common cause and compassion. On the one hand, women and minorities see the discrimination against them as groups more clearly than ever, and so tend to respond as alienated communities of interest that have no common bonds. On the other hand, middle- and lower-income whites, especially men, react to the reduction in their own economic opportunities by irrationally blaming feminism and affirmative action programs, as if these were responsible for the disappearance of entry-level manufacturing jobs, government employment, and retail expansion. Thus, one should greet the current tendency to portray white men as the unfairly victimized targets of left-wing hate groups by pointing out (as does Michael Lind) the long history of white supremacist attitudes informing public policy and economic life as well as the continuing position of predominance most white men have in American society. (Unfortunately, Lind thinks it necessary to balance this account with a hyperbolic jeremiad against affirmative action.) If reforms in society and education and government result in targeting the privileges white men have had for so long, it is done not out of a personal hatred of them for their gender or their race but out of a historical recognition and moral evaluation of the unjust distribution of social power and knowledge.

At colleges and universities a similar story unfolds. The momentum of the Civil Rights and women's movements of the 1960s created a variety of institutions and ideas, mostly on the periphery of the academic center, to remedy past intellectual injustices. Autonomous though usually precarious and underfunded programs in women's studies, black or African American studies, and similar innovations brought minority identity politics into campus administration and curriculum, which had long been the province of white identity politics. Throughout the Reagan and Bush years, however, the moneys and political support for these programs dried up, along with financial aid for the poor and underrepresented. Twenty-five years after the Civil Rights Act of 1964, black enrollment in higher education actually began to decline despite affirmative action programs. The fall into poverty of northern black industrial communities that lost their share of the wealth produced by urban manufacture (now exported to the Third World) had a devastating impact on the ability of blacks to attend college. By 1990, after a decade of expanding requirements, tuition increases, and cuts in financial aid, white students too began to feel the economic pinch, and massive numbers of white college students took part-time jobs to pay their way through school. Again, many whites unreasonably blamed affirmative action programs for the decline in college opportunities and course offerings rather than pointing the finger at the government officials who stole from the poor and middle class and gave to the rich. Young Americans of college age now stare hungrily at one another, seeing not friends or compatriots in a common culture but instead competitors in a grim struggle for money and power.

In debates on multiculturalism and the diversity of educational offerings, one sometimes encounters objections to the constant reiteration of "race, class, and gender" as seemingly the only categories requiring revised representation. Why, critics ask, should we restrict ourselves to this holy trinity? What about all the other, theoretically infinite, kinds of differences that separate people, such as region and religion? Why not affirmative action to ensure representation of evangelical Christians or stockbrokers or short people (the "vertically challenged," as some wags put it)? The answer lies, I think, in the connection between our knowledge about social groups and the relative power they have in a given culture. In the context of the United States, a strong argument has been made that acts of bigotry and discrimination against people on the basis of their race, class, and gender (including sexual orientation) are the most prevalent in our history and society. These groups — persons of color, women, the poor, gays and lesbians — are on the whole less socially powerful and more easily targeted than other groups. Although abstract ideas about justice and equality might suggest the arbitrariness of privileging these categories, a *historical* understanding of American society shows the dominant role these categories have played.[2] The fact that everyone can claim to be a victim of some prejudice does not mean that all have been *equally harmed* or that *degrees of oppression* are insignificant. Although it is important not to encourage exercises whereby people argue over who has been most oppressed, these disputes seem preferable to the relative silence about bigotry and discrimination that preceded them.

2. The best approach remains a comparative study that encompasses European cultural groups as well as those from Africa and Asia and Latin America; see, for example, Takaki, *A Different Mirror*, where, for example, accounts of indentured white servants and enslaved black Africans are compared with the stories of Irish maids, Chinese railworkers, and Mexican American agricultural laborers, among others.

The lack of power of specific social groups has been reflected in the way they have been represented in educational materials and institutions (if at all), and this misrepresentation (or lack of representation) in turn reproduces their social disempowerment. So the reiteration of "race, class, and gender" does not follow from some wrongheaded assertion that nonwhites, the working class, and women are the only categories of victimization, or that only these marginalized groups have cultural riches that require study and appreciation. Rather, the argument I am pursuing asserts that throughout America's history the traditions of cultural groups other than these have had relatively more access to representation; thus, such relatively well represented groups do not require exceptional efforts in order to gain a place in the national culture. In this way one can understand why questions of educational purpose and scholarship cannot be easily disentangled from political questions, especially when an education often provides the most ready access to the better-paid jobs and social power.

Cultural and economic assimilation in the United States has historically been relatively easy for those of European descent, more difficult for those of Hispanic descent, and virtually impossible for those of African descent. American Indians, of course, were removed beyond the pale and subjected to attempted genocide. Assimilation of Asian Americans remains problematic even as they form powerful economic groupings in California and Hawaii. Racial prejudice, then, the ancient human habit of making one's personal identity dependent on the illusion of superiority to someone else, continues to be decisive in American life and public policy. George Lipsitz summarizes those policies under the rubric of "the possessive investment in whiteness." It is a mistake to focus the issue of white privilege or white racism on slavery and its aftermath rather than on modern social policies that underwrite segregation or discrimination. These policies include federal housing and urban "renewal" programs that devastate low-income and minority communities, tax-break policies that favor white investors over minority workers, transportation plans that plow freeways through minority communities to enable the growth of white suburbs, loan discrimination that stifles minority home ownership and the desegregation of suburbia, and tax "reforms" that encourage the closure of factories and their movement overseas. Taken together, these policies add up to a giant affirmative action subsidy for whiteness, though their racial character is rarely acknowledged. Such policies bear much of the blame for the division of American society into ethno-racial enclaves. Meanwhile, this white policy of socioeconomic balkanization coincides with a demographic swing toward growth in those very sectors of the population that have been traditionally the most recalcitrant toward assimilation, since assimilation meant either accepting the superiority of Anglo-Saxon culture or melting into the pot of white European pluralism.[3] This demographic shift has contributed to the ever stronger tendency to see the nation as a conglomerate of distinct groups rather than as a social contract among highly individual and independent persons.

Indeed, many now question whether assimilation should be a goal at all, since it usually means the assimilation of less empowered groups to the cultural values and institutionalized powers of dominant groups. Cities such as Los Angeles, New York, and Chicago are increasingly made up of racially and ethnically distinct neighborhoods, composing together a kind of multicultural metropolis (a recent article on demographics in California was called "Los Angeles: Capital of the Third World," a title that suggests the white fear of hordes of racial Others descending on America in some remake of 1950s horror classics of xenophobia about "Them"). As the cultural critic Todd Gitlin sees it, there has been an almost complete reversal of the political landscape with respect to the old debate between universalism and particularism. Whereas in the eighteenth century, liberal progressives of the Enlightenment swore allegiance to an equal and common humanity transcending material particulars, today leftist reformers insist that political change must start with, and always respect, the unbridgeable differences between heterogeneous peoples. At this rate we will soon have difficulty finding anyone who was born on the Fourth of July, who thinks of himself or herself as simply "an American."

3. See Michael Lind's useful partitioning of America's cultural history into three phases: the Anglo-Saxon, the Pan-European, and the Multicultural. On the history of the notion of "cultural pluralism," see Sollors.

Obviously academic scholars can only indirectly affect the fundamental economic factors that are accelerating the breakdown of cultural consensus in the United States. But educators can work vigorously to change the policies and material practices of their own institutions; after all, professors should not protest injustice in faraway places while ignoring its persistence in their own backyards. Across the nation, the pressure on universities to make budgetary ends meet threatens to roll back innovative programs in area studies and to limit the hiring of younger scholars and nontraditional voices. Administrators may also be tempted to exploit further the services of poorly paid teaching assistants or part-time instructors who receive no benefits and are not protected by unions.

Still, most academics will continue, in their professional lives, to respond to the "culture wars" through the battle of books and ideas, whether in public forums or classroom syllabi or in the pages of journals and magazines. Here there are many strategies, many tasks. As intellectuals or cultural historians, we can object to the language of novelty commonly used about the "disuniting of America." It can be pointed out that the consensus about the American dream was never very comprehensive in the first place, and that acceptance of it was often not a matter of choice. We can also look positively at the multicultural and multinational demographics of the American population as something to be proud of and something requiring a new vision of the nation's history and purpose. Reversions to nationalistic patriotism, whether in the political sphere or in formulas for cultural history, should be received skeptically. Intellectuals have a responsibility to remind the public at large how such patriotism has historically been used as a weapon of violence against many of our own citizens and as an excuse for telling lies about our past.

At the same time, it remains indispensable to mark the limitations of identity politics and cultural separatism, since these repeat at the local level the same blindness that nationalism can perpetuate at the state level. Gitlin, Hollinger, Lind, and other liberal theorists are building a case for a "new nationalism" that would be "postethnic" and predicated on civic rather than religious or racial identity. However helpful, criticisms of identity politics should regularly remind the audience that the modern equation of race with nation is a dominant feature of modern European and Western thought, and that the invention of "whiteness" by Europeans and their American descendants is the key factor in the development of the contemporary problem of identity politics. Similarly, it was men, not women, who built the legal, religious, and educational institutions of male privilege, and so enshrined masculine identity politics in our laws, bibles, and textbooks. Rather than taking sides in disputes between fixed positions in the identity politics debates, we should be encouraging encounters that focus on how the ways we represent our differences affect the ways we value one another and the access each of us has to social and economic opportunities. We may want to challenge the centrality of "identity" itself in arguments about culture, for example, by considering the difference between "having" an identity and living by an ethos. At the colleges and universities, cultural difference cannot help but be a central focus of the agenda, though it should not become the pretext for naive pluralism or heated celebrations of ethnic traditions. Here the poststructuralist critique of identity proves useful; the uncritical assertion of the value of one's personal or cultural identity is not ultimately a sufficient response to those who have, on the basis of their own identity politics, repressed and denied one's identity. When we talk about rescuing those "differences within" that systems of totalizing identity whitewash away, that goes for the differences within the self as well as within the community or state.

As we explore different accounts of the "American," and different ways of being accountable to one another, each of us negotiates the rival demands of particular interests and universal principles. In making these hard choices we become ethical subjects, that is, subject to ethical quandaries that we may or may not resolve ethically. I call this moment ethical in part because in it I submit myself to the judgment of a principle larger than my own self-interest. I hold my cultural identity and its practices to the standard of justice, and ask how my mode of being affects the lives of others. Slavery and patriarchy were popular, after all, because they served the self-interest of a ruling class. What justifies struggles against that ruling class? Merely the desire of other classes, too, for power? Power to do what? To whom? To what end? These are questions, again, of "the good," and they cannot be reduced solely to questions of power. In a pure clash of forces for power, there is no reason to prefer either side.

Rather, a real political philosophy requires that I be able to argue that one arrangement of power is harmful, unjust, and immoral. Then even those who benefit from injustice can (in theory) be persuaded or constrained to give it up. This brings me back to the power of universal or idealizing rhetoric, whose virtues and limits have been tested by those who have appropriated the Declaration of Independence for causes that it was never originally meant to support.

• • •

As I shall show at greater length in the chapters that follow, one can dismantle the various interpretive models that were used in the past to fabricate the illusion of a singular "American" literature, as many critics over the last few years have done. Turning from theory to history, one can also show that the diversity of written texts produced in the American colonies and the United States always amounted to a contentious dialogue rather than adding up to a single voice of the national spirit. In the words of Paul Lauter in the *Heath Anthology of American Literature*: "From its start, the New World community was multi-racial and multi-cultural. . . . The New World, comprised of defined spheres of influence over territories claimed and counterclaimed by European sovereign powers, early offered signs of the necessary mingling of red, white, and black that remain as both a defining and a contested national vision" (18).[4] The United States became a postcolonial nation on that famous Fourth of July and went on to become a rarity — a former colony that would itself become an imperial colonial power. Throughout its history, however, this relative lack of a homogeneous ethno-racial, religious, or even linguistic origin, compounded by recurrent expansions of the nation's boundaries, meant that the United States would have to struggle to produce a common national culture, even if this meant violently repressing the differences within its borders. What I want to explore, then, is how this struggle for representation unfolded around a key document, the Declaration of Independence, whose meaning was constantly contested and revised. As the particulars of

4. In the first edition the sentence ends more hopefully, stating that these signs of mingling "remain its earliest, best promise."

American life changed, the viability of the universals in the Declaration were often tested, and the process also revealed the particular prejudices that lay behind the Declaration's idealistic rhetoric.

Since the Revolution of 1776, literary journalists, critics, and artists have repeatedly called for a uniquely "American" literature. All about them, however, that uniqueness was already taking the form of a polyvocal, even multilingual, writing that would continually resist formulation into a homogeneous canon. But, as Lauter has concisely demonstrated, literary critics at the colleges and universities largely succeeded during the period from 1920 to 1970 in drastically narrowing the canon of authors and works and in creating textbooks, curricula, departments, professional organizations, and interpretive studies based on that canon (*Canons and Contexts* 22–97). Throughout this era, from the early essays of Van Wyck Brooks through the decisive works of Vernon Louis Parrington, F. O. Matthiessen, Richard Chase, and Lionel Trilling (who, like Nathaniel Hawthorne, really was born on the Fourth of July), definitions of the American literary canon (in educational institutions as well as in mainstream periodicals, magazines, and newspapers) hinged on the critic's search for a usable past. Quite often this search was motivated by the desire to construct a set of authorizing cultural documents to give foundation to specific notions of a democratic culture or of America's exceptional mission (see Reising; Shumway).

In retrospect we can see how limited those notions were, especially as they tended to depend on an ideology of American individualism that emptied the human being of his or her material, historical features — especially ethno-racial, class, and gender differences. This ideology is understandable, however, since after all the American Revolution saw itself as a revolt against feudalism's policy of rigidly assigning human beings to fixed places in the social hierarchy. Rejecting this determinism for a philosophy of individualism and meritocratic competition was, in context, a liberating move, even if the new freedom was initially intended largely for the rising bourgeoisie. The tendency to focus on common human traits and conditions is also understandable when one considers the historic diversity of wave after wave of immigrants who, to this day, continue to alter the physical and cultural face of the United States. Born during the height of the European Enlightenment, the United States was founded on philosophical doctrines that emphasized the universal rather than the particular. This philosophy produced a legal system of justice predicated on the ethos of an abstract human subjectivity equally shared by all rational creatures. The ringing phrases of Thomas Jefferson's language in the Declaration of Independence forever linked the establishment of the nation to that humanistic idealism.[5]

"We hold these truths to be self-evident, that all men are created equal, that they are endowed by their Creator with certain unalienable Rights, that among these are Life, Liberty, and the pursuit of Happiness." The *subject* of the Declaration of Independence — grammatically and politically — is the rhetorical "we," produced in discourse and on paper before it appears in reality. This "we" creates the theatrical illusion of a preexistent body politic, a univocal subject who originates and speaks the revolutionary utterance. But as Jacques Derrida points out in his commentary on the Declaration, this utterance is what rhetoricians call a "performative" speech act: it performs an action as well as declaring a set of facts. "One cannot decide . . . whether independence is stated or produced by this utterance [since] this people does not exist, *before* this declaration, not *as such*. If it gives birth to itself, as free and independent subject, as possible signer, this can hold only in the act of the signature. The signature invents the signer" (10). Who signs, asks Derrida, and with what so-called proper name, the declarative act which founds an institution or a nation? The "we" of the American people is born during this performance. We become our own subjects, subject no longer to the king but to the higher "Laws of Nature and of Nature's God." Here one comes on the ambiguity of the terms "nation" and "state":

5. The faculties of rationality and the moral sense were often used to construct this subjectivity and to define those ethno-racial groups that were supposedly inferior. The essential study here is certainly Garry Wills, *Inventing America*. But Wills, in my judgment, often goes a bit far in exonerating Jefferson for his prejudices and racism (see chap. 15, for example, where Jefferson's often prurient remarks on the inferiority of Negroes are implausibly balanced by his sentimental respect for the moral sense of slaves). As I shall show, Wills exaggerates the "obscurity" into which the Declaration fell and underestimates the degree of influence its ideas had immediately among disenfranchised portions of the new American population.

"nation" can refer to a group of people united by common ancestry, locale, or belief, who may not have a political "state" in the legal sense. Although it can be argued that, in a cultural sense, an Anglo-Saxon American nation had already developed by 1776, Jefferson's "we" refers less to a historical population than to a proposed political position (one, not incidentally, that many Americans at the time opposed). The Declaration negotiates the transformation of a nation into a state; insofar as the nation was a cultural entity that excluded some by virtue of race and discriminated against others by virtue of class or gender, the new state replicated the nation's biases, even as it wrote into its documents principles that seemed to clash with those biases.

As Jay Fliegelman points out in *Declaring Independence: Jefferson, Natural Language, and the Culture of Performance*, the Declaration represents the Revolution as both an unavoidable necessity *and* an act of free will. The language of the Declaration exhibits an uneasy dialectic between mechanical determinism and individual agency characteristic of the period.[6] The rhetoric of the Declaration suggests that the people are passive or act only when forced. The language speaks of what it is "necessary for one people" to do after such "patient sufferance" of the willful actions against them of the king. By making their invention of their own rebellious subjectivity sound like a necessity imposed upon them, the colonists mitigate their guilt and obscure the artificial character of the union they declare. The coherence of this "people" as a preexisting "nation" is tenuous at best.

In this "UNANIMOUS DECLARATION" we hear of "one people," of "the Right of the People" and "their duty" to — among other things — commit treason. Although the agency of human action narrated by the Declaration anthropomorphizes the body politic, imagining it as a collective of different persons, this subject nonetheless speaks with one voice, as if it were a particular individual with rights and duties. Was this universalizing presumption ethical, especially considering how many particular people had no voice in this

6. Fliegelman's brilliant book reached me some two years and three drafts into this chapter. I was glad to find, at least in my own view, considerable agreement in our readings; in correspondence he made a number of expert suggestions, though I was not able to incorporate all of them.

utterance? "Jefferson's statement of equality" in the sense of being equally made by God with moral faculties, writes Fliegelman, "was far from a racial call for social equality" (197). The Declaration postulated an abstractly equal and universal human subjectivity despite the historical exclusion from it of Indians, the enslaved, women, and those men who did not own property. The words of the Declaration have continued to haunt the moral and political life of America, and subsequent generations have both embraced and repudiated them.[7] At the origin of the United States, then, we find an ethically troubling contradiction between enabling fictions of universalism and stubborn realities of particularity and exclusion. What the next two centuries would bring was not simply a history of hypocrisy, however, but a series of subversive appropriations, as those who were left out of the original Declaration used its own utopian terms both to challenge and to expand the practices of American democracy.

The original draft of Jefferson's Declaration contained a long, hypocritical, and self-serving condemnation of the king's encouragement of the international slave trade, and of the Crown's policy of offering manumission to slaves who rebelled against their rebellious masters. But even Jefferson and his colleagues quickly recognized the folly of citing the king's offer of freedom for the enslaved as an example of the tyranny they opposed; the passage was dropped, though a veiled reference to the Crown's instigation of "domestic insurrections" was inserted (see Wills, *Inventing America* chap. 5; Fliegelman 189–200). When the Constitution of the United States was eventually negotiated, it counted enslaved Africans as two-thirds of a person for the purpose of determining the representation of districts and states in the Congress (while this increased the political power of the southern states, it still gave an advantage to the northern ones which would have been lost had the slaves been counted as whole persons). These enslaved Africans, of course, had no vote themselves; nor did women and most unpropertied men for that matter.

7. As Larry E. Tise argues, a strong case can be made that the political theory of the Declaration of Independence represented a minority opinion and an aberration in the mainstream of American thought, and that by the first decades of the nineteenth century a new, conservative consensus had taken hold which repudiated the assumptions of Jefferson's language.

The Declaration and the Constitution presented Americanness as a revolutionary identity or ethos for all, but the reality and power of citizenship were in practice restricted.

The rhetoric of the Declaration became something of a template for generations of reformers to come. Various classes who saw themselves as excluded from the original Declaration wrote their own, citing and revising Jefferson's language so as to apply it to their own cause. Philip Foner documents how early organizers of the labor and trades union movements in Jacksonian America repeatedly used the Revolution's language in a series of orations and pamphlets. "By the 1820s and 1830s," reports Foner, "the Fourth of July had become fixed as the working-class day of celebration." Although a day for banquets and parades, it was also a time "for dramatizing the demands of the working class, for rewriting the Declaration of Independence to restore the rights employers 'have robbed us of,' and a day for toasts like: 'The Working Men — the legitimate children of '76; their sires left them the legacy of freedom and equality. They are now of age, and are laboring to guarantee the principles of the Revolution'"(1–2).

In these new declarations, the tyranny of King George is replaced by the tyranny of landlords, manufacturers, monopolists, capitalists, and the wealthy. "The Working Men's Declaration of Independence" (1829) states that "the laws and municipal ordinances and regulations . . . have heretofore been ordained on such principles, as have deprived nine tenths of the members of the body politic, who are *not* wealthy, of the *equal means* to enjoy '*life, liberty and the pursuit of happiness,*' which the *rich* enjoy exclusively; but the federative compact intended to secure to all, indiscriminately" (Foner 49). After quoting the self-evident truths articulated by "the Fathers of our Country," the "Declaration of Rights of the Trades' Union of Boston and Vicinity" (1834) protests against "laws which have a tendency to raise any peculiar class above their fellow citizens," asserting that "labor, being the legitimate and only real source of wealth, and the laboring classes the majority and real strength of every country, their interests and happiness ought to be the principal care of government" (Foner 53). Lewis Masquerier, in "Declaration of Independence of the Producing from the Non-Producing Class" (1844), opens with this revision of Jefferson:

When in the course of human events, the producers of property have been reduced to the lowest state of degradation and misery by the almost universal usurpation of all property and power by a non-producing, tyrannical, and aristocratic class, a decent respect for the opinions of mankind requires that they should declare the causes which impel them to cease ultimately being tenants to land usurping and non-producing lords; in being journeymen to masters, shoppers, and manufacturers, to produce fabrics to which they are mostly entitled themselves, and in being electors to elevate officers of parties and cliques instead of those of their own class. (Foner 66).

Similar sentiments are expressed in other documents of the labor movement extending from before the Civil War into the latter part of the twentieth century.

These texts demonstrate clearly that members of the white American working class discerned the injustice of their exclusion from the practice of liberty, and did so by upholding a document written by representatives of the wealthy landowning and mercantile elites. The extension of the franchise and of political freedoms to white working men is usually narrated as central to the Jacksonian period and a landmark in the growth of democracy. Labor's successes in the era were limited, however, in part because of racism (see Roediger). The ideology of whiteness served as one of the unifying forces among the laboring classes, binding ethnics of European extraction together in a common economic and social fear of blacks. Thus, no larger working class alliance across racial barriers came about, leaving the propertied elites both North and South firmly in charge. Capable of universalizing the Declaration's words to include the unpropertied man and the "wage slave," the rhetoric of the workers never took the next step of calling for the abolition of Negro slavery. Foner notes that "in all of the Fourth of July celebrations by labor groups from the 1790s" to 1845, no labor spokesman made reference to slavery (16). White working men in the North would continue to express hostility to emancipation right up through the draft riots of the Civil War. The failure to connect trade union agitation with abolitionism deserves more analysis, especially in comparison to the long history of black abolitionist citations of the Declaration and to the analogy drawn by women between their condition and that of the slaves.

Even before 1776 the blacks enslaved in Massachusetts were using the language of the Enlightenment, protesting that "we have in common with all other men a naturel [sic] right to our freedoms." In a subsequent petition of January 1777, enslaved Africans in Massachusetts were already appropriating the Declaration of Independence and Jefferson's phrases as they made two claims that would characterize abolitionist (and later women's rights) literature: that African Americans were entitled to equal status as human beings, and that the oppression of African Americans vividly resembled the oppression suffered by the colonies at the hands of King George. These petitioners claimed to "have in common with all other men a Natural and Unaliable Right to that freedom which the Grat parent of the Unavers hath Bestowed equalley on all menkind and which they have Never forfeited by any Compact or agreement whatever"; they further expressed "their Astonishment that It have Never Bin Considred that Every Principle from which America has Acted in the Cours of their unhappy Difficultes with Great Briton Pleads Stronger than A thousand arguments in favours of your petitioners" seeking freedom from slavery (Aptheker 8, 10).

Black and white abolitionists throughout the early 1800s continued to throw the slave owner Jefferson's words back in the face of the political establishment and to make that one sentence ("We hold these truths to be self-evident, that all men are created equal") the most often and ironically quoted text in abolitionist literature. David Walker's 1829 *Appeal to the Coloured Citizens of the World*, perhaps the most fiery antislavery pamphlet before the speeches of Frederick Douglass, pointedly singled out Jefferson for analytical ridicule. Walker responded at length to the assertion of the racial inferiority of blacks in Jefferson's *Notes on the State of Virginia*. He also quoted the first two paragraphs of the Declaration verbatim and asked: "Compare your own language . . . with your cruelties and murders inflicted by your cruel and unmerciful fathers and yourselves on our fathers and on us. . . . I ask you candidly, was your sufferings under Great Britain, one hundredth part as cruel and tyrannical as you have rendered ours under you?" (75). When in 1853 William Wells Brown wrote the first novel by an African American, he called it

Clotel, or The President's Daughter. Brown based his story on the rumors that Jefferson had fathered two mulatto slave daughters who were subsequently sold south. The epigraph on Brown's title page was, of course, Jefferson's by then notorious sentence about equality from the Declaration of Independence.

This tradition of antislavery responses to the Declaration perhaps reached its climax in Frederick Douglass's spectacular oration "What to the Slave is the Fourth of July?" An escaped slave and abolitionist leader, Douglass pointedly delivered his speech on the *fifth* of July 1852:

> What to the American slave is your Fourth of July? I answer, a day that reveals to him more than all other days of the year, the gross injustice and cruelty to which he is the constant victim. To him your celebration is a sham; your boasted liberty an unholy license; your national greatness, swelling vanity; your sounds of rejoicing are empty and heartless; your denunciation of tyrants, brass-fronted impudence; your shouts of liberty and equality, hollow mockery; your prayers and hymns, your sermons and thanksgivings, with all your religious parade and solemnity, are to him mere bombast, fraud, deception, impiety, and hypocrisy — a thin veil to cover up crimes which would disgrace a nation of savages. There is not a nation of the earth guilty of practices more shocking and bloody than are the people of these United States. (Aptheker 334)[8]

Douglass's classically influenced rhetorical style carefully balances the political and moral syntax: general or universal ideals are juxtaposed to the failure by whites to realize them in practice. This failure is placed squarely on the shoulders of "the people of these United States" who have committed these "crimes." He reverses the racial stereotypes in branding the whites "a nation of savages," and

---

8. For an account of the speech's context, see McFeely 172–73. For the complete text of the address, see Blassingame, *Douglass Papers* 2:359–88. The tradition of ironically citing the Declaration continued into the twentieth century, as can be seen in depictions of the Fourth of July in Audre Lorde's *Zami* and Alice Walker's *The Color Purple.* Martin Luther King, Jr.'s, invocation of the Declaration is examined later in this chapter.

his reiteration of the accusatory "you" puts whites in their place, as Douglass occupies the high ground of judgment. As is characteristic of antebellum sentimental discourse, Douglass indicts whites for a failure of feeling as well as of action. Invoking the universal languages of political liberty and ethical behavior, he focuses our attention on the particular difference race makes in America.

It was no accident that Frederick Douglass gave his speech in response to an invitation from the Rochester Ladies' Anti-Slavery Society. For decades the causes of women's rights and antislavery had been closely linked, as women played a key role in advancing the work of abolitionism in the North. Indeed, the association of the condition of women with that of the enslaved goes back at least to 1776. In a famous exchange of letters during the months prior to the signing of the Declaration, Abigail and John Adams gave rare witness in writing to a debate that doubtless raged in many households. "I long to hear that you have declared an independancy," wrote Abigail, " — and by the way in the new Code of Laws which I suppose it will be necessary for you to make I desire you would Remember the Ladies." Observing to her husband that "your Sex are Naturally Tyrannical," she asked for specific laws to protect women from the "cruelty and indignity" suffered under the "unlimited power" of husbands: "If perticuliar care and attention is not paid to the Laidies we are determined to foment a Rebelion, and will not hold ourselves bound by any Laws in which we have no voice, or Representation" (121).

John Adams responded, "As to your extraordinary Code of Laws, I cannot but laugh." Exploiting the witty tone of Abigail's letter to his own end, he noted that the revolutionaries had been accused of fomenting a general anarchy and a disruption of traditional social hierarchies: the Tories claimed that children, apprentices, students, Indians, and Negroes all grew "insolent to their Masters." "But your letter," John continued, "was the first Intimation that another Tribe more numerous and powerfull than all the rest were grown discontented." He went on to say, "We know better than to repeal our Masculine systems," and he repeated the myth that men were the victims of what he called the "Despotism of the Peticoat." He (perhaps) jokingly accused King George's government of instigating rebellion among the women as it did among "Tories, Landjobbers, Trimmers, Bigots, Canadians, Indians, Negros, Hanoverians, Hessians, Russians,

Irish Roman Catholicks, Scotch Renegadoes" (122–23). By this argument, the same made by Jefferson in the Declaration's struck passage on slavery, the Founding Fathers meant to declare their independence from women as well as from the king. Their construction of the American political ethos carefully separated a masculine claim to inalienable (property) rights from claims made by the groups whose clamoring for representation they thought ought to be squelched. John Adams's sarcastic linking of women's claims to those of Negroes, Indians, and other oppressed groups would, of course, return as a serious political argument in the hands of feminists and abolitionists in the nineteenth century, and remains a logical connection for many cultural analysts to this day. Confirming John Adams's fear, polemicists from the American Indian tribes were also adept at invoking the white man's Revolution and Declaration for their own purposes. In his 1834 *Indian Nullification of the Unconstitutional Laws of Massachusetts Relative to the Marshpee Tribe*, William Apess (himself a Pequot) denounced the expropriation of Marshpee lands and resources by invoking the comparative memory of 1776: "I will ask him [the white man] how, if he values his own liberty, he would or could rest quiet under such laws. I ask the Inhabitants of New England generally how their fathers bore laws, much less oppressive, when imposed upon them by a foreign government" (O'Connell 211).

By the late 1820s, women were increasingly apt to compare their situation to that of the enslaved, all the more so when women's attempts to speak in public and exercise political power were met with contempt, ridicule, and violence. One of the first of these women, Angelina Grimké, herself the daughter of a slave owner, wrote Catharine Beecher in 1837 that "the investigation of the rights of the slave has led me to a better understanding of my own." Employing the rhetoric of sentiment, domesticity, and Christianity, Grimké established equality on the basis of morality: "Human beings have *rights*, because they are *moral* beings: the rights of *all* men grow out of their moral nature; and as all men have the same moral nature, they have essentially the same rights. . . . My doctrine, then, is that whatever it is morally right for man to do, it is morally right for woman to do" (Lauter, *Heath* 1866). This radical feminist assertion of the ethos of a common moral nature aims to stop the particular discrimination against the character of women and blacks; her moral egalitarianism would theoretically prevent the use of character as a justification for subordination by race or gender. In 1845 Margaret Fuller underscored how America's declaration of "national independence be blurred by the servility of individuals," and she too drew the by then standard analogy between women and the enslaved: "As the friend of the negro assumes that one man cannot by right hold another in bondage, so should the friend of Woman assume that Man cannot by right lay even well-meant restrictions on Woman" (Chevigny 243, 248).

As Barbara Bardes and Suzanne Gossett point out in *Declarations of Independence: Women and Political Power in Nineteenth-Century American Fiction*, women's rights activists and women novelists in the nineteenth century often took up Jefferson's rhetoric for their own subversive purposes. The participants in the historic 1848 Women's Rights Convention in Seneca Falls (which Frederick Douglass attended) left this account of preparing their manifesto, which they would call the Declaration of Sentiments:

> And the humiliating fact may as well now be recorded that before taking the initiative step, those ladies resigned themselves to a faithful perusal of various masculine productions. The reports of Peace, Temperance, and Anti-Slavery conventions were examined, but all alike seemed too tame and pacific for the inauguration of a rebellion such as the world had never before seen. . . . After much delay, one of the circle [Elizabeth Cady Stanton] took up the Declaration of 1776, and read it aloud with much spirit and emphasis, and it was at once decided to adopt the historic document, with some slight changes such as substituting "all men" for "King George." (Buhle and Buhle 92)

In substituting "all men" for "King George," the women turned the strategy of universalization to their own ends — the same strategy that had left them out of the original Declaration when the men's reference to "men" obscured their exclusion of women. To these rebellious ladies, all men were King George. This feminist strategy recast the figure of the oppressor from the particular tyrant King George to the universal tyranny of men over women. And in *their* Declaration the women boldly rewrote Jefferson's most famous line:

"We hold these truths to be self-evident: that all men and women are created equal." By rewriting, with a significant difference, the words of the founding document of the nation's political and cultural identity, the women of Seneca Falls gave voice to something repressed at the nation's origin, even something whose repression was constitutive of that origin. Their Declaration became an uncanny return of the repressed, producing a mocking echo within the univocal expression of American truth, replacing history with her-story. The women's version stated: "The history of mankind is a history of repeated injuries and usurpations on the part of man toward woman, having in direct object the establishment of an absolute tyranny over her" (Buhle and Buhle 94). The women of Seneca Falls exposed the masculine ethos of the Founding Fathers even as they invoked the value of liberty (not least of all in the liberties they took with Jefferson's text).

By the 1850s an ironic reference to the Declaration of Independence was standard in the rhetoric of the women's rights movement. Sara Parton, who under the pen name Fanny Fern became perhaps the most famous woman journalist of her day, delighted in satirizing the injustices of patriarchal tyranny — be they in the bedroom and parlor or the houses of prostitution and publishing. In a column of July 30, 1859, for the *New York Ledger*, Parton wrote as if in conscious imitation of Douglass as she took up the theme of women's relation to the promises of the Founding Fathers. Characteristic of her style, the column features the first-person voice of an American woman who speaks up:

"FOURTH OF JULY." Well — I don't feel patriotic. Perhaps I might if they would stop that deafening racket. Washington was very well, if he *couldn't* spell, and I'm glad we are all free; but as a woman — I shouldn't know it, didn't some orator tell me. Can I go out of an evening without a hat at my side? Can I go out with one on my head without danger of a station-house? Can I clap my hands at some public speaker when I am nearly bursting with delight? Can I signify the contrary when my hair stands on end with vexation? Can I stand up in the cars "like a gentleman" without being immediately invited "to sit down"? . . . Can I go to see anything *pleasant*, like an execution or a dissection? . . . Can I be a

Senator, that I may hurry up that millennial International Copyright Law? Can I *even* be President? Bah — you know I can't. "*Free!*" Humph! (Fern 314–15)

Fanny Fern didn't feel patriotic because, in many detailed ways, she did not live in the land of the free. The nation created by the Declaration treats her like a criminal and a child, denying her the most mundane as well as sublime rights. With characteristic wit, Fern makes it amply clear that her freedom is sharply restricted by gender: she cannot go "out of an evening without a hat" (that is, without a male escort), and she cannot go out wearing a man's hat without fear of arrest. The proper sex roles are literally policed, though Fern has fun pointing out what a superficial costume gender difference may be, if all it comes down to is what hats we wear. By playing with that well-recognized pun, however, Fern also prompts readers to reconsider seriously the ways we dress up our differences, who controls the show, and the punishments inflicted when the disempowered try to assert their freedom. Freedom of dress and freedom of address — of speech, or bodily movement, of social location — walk hand in hand. Dress how she might, and attend however many Fourth of July addresses she can bear, Fern's address will never be 1600 Pennsylvania Avenue. The only space of free address Fern can carve out is on the page, where her irreverent authority of experience is worn stylishly. Such cultural literacy as Fern commands serves her well in judging the Founding Fathers: "Washington was very well, if he *couldn't* spell."

In her commentary on this column, Lauren Berlant argues that "to Fern, citizenship is not an abstract condition or privilege: it is a relay to protection and legitimation under the law and in the public sphere, which includes the world of the arts and the more banal experience of the body in the marketplace," including "the absurdity of the degree to which society regulates juridically what women wear and what they say" (442). In contrast to the Enlightenment notion of a universal political citizen with equal rights, Fern portrays the specific ways that society and the law address women and their bodies, disciplining their freedom with an oppressive protective custody. Implicitly, as some feminist legal scholars argue today, women's freedom cannot result from the simple application to them of a doctrine of rights developed on the model of a masculine citizen but must instead be crafted to address the specifics of women's condition in a patriarchal society. Whereas "freedom" remains a universal abstract token of women's desire, the realization of freedom (or of its absence) takes place only in particulars — in the wearing or not wearing of certain hats, in the public display of emotion, in preferring to stand on an omnibus, in watching an execution or dissection, in getting paid for one's work, in being president. In a democracy, part of our ethical responsibility (by which I mean our responsibility to others) involves asking what freedom will look like for particular citizens, not simply for the citizen in the abstract. (See also Fern's piece titled "A Little Bunker Hill," in which she comments about the general demand for rights, "I hope no female sister will be such a novice as to suppose it refers to any but *masculine* rights" [243].)

For white women in antebellum America, it was property rights, not the vote, that dominated the agenda as these women considered the particulars of their lack of freedom.[9] Under the legal doctrine of coverture, women lost their property rights under marriage, even their rights to their children. Upper- and middle-class women found this an increasingly restrictive and shameful state of affairs, as did lower-class women who were beginning to receive wages for labor (such as shoebindery and needlework) that had once been remunerated through barter. The late 1840s saw the first legislative acts guaranteeing property rights for married women. At the same time, women in the manufacturing industries continued to complain about the artificially low wages paid them under the ethos of domestic ideology which defined women first as wives and mothers: women were paid only those wages calculated to compensate the family for time taken from domestic chores, while men were paid under the "head of household" rubric, and so domestic ideology blocked any notion of equal pay for equal work. Women could not be independent of the patriarchal home without a wage, but if they left the

9. See Bardes and Gossett, *Declarations of Independence*, chap. 3 ("Women and Property Rights"). They conclude by observing that the married women's property laws passed at midcentury were focused mainly on land. These primarily benefited wealthier women and did little to mitigate the economic exploitation of wage-laboring women.

home for outside work, they found themselves paid as if they were wives or mothers or daughters. True citizenship for women would mean the right to hold property equally and the achievement of a just wage. Any "political" rights granted in the absence of these reforms was of little worth and deceptive, for it would throw a cloak of respectable universal citizenship over the particular reality of women's inequality in a patriarchal society. The claim of women to the universal principles of freedom and equality, however, provided a rhetorical and utopian lever by which to move men off the pedestal of privilege they had erected for themselves.

What the labor, antislavery, and women's rights literature demonstrates is that every attempt to rectify a past injustice involves some appeal to universality. As one might expect, these claims usually produce more rather than less social and cultural discord along with any actual progress they achieve in the treatment of individuals. When working-class men, women, and African Americans appropriate Jefferson's voice, they decenter the national rhetoric by speaking it through an unauthorized body.[10] This tactical appropriation of language and ideas seems to express the extension of universality to the formerly excluded subject, but the ironic embodiment this entails seems to underscore the limits of pluralism. Americans previously excluded by prejudice or exploitation cannot lay claim to equal rights in the abstract without eventually upsetting the practical distribution of social power and cultural authority. Equal rights cannot be achieved painlessly by rhetorical or legislative fiat; injustice has meant that some persons have had their bodies, wealth, and rights

10. History has a way of continuing to ignore these voices. In his marvelous volume *Lincoln at Gettysburg*, Garry Wills focuses most of his attention on the centrality of the Declaration of Independence to Lincoln's political thought. He presents detailed reviews of how white politicians in the era appropriated Jefferson's document. Unaccountably, there is no mention of Walker, Douglass, the Declaration of Sentiments, or any other instances from the countertradition I have sketched. Wills's analysis of how Lincoln interprets the Declaration as an idealistic promise would have been strengthened (and made more historically accurate) had he included a more diverse set of sources for his study. Lincoln's interpretation appears less novel when one considers how long it had been articulated by African Americans protesting slavery.

taken from them, and undoing this injustice means depriving a once-dominant group of the privileges and resources it has taken for granted as its own rights. This redistribution of wealth and power can also be formulated in moral terms, as a general ethos of justice to which one submits regardless of one's own particular self-interest.

In raising the question of the good, I mean to suggest that cultural criticism, to be worth the effort, should have an affirmative dimension. Certainly such affirmation may take complex, even ironic forms, as my discussion of the subversive affirmations of the Declaration of Independence has demonstrated. Ralph Ellison continues this tradition in the "Epilogue" to *Invisible Man*, where his narrator gives this final gloss to his grandfather's deathbed injunction to "overcome 'em [whites] with yeses, undermine 'em with grins, agree 'em to death and destruction" (16):

> Could he have meant — hell, he *must* have meant the principle, that we were to affirm the principle on which the country was built and not the men, or at least not the men who did the violence. . . . Did he mean to affirm the principle, which they themselves had dreamed into being out of the chaos and darkness of the feudal past, and which they had violated and compromised to the point of absurdity even in their own corrupt minds? Or did he mean that we had to take the responsibility for all of it, for the men as well as the principle . . . ? Was it that we of all, we, most of all, had to affirm the principle, the plan in whose name we had been brutalized and sacrificed? (574)

Ellison's affirmation of the white master's "plan in whose name we had been brutalized and sacrificed" is bound to strike many today as naive if not self-destructive. But is Ellison's idealism — his affirmation of principles despite particular individual failures to live up to them — really so ineffectual a course or so lacking in theoretical strength or practical justification? There has been, I think, too little admission by the left today (at least on campus) that its principles remain indebted to the tradition of the Declaration of Independence, especially as appropriated and extended by successive generations since Abigail Adams and David Walker and William Apess. Uneasiness about being seen as oppressively "patriotic" or "nationalist" in the wake of the 1960s and the Vietnam War explains some of this hesitance, as does the influence of Marxism on academics, among whom it helped foster an atmosphere hostile to liberalism and suspicious of hypocritical pieties about equal rights, justice, and democracy. Writers who unabashedly espoused belief in American possibilities suffered harsh attack, as was the case with Ellison. Recalling Ellison at the current moment presents an interesting opportunity to reflect on identity politics and American culture, and on conflicts between intellectual, artistic, and political commitments, as Jerry Watts notes in his study of Ellison in *Heroism and the Black Intellectual* (see also Wonham, "Introduction"). Many of Ellison's views might be dubbed "politically incorrect," and he has indeed been taken to task by the left and by proponents of the Black Aesthetic and Black Nationalism ever since the publication in 1952 of *Invisible Man*. The criticisms have merit, but one hopes that the days of having to choose between Ellison and Wright (or between Martin Luther King and Malcolm X) are past.

What makes Ellison newly fascinating is his stance as a hybrid character. While grounding his fiction and essays in the black experience — in blues and folklore — Ellison freely adapted techniques and themes from white writers he praised, including Malraux, Joyce, Hemingway, and Eliot. He saw "American" culture, especially in music and literature, as having always been shaped by the contributions of African Americans, so that to speak of American culture as distinct from black culture (or vice versa) made little sense. This position did not endear Ellison to many in the black community, who, even if they acknowledged the truth of his position, could nonetheless rightly argue that African Americans and their art had been regularly discriminated against and violated, to the point where it made no sense not to speak of a difference between white and black cultural experience. And whatever cultural achievements the black community could boast in no way mitigated the extremes of poverty and violence to which it was subjected. Nonetheless, Ellison seems clearly the forerunner of Toni Morrison, who in *Playing in the Dark* demonstrates extensively how white literature is haunted by an Africanist presence.[11]

11. For further scholarship in this direction, see Wonham.

Ellison's gamble on the tactics of integration and subversive appropriation was a dangerous one, and is obviously still controversial no matter who takes it up. Yet, in the current swing away from essentialism and identity politics, Ellison's decision to say yes to multiple and contradictory versions of America might offer fresh lessons. The Ellison controversy recalls other such debates over the question who is an authentically black (or Jewish or Indian or feminist) writer? Ellison's move away from Marxism and social determinism toward an existentialism of the blues emphasized the power of choice, or agency, in a way that resonates in the aftermath of the determinism spawned by structuralism and social constructionism. Watts cautions, however, that "in his public statements Ellison will sometimes offer a perfunctory mention of the dire plight of many blacks before he proceeds into a celebration of black American creative endurance and American possibility. . . . Ellison utilizes hegemonic American democratic rhetoric as well as the resilient hopeful outlooks of many black Americans to divert his attention from the most debilitating aspects of black existence in America" (108). Ellison's championing of the blues and folklore can come to seem like other paeans to popular culture, that is, as an account that overestimates the "resistance" power of popular culture and mistakes the artistic expression of oppression for the practical undoing of its material and political causes.

Ellison's "yes" to American democracy never translated into political action, as his critics in the 1960s were quick to point out. The freedom imagined in *Invisible Man* becomes so universal a principle of enlightenment (recall the room of bulbs and the subversive appropriation of the power grid) that it sometimes fails to stay connected to the particulars of the black experience in America. When the Civil Rights movement sought to take to the streets with that "yes" as a weapon of political action, it continued to invoke Jefferson's words. Martin Luther King, Jr., takes up the theme of the Declaration during his "I Have a Dream" speech at the 1963 March on Washington, combining the oratorical authority of Douglass's cry against injustice with Ellison's idealistic affirmation.[12]

12. The speech King delivered was based on a carefully written and revised text, though King appeared to depart from it when he improvised the

Speaking from the steps of the Lincoln Memorial, King begins by recalling the Gettysburg Address:

> Five score years ago, a great American, in whose symbolic shadow we stand today, signed the Emancipation Proclamation. This momentous decree came as a great beacon light of hope to millions of Negro slaves who had been seared in the flames of withering injustice. It came as a joyous daybreak to end the long night of their captivity. But one hundred years later, the Negro still is not free; one hundred years later, the life of the Negro is still sadly crippled by the manacles of segregation and the chains of discrimination; one hundred years later, the Negro lives on a lonely island of poverty in the midst of a vast ocean of material prosperity; one hundred years later, the Negro is still languished in the corners of American society and finds himself in exile in his own land.

So much reminds us of Douglass: the cadence, the imagery, the syntactic parallelisms, the evocation of the sermon and the jeremiad. Strategically, though, what interests us is King's implicit comparison of his speech to Lincoln's Gettysburg Address, perhaps the most famous instance of American democratic rhetoric after the Declaration. King understands that the Civil Rights movement is a continu-

---

final section containing the "I have a dream" passages. This and other sections, however, represented reworkings of material King had been using for a number of years. Published versions of the speech are based on the delivered one, though the speech has often been reprinted with minor discrepancies. Some of these originate in the first publication of the speech in the *Negro History Bulletin*, which presumably drew on the prepared as well as the delivered text. For background and analyses, see the essays collected in Calloway-Thomas and Lucaites. The edition of 1993 authorized by King's wife and daughter carries this note: "Disclaimer: The words that appear here are the original words written by Martin Luther King, Jr., and are slightly different from the words Reverend King spoke on August 28, 1963." But King and his biographers confirmed that the latter part of the speech departed from the "original" written text; perhaps the Kings are referring to the written version King gave to the *Negro History Bulletin*. A still different version, closer to but not exactly the same as the delivered one, is available from the Martin Luther King, Jr., Papers Project Web site at Stanford University. I have used this version and checked it against videotape of the speech.

ation of the Civil War by other means. Lincoln had followed (reluctantly) the abolitionist tradition of applying the Declaration and its rights to an unintended beneficiary: the enslaved Africans of America (see Wills, *Lincoln*). The Gettysburg Address expresses that extension by first quoting Jefferson's lines: "Four score and seven years ago our fathers brought forth, upon this continent, a new nation, conceived in liberty, and dedicated to the proposition that 'all men are created equal'" (punctuation follows first manuscript copy). Unless we read the address within this context, as one more invocation of Jefferson in a line stretching back through Douglass and William Wells Brown and David Walker, we may miss how pointedly Lincoln's speech in fact refers to the liberation of African Americans. In citing Lincoln, or in appropriating him subversively, King reclaims the Gettysburg Address for the purposes of the Civil Rights movement, even as he goes on to iterate the undone work of reconstruction.

In once more citing Jefferson, however, King does not restrict his language to the rhetoric of democracy. Instead, his often biblical imagery suddenly takes a very material turn, as he reminds his audience that the "riches of freedom" are counted in money as well as votes:

> When the architects of our republic wrote the magnificent words of the Constitution and the Declaration of Independence, they were signing a promissory note to which every American was to fall heir. This note was a promise that all men, yes, black men as well as white men, would be guaranteed the unalienable rights of life, liberty, and the pursuit of happiness. It is obvious today that America has defaulted on this promissory note in so far as her citizens of color are concerned. Instead of honoring this sacred obligation, America has given the Negro people a bad check; a check which has come back marked "insufficient funds."

King circumvents the intentionalist reading of the Declaration and the Constitution (documents which certainly did not intend to extend the freedoms of citizenship to people of color) by reconstruing them as "promissory notes," or writings of a utopian cast. This recasting puts the Founding Fathers and their heirs under an obligation which, however morally and politically right, does not strictly follow from the original documents. But from Abigail Adams to Abraham Lincoln to King, this has become standard procedure in uses of the Declaration. More interesting is King's rhetorical troping of the Declaration and Constitution as "promissory notes," economic as well as political obligations. Although accounts of the Civil Rights movement sometimes divide its emphases into first a legal and then an economic phase, King's speech shows that black Americans always saw the link between the two, as the boycott in Birmingham earlier that year demonstrated.

The most often quoted passage of King's speech is that now titular paragraph in which he tells us that "I still have a dream. It is a dream deeply rooted in the American dream. I have a dream that one day this nation will rise up and live out the true meaning of its creed. 'We hold these truths to be self-evident, that all men are created equal.'" Playing (or signifyin') on that most clichéd of phrases ("the American dream"), King's reiterated "I have a dream" comes to have some of the same aggressive, ironic, even caustic, force one can hear in Walker, Fern, and Douglass (though in performance the speech stuck to the tones of righteousness and avoided pronouncing the bitterness that belonged to its content). In asserting that he, too, has a dream, King both contests the exclusion of African Americans from the American dream and insists rhetorically on their place within it (a place that has often been imagined by whites as the scene of a haunting nightmare). The integrationist, appropriative, and universalizing terms of King's dream of racial harmony and transcendence ("I have a dream that my four little children will one day live in a nation where they will not be judged by the color of their skin, but by the content of their character") so expertly express the dogmas of official American idealism that he leaves the white audience watching on TV with few authorized means of resistance (though plenty of Americans from George Wallace to the Congress were not persuaded). At the same time, his image of the promissory note implies an ambiguity in "the American dream": is it a dream of civil and political freedoms or a dream of economic possibilities? Given the economic infrastructure of racism, can it be both? Since a promise belongs to the realm of moral action, what kind of ethos does the "promissory note" of "the American dream" require? To whom was that note issued? And what will it take to pay the debt? Do we have the economic, cultural, and spiritual funds, or are they insufficient?

The shape of multicultural America's dilemmas in the subsequent decades has its roots in these questions.

King would come down from the mountain only to be assassinated while assisting a sanitation workers' strike in Memphis as part of his "poor people's campaign." By 1968 his "American" credentials were in dispute because of his opposition to the Vietnam War and his emphasis on economic issues rather than civil rights. Criticism from black militants and harassment from J. Edgar Hoover's FBI further eroded King's capacity to hold together an American dream capacious enough to unite people across races.[13] For his part, Ellison never did finish his much-awaited second novel. The "yes" Ellison pronounced in *Invisible Man* gave voice to a dream he found it hard to fulfill, as if the energy expended in upholding his *belief* in freedom robbed him of what force he needed to achieve something more in art (or politics). Ellison did write a series of powerful and problematic essays on literature, art, and cultural politics (collected in *Shadow and Act* and *Going into the Territory*) which, together with *Invisible Man*, deeply influenced the development of African American criticism and such practitioners as Houston Baker and Henry Louis Gates, Jr. In retrospect, however, it is not surprising that it was the Black Nationalist, Black Aesthetic, and women's liberation movements that predominated in black cultural and literary studies from the 1960s to the 1990s, rather than any vision growing out of the work of King and Ellison (who are less and less often mentioned).

13. In his account of King's place in the transition from the Civil Rights movement to identity politics and multiculturalism, Todd Gitlin claims that "King was the personification of faith and possibility: the incarnation of a black leadership that might build bridges from the movement against segregation to a successor movement against poverty and the inequality of wealth." Had he lived, King, no matter the setbacks he might have suffered, "would still have lingered as a unifying presence, as goad and conscience, as a living link with the America of Paine, Thoreau, Douglass, and Lincoln" (131). Gitlin projects onto King a "what if" narrative that overestimates the powers of heroes and underestimates the impersonal forces of politics and economics. It is an insult to the African American community to suggest that the failure of its leaders is to blame for the lack of dramatic progress in desegregation.

In the dialectic of cultural struggle, their work in the arenas of political idealism and artistic universalism would, inevitably, have to make way for the claims of the particular and the material — of the *differences* that came to be the chief theme of contemporary cultural studies.

Of course, King and Ellison were always there alongside Malcolm X, Alice Walker, Amiri Baraka, Toni Morrison, Jesse Jackson, Audre Lorde, Albert Murray, Cornel West, and the others. It has just been difficult of late to know where to place them, since the liberal tradition they belong to has been subject to so much critique in the less idealistic years since King's death. In trying to move the dialectic again and so to pick up the thread of their legacies, I think we can borrow profitably on the promissory note of the tradition, as I have tried to show. The various calls for a "rainbow coalition," for "intercultural dialogue" and "the politics of recognition," for "multiculturalism" and even a "postethnic America" are symptomatic of an effort to declare a new "we the people," though there remains good reason to fear any rush to revive patriotic community unless it is built on a foundation of historical memory and mutual care.

Ellison's relevance to the 1990s culture wars can be traced to his stubborn insistence on the "melting pot" as an apt metaphor for American identity. Resisting separatist tendencies in the 1970s, Ellison opens *Going into the Territory* by arguing forcefully that American culture has always been an integrative, appropriate mixture of diverse traditions. "Indeed," he writes, "it was through this process of cultural appropriation (and misappropriation) that Englishmen, Europeans, Africans, and Asians *became Americans*" (17). "American ness" by this light means the practice of freedom in cultural as well as political matters; indeed, it means a faith that the pursuit of freedom in each area is vital to the other. The failure of dominant institutions to live up to the ideals of the nation's founding documents does not, in Ellison's eye, blot out the continuous achievement of freedom by American artists, writers, thinkers, and musicians of every ethnic and racial background as they improvise together. Jazz is thus Ellison's constant model for how the performers of cultural pluralism appropriate and misappropriate from one another to sound the note of American unity-in-diversity.

Democracy realizes itself, in his account, more rapidly in culture than in the less pliable domain of politics. Ellison celebrates an American "vernacular" culture cobbled together by people exercising their freedom (albeit often against the rules of society, convention, and law). The territory in his title refers literally to Oklahoma, where black and Indian and white mixed in a cultural upheaval producing jazz and his own fiction. Ellison's vernacular territory resembles the borderlands of hybridity now so often theorized by cultural critics. This similarity in turn raises the question how to differentiate Ellison's integrative view of cultural identity from current accounts growing out of multiculturalism. Although Ellison's description of the "mixed and pluralistic" character of American cultural identity is hard to refute, it fails adequately to address social, juridical, and institutional segregation by race and gender in the United States. Ellison's idealizing use of jazz as metaphor of Americanness, after all, should not make us forget the discrimination and exploitation suffered by real jazz musicians and singers such as Bessie Smith, or the continued inequality of power between American whites and people of color, even in the cultural sphere (where white domination of the production system continues). The reaction against integrationism after the 1960s should not, then, be interpreted as a denial of the hybrid character of American cultural identity. This reaction signals rather a frustration with the lack of integration, or at least of justice, in other arenas of American life, as well as with the ongoing resistance of American cultural institutions (such as the university) to representing the diversity of our Americanness.

Meditating in *Shadow and Act* on the black writer's contradictory relation to the American dream and its fictional tradition, Ellison observes that "though as passionate believers in democracy Negroes identify themselves with the broader American ideals, their sense of reality springs, in part, from an American experience which most white men not only have not had, but one with which they are reluctant to identify themselves even when presented in forms of the imagination" (25). As I see it, the tradition of radical reform in American literary and cultural studies says yes to democracy in just the double-edged way Ellison describes. This affirmation obligates us to engage in complex and difficult acts of identification, empathy, and imagination. On occasion we need to affirm that which we have not experienced or, in politics, say yes even when the Supreme Court, from *Dred Scott* to yesterday, says no. Although the America of which many dream has yet to be born, and may exceed the boundary of any nation-state, the outlines of its ethos have already begun to form as the cultural struggles of the late twentieth century take their next turns. One of those is the "ethical turn" now apparent in various arenas, from academic theory to the political marketplace. In Chapter 3 I want to explore this turn further by connecting the development of multiculturalism since the 1960s with the idea of the ethical. If an ethos is a way of life, combining the certainties of knowledge with the uncertainties of ideals and beliefs, what ethos follows from today's struggles for representation? Looking back to 1776 and beyond 1996, I think this ethos could be one that is accountable to history's horrors, that dreams of a community of stories, that is merciless in exposing the practices of injustice, that emphasizes the accountability of individuals to one another, and that acknowledges that power without a vision of the good is a hollow goal to seek.

• • •

My reading of the Declaration's literary history emerged from my classrooms, including survey courses in American literature and two specialized seminars, "Slavery and American Literature" and "Fictions of Multiculturalism." What I have tried to illustrate in my approach is a pedagogy that negotiates between the counterclaims of separatism and universalism. On the one hand, the appropriation of Jefferson by African American writers forms a distinct lineage that belongs to the rich history of African American literature. That literature needs to be studied independently and as a coherent whole, as a *tradition* in which each writer is best understood and appreciated within the comparative and historical context shaped by the others. David Walker sheds light on Douglass, who in turn forms the standard for measuring Ellison and King. Without this context we might attribute more originality to one of them than he deserves, or appreciate less the importance of their use of the Declaration's words. There is a dialogue among them that can be discovered only if sufficient intelligence and resources and curricular time are devoted to the study of the African American tradition.

On the other hand, these appropriations of Jefferson put the African American tradition in dialogue with the European American tradition. It is not simply a matter of abstractly comparing Jefferson with Walker, or Douglass with Lincoln, however. The conversations between these texts belong to the actual history of their production, and not only to our retrospective perception. Walker wrote in response to Jefferson and his tradition, and Lincoln spoke in response to Douglass and his tradition. An accurate account of American literary history requires that we reconstitute these actual dialogues among writers to appreciate better how texts come into being and how they work in the cultures that produce them. To study Lincoln's Gettysburg Address without comparison to the tradition of African American writing on the Declaration is to miss a key ingredient in the formation of Lincoln's speech. It would be bad history and bad literary criticism to do so, just as we miss something essential about King's "I Have a Dream" speech if we neglect to trace its dialogue with Lincoln and Douglass and Jefferson. When we add the tradition of women writers to the mix, and begin comparing Walker and Douglass with Fern and the Seneca Falls activists, another dimension of cultural history and interpretation challenges us as well, though again we best approach this comparison with some solid independent study of the history of the women's rights movement and of feminist literary theory. Adding the history of working-class writing to the mix further complicates the story. In so expanding the universe of literary study, however, we do not proceed by first applying an ahistorical measure of aesthetic greatness or cultural value. Rather, scholarship seeks to do justice to the actual particulars of cultural history as lived by the diversity of men and women who expressed their struggles through it.

In Chapter 5 I will propose in some detail ways in which we can take a comparative approach to writing in the United States, one that would encourage us to do more than pronounce an aesthetic pledge of allegiance when asked: What is an American writer? Here I wish merely to prefigure that argument by pointing out that the theoretical and historical discussion of American identity and cultural politics offered in the present chapter was actually based on the practice of such a comparative approach. Indeed, some of it comes right out of classroom time spent in just such comparisons, or in following students as they transgressed the boundaries of genres, races, and traditions to make connections I had not foreseen. As the writings I assigned grew more and more diverse in an effort to keep up with these connections, I found myself moving from the debate over the American canon into the debate over multiculturalism.

t h r e e **Taking Multiculturalism Personally**

ince its beginning in the 1970s, the movement known as multiculturalism has taken two distinct directions.[1] One type of multiculturalism celebrates the diversity of cultural groups. Sometimes called ethnic revitalization, this multiculturalism seeks to preserve the cultural practices of specific groups and to resist the push toward assimilation. It sees the identities of individuals as primarily cultural, determined by their membership in a group, and not as the expression of a unique self-consciousness. Oriented by identity politics, this multiculturalism

---

1. The scholarly and critical literature on the topic continues to expand beyond anyone's capacity to keep up. For helpful summaries, see Banks and Lynch; Erickson; James and Jeffcoate; McCarthy; McCarthy and Crichlow viii–xxviii.

rejects the individualistic model of personhood and instead stresses the analysis of communal expressive traditions. The forms and values of these traditions, in turn, become the focus of curriculum reform. Pedagogy is responsible for developing a competence in the student, such that he or she can understand various cultures and appreciate their achievements. This competence may even lead to the student's choosing to join in that culture's practices, though this choice may be seen as a social faux pas and as a violation of the decorum of essentialism. For marginalized groups, an appreciation of their culture can enhance students' sense of self-worth and so reverse the effects of bigotry and discrimination. In ideological terms this multiculturalism may be called pluralist, since it emphasizes the characteristics of individual cultures rather than stressing the social or political relationships between them.

This first type of multiculturalism is said by some to paint a false picture of harmonious diversity and so to obscure the structures of exploitation and injustice that may actually define the differences between groups. We should not be surprised by this debate within the ranks, since multiculturalism stems in part from the political movements of the 1960s, such as the struggles of women, the poor and working classes, racial minority groups, and gay men and lesbians. Thus, the second type (or tendency) of multiculturalism is oppositional rather than pluralist (see, for example, Carby; Giroux, "Post-Colonial"; Morton and Zavarzadeh; Roman; and Wallace). It is less interested in celebrating difference than in resisting oppression. Sometimes called radical, critical, or strong multiculturalism, this branch of the movement targets the unequal distribution of power in society.[2] Rather than accepting the borders between cultural groups, it insists on analyzing how cultural divisions are constructed historically through racist policies or other institutionalizations of oppression. It maintains that cultural difference cannot be taught meaningfully without studying the structure of social inequalities outside the classroom, and it advocates using pedagogy as a means toward transforming those larger social realities. Radical multiculturalists would

2. See Kanpol and McLaren's *Critical Multiculturalism* for representative work in this area. The essays collected in Gordon and Newfield's *Mapping Multiculturalism* also challenge new orthodoxies in provocative ways.

not be satisfied with teaching the appreciation of African American cultural forms, for example, but would look for reasons why African Americans so often sing the blues. Proponents of this multiculturalism stress the specific class relations between dominant and subordinate groups within local, national, or global contexts. In some cases these oppositional critics move away from the focus on culture, rejecting it as an ideological distraction from the material conditions and political arrangements that determine the shape of our lives.

Such oppositional strategies for multiculturalism make crucial contributions, and I have found myself identifying with or endorsing many of their arguments. But I also feel that they tend toward versions of economic or political determinism that are ultimately no more satisfying than models that examine culture only as a set of personal aesthetic practices. As Cameron McCarthy argues in *Race and Curriculum*, we need "an alternative formulation that attempts to avoid privileging either 'cultural values' or 'economic structures' as 'the' exclusive or unitary source of racial inequality in schooling" (5). (For various attempts at such formulations, see the essays collected in McCarthy and Crichlow.) McCarthy's call for an alternative to the impasse between economic determinism and cultural determinism will sound familiar to those who have followed countless similar debates within Marxist, poststructuralist, and cultural studies circles. What emerges from those conflicts is usually a stronger emphasis on the problem of *agency*: despite the much heralded "death of the subject" and other requiems for humanism, critical theorists have rediscovered that the individual subject or person remains the vital and often unpredictable agent who realizes and mediates the claims of the economic and the cultural.

This renewed concern with personal agency seems to me part of a larger consensus that essentialism — whether used to define the homogeneous essence of a group or the singular nature of a person — must give way to more complex descriptions that accommodate the differences *within* groups and persons. (Here we can recall the positions articulated by Epstein, Escoffier, and Said reviewed in Chapter 1.) McCarthy's "alternative" will then require that we think hard about what multiculturalism teaches us about agency, identity, personhood, and individuality. If these are irreducible to either economics or culture, and if every person always occupies numerous contradictory social positions, then to proceed we need a third way, so to speak, one that conceives of agency as an *ethical* condition or that provides a complex description of *ethos* as a person's way of life. While multiculturalism should continue to advocate an antiracist, postcolonial, and resistant politics of the marginalized, it should also lead to ethical questions that cannot be entirely subordinated to identity politics or the analysis of ideology and political economy.

• • •

What is striking about the debate among the various multiculturalists is the common assumption they make about the "personal": identity in most of these theoretical or even practical accounts is defined and determined by totalizing social structures such as culture or economy. Given this preference for a social constructionist approach to human identities, any reference to persons or individuals tends to sound like a throwback to the discredited discourse of Enlightenment liberalism, whose image of the universal man turned out to be the reflection of a few European and American white guys. Words such as "humanism" and "individualism" are now regularly prefaced with discrediting adjectives such as "bourgeois" or "Western," which in many contexts they probably deserve. But if one grants that even the choice between economism and culturalism remains precisely a *choice*, something in part determined by the person rather than the system, then we need to account for the kind and quality of freedom that agents have, and the responsibilities that these freedoms might entail. In sum, I think we need an alternative formulation that avoids privileging either the social constructionist or liberal pluralist accounts of personhood in a multicultural society.

It is often said, sometimes in a tone of accusation, that the white masters of postmodernism or poststructuralism promoted the disappearance of the subject and the author at the very moment when the disenfranchised were finally gaining a powerful voice. Barbara Christian made this charge in her widely read article "The Race for Theory":

> I feel that the new emphasis on literary critical theory is as hegemonic as the world it attacks. I see the language it creates as one that mystifies rather than clarifies our condition, making it possible for

a few people who know that particular language to control the critical scene. That language surfaced, interestingly enough, just when the literature of peoples of color, black women, Latin Americans, and Africans began to move to "the center." . . . Now I am being told that philosophers are the ones who write literature; that authors are dead, irrelevant, mere vessels through which their narratives ooze; that they do not work nor have they the faintest idea what they are doing — rather, they produce texts as disembodied as the angels. (71–72).[3]

Jon Michael Spencer sees theoretical critiques of ideas about race as belonging to a "pattern in our public discourse that is aimed in part at reversing the impetus to implement multicultural education," a discourse "coming from intellectuals involved in what I call *the postmodern conspiracy to explode racial identity*" (2).[4] The debate over whether this kind of theory is dangerous has played itself out not only in African American studies but in Native American, Asian American, and gay and lesbian studies as well, since each of them is invested to some degree in the politics of identity.

Pamela Caughie defends the postmodern approach to race and the multicultural classroom by finding an allegory for them in Nella Larsen's novel *Passing*. There, as in so much African American literature of the early twentieth century, the color line is blurred as racial identity keeps exploding in people's faces (so to speak). Different characters negotiate their passages back and forth across the color line, encountering questions of ethics and agency along the way. In the scene of recognition that opens the novel, two passing women discover each other across this line; but as the novel develops, their discovery only deepens the question of what we can know of someone else by virtue of racial categorization. As the other person's gaze fixes us with a definition of our racial identity, a complex transference of values and meanings takes place. That other person may attribute to me qualities and experiences that, in fact, I can lay claim to

3. I cite the 1988 revised version of her essay, which originally appeared in 1987 in *Cultural Critique*. The argument is echoed in Gates, "Master's Pieces."

4. An interesting forum in response to Spencer's essay appeared in *The Black Scholar* 23 (1993): 50–80.

only partly if at all, since my racial subject position does not exhaust my personal identity. The uncertainties of "racial identity" make it difficult to resort to the "authority of experience" as a way of establishing the essential limits for identity categories, especially as we see the degree to which such authority gets granted by a kind of transference not unlike the transference that gives (or denies) authority to the racialized body in the classroom. The white teacher's authority, notes Caughie, which is usually the product of a transference modeled on the family (in which the student's gaze fixes the instructor as parent), is undermined when the issue of race comes up. Black students are less likely to produce her authority through such a transference, more likely to produce it as a component of the teacher's privileged racial or class position. But as authority gets passed around the classroom on the basis of supposedly sure markers of racial identity, it quickly becomes apparent that this one difference is not enough of a difference: the acceptance of the transference can become a kind of passing. Taking up the authority of a supposed racial experience may amount to covering over differences of sex or class, region or age or religion. The result of such well-intentioned honoring of the authority of experience may be just as bad as the pedagogical moment when the white class looks to the one black student to find out what all African Americans think.

Writing from the standpoint of an African American teacher familiar with such looks, Cheryl Johnson similarly concludes that "we are all cross-dressers." As her students' gaze positions her according to socially constructed meanings she cannot control, Johnson undergoes a postmodern explosion of her racial identity that, bizarrely, almost makes her feel as if she is passing: "Do students empower me as an absolute authority on black womanhood (and, therefore, the literature of black women) because my *experience* of this gives me an infallible handle on the 'true meaning' of the text? Am I 'read' as a representation of essentialized black womanhood, and if so, what is that 'reading,' and how much do I participate in or contribute to students' ideas about the nature of black women?" (410).[5] Johnson goes on to recount two incidents in which white students were unable to

5. "Does the black face of the Afro-American critic," asks Michael Awkward, "actually lead to qualitatively superior or perceptively different read-

finish reading black texts because they took them *too* personally: these students associated the violence and sexual abuse in the novels with personal experiences to which they bore only a faint resemblance. Worse, they confided in Johnson and expected her compassion because of their own stereotypes about the nature of black women. Onto her they transferred certain qualities they presumed belonged to her by virtue of her racial and gender identities, and felt they were honoring and respecting her in the process. The misreading of the text and of the teacher was, it seems, the result of mistaking people for subject positions, and vice versa. (For more on the situation of the black woman as teacher, see hooks).

Although I think that Christian and Spencer are partly right, then, I agree with Caughie and Johnson that much can go wrong when identity politics enters the classroom as if it were a reliable epistemology. This white teacher and this black teacher (both of them, however, feminists) document the misperceptions generated when the cultural subjectivity of race completely overshadows the multiple differences of our positions and the idiosyncrasies of our individual lives. It remains fair to point out that in their own critiques of universalizing stereotypes, the liberation movements also replaced the particulars of personal identity with the generalities of cultural subjectivities. Social constructionism goes hand in hand with multiculturalism, as both define the individual as the expression of the cultural practices of sociohistorical groups. The poststructuralist cry that "language speaks man" finds an eerie echo in the articulations of how race and ethnicity, sexuality and gender, class and nation speak the person.

Yet multiculturalism and the liberation movements often associated with it continue to exhibit discomfort about replacing persons with subject positions. The experience, the literature, and the theorizing on multiculturalism insistently bring out the stubborn

---

ings of the black text than ones offered by scholars with paler faces? In what ways is Afro-American insistence on the authority of experience comparable to the similar appeals of American feminist critics who originated the phrase and made it their interpretive catchword?" (28). Awkward's book provides an insightful discussion of these questions, especially as regards men's relation to feminism and the white critic's relation to African American literature.

tensions between persons and positions. For example, cultural identity as I live it is not a matter of choosing between a personal essence and a social construction. These are hypothetical entities in dialectical relationship to each other, and the shape their conversation takes over time constitutes the character of my person. *Agency* is one metaphor to name this dialectic: agency appears in the way I take a social construction personally, as my duty, my responsibility, my ethos, my law, my enemy, or my love. *Agency* also names the tendency of cultural practices to become reified and bureaucratized, to become agencies in the institutional sense. Such an agency can make people its instrumental agents, robbing them of their persons in the process of making them its subjects.

I think it could be healthy to insist on the difference between persons and cultural identities. The difference between me and my cultural identity creates opportunities for change. Taking these opportunities as occasions for agency, I also end up taking some responsibility for what happens as a result. If my cultural identity and I were the same, and if I imagined that identity as homogeneous and univocal, then my actions and beliefs would follow in strict accord. I would be on automatic, so to speak. Of course, the multiplicity of my cultural identities and their lack of any totalizing framework ensure that this never occurs. My positions, by virtue of race or class or gender or sexual orientation or age or nation or political ideology or professional vocation, include many contradictions, making me frequently the dominant, sometimes the marginalized, and quite often just the muddled one in the middle.

Negotiating the internal conflict of cultural identities requires as much or more energy and theoretical savvy than negotiating the differences between social groups or cultural formations. These groups and formations are not grounded in singular essences; they are coalitions and affiliations whose appearance of identity comes into being through history, strategy, and struggle. Categories such as heterosexual or white or Jewish American or middle class are not natural or divine divisions but rather the products of history. This does not make them false, unimportant, or unnecessary, but it does mean that I had better accept some responsibility for them, whether I wish to advocate or deconstruct them. The solidity of these categories remains fragile and transient, as the history of these and other group formations demonstrates. As McCarthy notes, "An essentialist approach to race typically ignores or flattens out the differences within minority groups while at the same time insulating the problem of race inequality from issues of class and sexual oppression" (118). What we have learned from Foucault and others about the "invention" of "homosexuality" as an identity category may be applied to the history of words such as "white" and "middle class" as well (see Omi and Winant). Such words not only name but also help shape the groups to which they are attached. Like any name or noun, these categorical labels create universals at the expense of particular differences, which are forgotten in the process.

The differences between the Dutch, German, English, French, Swiss, Russian, and Italian are forgotten, largely for political reasons, when the panethnic category "white" subsumes them all. Likewise the category "middle class" obscures the real differences between men and women, gays and straights, whites and blacks who otherwise share a common socioeconomic bracket. The differences within particular categories are suspended, then, when the identity of the group gets constructed. These suspended differences, in turn, are always potentially the source of fracture and realignment as people respond to new claims on their passions and allegiances. "Person" is another name for the individual who is the remainder of this process, the leftover when totality fails, or the agent who negotiates the new contract. "Ethics" is one name for the way this person self-consciously conducts these negotiations, and "ethos" is a name for the way of life such conduct reinforces or makes possible.

There is often something a bit suspect about the plea not to "take it personally." In the case of multiculturalism, the plea would seem especially odd, given the roots of multiculturalism in the grounds of identity politics. But is a cultural identity personal? The problem of taking multiculturalism personally comes back to this puzzling question. I want to dwell for a moment on the possibility that identity and the personal are not the same thing. If they were, how could an individual experience the crisis of wondering whether to take being Hispanic or Asian, male or female, Christian or Muslim personally? To pose cultural identity in the form of a question, as something that someone can choose to take or reject, as something that may be adopted or imposed, already introduces an element of agency, freedom, or voluntarism that strict essentialists or determinists reject. I think the resilience of the idiomatic question testifies to a practical belief that agency is both real and desirable, even if this means being vulnerable to ideological manipulation and one's own naïveté.

Within the practices of education, multiculturalism assumes some degree of personal agency in its teachers and students. Teachers are expected to take multiculturalism seriously, if not personally, and to change their syllabi, their classroom behavior, and their administrative goals accordingly. Students are expected to consider the possibility that the cultural values and practices of their group may be either the ideological mask of a will-to-power or the encoded expression of a people's resistance, outrage, and pride. Whether in the case of teachers or students, multiculturalism opens a gap between personal selfhood and cultural identity, and this is to the good. Taking multiculturalism personally ought to be an ethical injunction for every teacher, scholar, and student today, though obviously the effects of this ethic will vary dramatically depending on the person involved. For people like me, this ethic should be a kind of categorical imperative of pedagogy, for it insists on treating the Other as an end and not a means. Trying to formulate and live by this ethic forces me to confront confusing and painful truths about myself and my profession.

• • •

Me, I got a late start taking multiculturalism personally. It was the early 1980s. I was teaching survey courses in American literature and had begun to introduce culturally diverse works into the canon of my syllabus, partly in response to the racial makeup of my classes at the University of Alabama (for more on this experience, see Chapter 4). Being from a suburb of Los Angeles, and having spent the previous eight years in relatively elite institutions of higher education, I was not accustomed to much in the way of racial diversity. Now I was teaching just down the street from the steps where Governor George Wallace had stood, only twenty years before, in defiance of federal orders to desegregate the university. By the early 1980s some 10 percent of the undergraduate population there was African American, a proportion that regularly showed up in my survey classes.

The course tried to represent the heterogeneous groups who have given their radically different answers to Crèvecoeur's question "What is an American?" As the list of categories multiplied — American Indian, African American, Asian American, Polish American, Irish American, Jewish American — I felt left out. Who were *my* people? More uncomfortably, what was I doing trying to represent these Others anyway? Couldn't they speak for themselves? What was my ethical relation to this professional and pedagogical practice? Given the manifest failure of the institution to provide the marginalized with access to speech or representation, what was my responsibility? According to some of my African American students, my responsibility certainly did not include designating them as the spokespersons for the race. The job of analyzing and denouncing racism in a classroom dominated by whites was, for them, the white man's job, since he had invented race in the first place.

Identity politics and its discontents started following me home at night. Child of a secular Jewish father and a lapsed Mormon mother, I found myself puzzling over my own cultural identity. Did I have a race or ethnicity? A gender or a sexual orientation? A class or a nationality? Was my cultural identity singular or plural? And was it something I got by inheritance and imposition, or something I could choose and alter at my will? Perhaps most important, why hadn't I worried about all of this before? Who was I that I hadn't had a cultural identity crisis? Why had I suddenly become a white man? Was it only because I now lived in Alabama? Or had I been an invisible man to myself for all the years before?

Of course I had had lots of identity crises in the past, but none that turned so specifically on how cultural categories determine experiences of identity. Being a child of the radical 1960s, I had long since taken it for granted that my primary social identity was that of an oppositional intellectual. Hadn't I chosen a marginal and unprofitable major in college? Hadn't I consciously rejected materialism and sought higher values in art and philosophy? Hadn't I, to my father's bewilderment, decided to teach literature as a career and ended up in Tuscaloosa? Even if I had become a professional, I could take some pride in being a relatively ill paid, unrespected, uninfluential, and routinely alienated person. I thought of the cultural politics of my identity in conventional terms, positioning myself as the enemy of variously named forces of right-wing evil. Surely the night riders of the Klan and I had nothing in common and could never be identified with each other. I clung stubbornly to the utopian dream of my own person, not recognizing how I too wore the white sheet wherever I walked. By this I do not mean that I finally realized the moral equivalency of my racism with that of the Klan; rather, I realized that guilt was not really the point, since whether I wished it or not, my whiteness made a difference in how I was treated. Onto my whiteness was transferred a host of qualities and privileges, or fears and hostilities, to which I had to become accountable.

Those years led me to write an essay on American literature and multiculturalism, in which I added my voice to those of the canon busters. My professional identity began to change from that of a "theorist" publishing in *diacritics* to a teacher of literature writing for *College English*. Was this shift simply determined by the marketplace — in ideas and in jobs — or was it the result of experience and choice? Had I simply jumped from one kind of opportunism to another? The more I imagined that my professional choices had political and even moral claims, the more uncomfortable I felt, even as I enjoyed the rhetoric of polemic that these claims made possible. Professors were supposed to be useless, irrelevant, or at best ineffectual and harmless, and this went double for liberal white men. Was multiculturalism an ethical way of life for the professor, and did it have anything to do with the way I lived my "real" life?

There was only one thing left to do: offer a class about the problem. I decided to design a course called "Fictions of Multiculturalism," which I have offered regularly since then. The readings include modern prose fiction by a culturally diverse group of writers as well as critical and theoretical essays on multiculturalism and pedagogy. Institutionally, the course fulfills my university's new cultural diversity requirement, so the enrollment includes students from a variety of majors. Fortunately it has also drawn a culturally diverse student population, at least relatively speaking, as mine is a predominantly white working-class campus.

In its design, syllabus, and classroom approach, the course is intended to ask students both to take responsibility for their own cultural identities and to practice forming relationships with people who do not share their subject position, values, skin color, religion, and so on. In the multicultural classroom, the authority of one person's experience quickly runs up against that of someone else, so that the limits of such authority may be usefully marked and analyzed. Clashes of cultural identity, however, do not always yield to a happy pluralism or cheerful tolerance. On the contrary, the differences between cultural groups are often fundamental, sometimes deadly, and are better brought into the open than repressed (at least in the classroom). Multicultural pedagogy inevitably confronts the problem of how a social structure can successfully accommodate persons who find the beliefs or truths of others to be intolerable and unacceptable.

To get my students to take multiculturalism personally, I first ask them to write an analysis of their own cultural identity, which, it turns out, is very different from writing a personal essay expressing one's self. We use this paper and the first few readings (pieces such as Adrienne Rich's "Split at the Root" and June Jordan's "Flight to the Bahamas") to explore what a cultural identity might be, where we might get one, and how we might feel about the ones we have or that others have. The notion of cultural identity strikes many of the students as strange. In the context of American individualism, the concept of cultural identity seems anomalous: identity is supposed to be personal, idiosyncratic, something we don't share with anyone else. Seeing one's *self* as a cultural identity tends to erode the feeling of uniqueness so prized in American culture and so important to the process of assimilation. Assimilation results, the story goes, when an American self emerges after the immigrant casts off the cultural identity and trappings brought from another land.

This gets us to the paradox that the assignment aims to bring to the surface. Dominant American culture defines the person as essentially private and thus as lacking a cultural identity, for a cultural identity would be a restraint on individual freedom, a straitjacket of convention, a prescription of inauthenticity. A cultural identity would limit what a person wore, ate, said, kissed, worshipped, wrote, bought, or sold. Modern entrepreneurial individualism, or consumer identity, considers cultural practices strictly as commodities, as entirely relative to the fundamental project of the self's acquisitive freedom. Histories of the United States regularly narrate American selfhood in terms of European tyranny versus American freedom, the cultural conservatism of the Old World versus the open modernity of the New. In traditional accounts, having a cultural identity tends to be associated, then, with people from the Old World or with racial minorities. "Americans," by contrast, are supposed to be those people who have abandoned the outdated garments of an old cultural identity to stand naked and reborn in the perpetual future that is America. Of course, when your cultural identity by virtue of gender or skin color cannot be stripped off like an unfashionable wardrobe, your opportunities for assimilation may be drastically narrowed.

It is no surprise, then, that many of my puzzled students end up writing about how they do not have a cultural identity. Some proudly announce that they are "just Americans," while others more wistfully describe themselves as "merely normal." This perception of the self as "American" and "normal" usually involves an implicit or explicit comparison to others whom the student identifies as having a cultural identity. These people with cultural identities are usually African, Asian, Latino, or Native Americans. They are described as having special cultural characteristics, unique food and music, strange languages, different beliefs. And, not incidentally, their skin is usually darker.

Not surprisingly, the lost students I am describing are the descendants of European immigrants, especially those in the third and fourth generations. They are most likely to see themselves as the norm and to see other groups as special, particular, or deviant. Having lost many of the ethnic characteristics that differentiated the quite diverse European populations who settled and assimilated in the United States, these students have also assimilated the notion that freeing oneself of cultural peculiarities is essential to becoming a normal, prosperous American. They do not see their own clothes, food, beliefs, values, or music as constituting a distinctive culture, just as they do not see themselves as having a cultural rather than an individual identity. As one might expect, the exceptions are children of first- or second-generation immigrants whose families and neighborhoods have consciously preserved linguistic, religious, culinary, and social practices identified with the "old country."

Students from non-European backgrounds have much less trouble with the assignment, since they are accustomed to being seen, and seeing themselves, as having a cultural identity that is "different." Although these students never fit into neat boxes, and their personal experiences and senses of identity vary enormously, almost all share a daily consciousness of having to negotiate between their sense of being a person and their sense of belonging to a group. Their person, they feel, is often not identifiable with the symbolic figures that populate the dominant mainstream culture. They rarely see people like themselves on TV, except perhaps during police dramas or the local news. By contrast, persons who see themselves as very similar to the dominant cultural imaginary do not experience themselves as having a cultural identity, since in their eyes they are not "different." The universalization of their cultural presuppositions whitewashes them, allowing them to mistake the cultural for the personal and making them invisible to themselves.

I should note how gender skews this pedagogical exercise. As one might guess, many women students define their cultural identity in terms of their gender. They discuss how important their condition or experience of gender has been in shaping their ideas, feelings, and values. This assertion tends to come more strongly from self-identified feminists, but it also comes from women of various political stripes. In the first two semesters, which included over seventy students, I never had a male student write about the importance of gender to his cultural identity. Just as the children of European immigrants tend not to see their skin as having color or their values as being culturally specific, men tend to dissociate their gender from their individuality. I found this pattern extraordinary, knowing as I do how much time men spend talking about and asserting their masculinity. Yet, probably in part because of the nature of the course and the presumed values of the instructor, none of the men wrote about how growing up male had affected his identity.

The results in the area of sexual orientation were similar. Given the prejudice and legal prohibitions against homosexuality in our society, it is understandable that only one person explicitly identified herself as lesbian or gay through the assignment. (One other discussed her recent exploration of bisexuality.) And why should a gay or lesbian student come out to classmates? Is it any of their business? Is sexual orientation a private, personal identity rather than a social or cultural identity? Here the ethical puzzles for the instructor are daunting.[6] On the one hand, I want to make my classroom a place that supports the expression of formerly silenced subjectivities, and I want that expression to alter the prejudices of other students. On the other hand, what right have I to make the sexual orientation of my students a matter of pedagogical manipulation? Is this the business of the professor? Can the professor, given his business, avoid professing biases and values in regard to sexuality or race or other social divisions merely by remaining quiet about them? And who is to say that sexual orientation is an identity waiting to "come out" anyway? Many, if not most, college students are still trying to figure out their sexual identity, as they come to learn that sexual identity is a complex process of changes that do not stop with puberty or early adulthood or even middle age and marriage. The puzzles here are clearly different than in the cases of race and gender, where the body usually gives people's identities away without their being able to choose whether to "come out." Yet, even then, my ethical dilemma seems different in terms of dealing with people depending on whether their position is privileged or subordinated. Rightly or wrongly, I have not felt much restraint about putting the race of white people or the sexuality of straight men before the class as a subject for critique, and I regularly push students in these categories toward a more public reckoning with the relationship between their personal and their group identities. With privileges come responsibilities.

The results of the initial assignment, in any case, provide a chance to analyze which kinds of identity seem to have ready access to public representation and what particular problems people face when speaking about different identity positions. In realizing the kinds of privileges or oppressions that our cultural identities entail, whether we choose them or not, students get a better understanding of the importance of history and may relent a bit in their insistence that they are not affected by or responsible for anything that happened before they were born.

One consequence of the assignment was to drive a wedge between "race" and "culture." The students who felt that they did not have a common culture belonged to the category that race discourse dubs

6. See Mary Elliott's "Coming Out in the Classroom" for a helpful exploration of these issues.

"white." I have argued that this feeling is in part ideologically motivated, a blind spot of privilege and social dominance. But I also want to argue that in a way these students are right. Strictly speaking, there is no such thing as white culture. Culture makes sense in terms of ethnic groups and geographic populations, but it makes less sense when oriented solely by skin pigmentation. Historically, the term "white" was invented in the seventeenth and eighteenth centuries to provide Europeans, especially Europeans settling in the American colonies, with a word for their difference from Africans and Native Americans. As the scholarship of Afrocentrism demonstrates, "white" stands for a politically constructed group grounded in a mythical Greco-Roman classicism.

"White" designates the supposed common culture binding diverse European immigrants. Since their ethnic and national groups do not constitute a common culture, historiography had to invent one for them to help justify the project of colonialism and the institution of slavery. In fact, "white" replaces ethnic taxonomies with a racial one, producing real confusion and misrecognition when the children of European immigrants compare their family tales of by-our-bootstraps upward mobility to the bleak fortunes of African Americans, as if being a Polish or Italian or Irish immigrant were in some way commensurable with being a member of an outcast racial class (see Sleeter, whose fascinating interviews with white teachers of multiculturalism produced results not unlike those my assignment uncovered). "White" is a political category, not a cultural one (yes, I know how difficult it is to draw these lines, but here it seems crucial to do so). What holds white people together is not a common language, religion, cuisine, literature, or philosophy, but rather a political arrangement that distributes power and resources by skin color. By replacing a specific ethnicity with the metaphor of a colorless color, "white" has the effect of making everyone else "different." But, as Leslie Roman reminds us, "white is a color!" This makes the "ambivalent and oxymoronic phrase 'people of color'" troublesome. "Given the tendency of the multicultural discourse to celebrate diversity without adequately analyzing power differentials among groups positioned by racial categorizations and inequalities, the phrase 'people of color' still implies that white culture is the *hidden norm*" (71). But I think Roman's reference to "white culture" here is misleading, since "white" came into use as a way of replacing cultural differences with racial differences.

Now, it may be argued that everything I have said about "white" applies to "black" just as well. The switch from "black" to "African American" could be offered as proof of this, since it indicates a switch from racial to ethnic or geographical or descent categorizations that have more solid footing than color distinctions when it comes to cultural formations. This is very tricky territory, for political and ethical as well as other reasons. I would venture to observe, however, that when "whiteness" and "blackness" were put to use as cultural terms, "black" (or "Negro" or "colored") had the effect of denying the cultural value of African ancestry, and so de-ethnicized African Americans in a dehumanizing fashion. Over time, this population lived through experiences as "blacks" that became the subject of their art, literature, music, and religion, so that race and culture became *joined* in the recognition of a vibrant black culture. While "white" functioned somewhat analogously, especially when it centered on Anglo-Saxon and Protestant ethnicity, its cultural borders kept shifting as the family of whiteness grew (to include the Irish and the Italians and the Jews, for example). In this case it seemed that no particular feature reigned except non-blackness (or non-redness or non-brownness or non-yellowness). Attempts to assert proudly the existence of a white culture are as old as the republic, but these are considered odd fringe movements embarrassing to the dominant culture's ethic of universalism. Although there may be a white culture, it has difficulty naming itself, for such a naming would immediately contradict the universalism of its ethos. Black culture, by contrast, names the capacity of a disempowered group to gain voice and autonomy despite its exclusion — names a capacity to universalize from an unchosen site of particular marginalization (see Marable). Whereas white culture cannot assert itself without proclaiming the inferiority of others or becoming entangled in the history of its own sins, black culture is under no such constraint. Of course, since in the United States these two cultures are in practice inseparably linked, it is finally impossible to theorize (much less participate in) one without becoming accountable to the other.

No wonder my students were confused. To be a white person is to have certain advantages and distinctions, socially and politically and economically; but being white does not provide a person with a culture. Indeed, the discourse of race separates whites from their own culture, insofar as it lies to them about how profoundly the work and art of racially subordinated people has shaped American culture. "The sequestered suburban white student is uninformed," writes William Pinar, "unless he or she comes to understand how, culturally, he or she is also African American," and this means more than admitting one's infatuation with rap music or Alice Walker (63). There is, I think, an American culture, but it is not defined by ethnic groups or racial distinctions. Rather, it is grounded in economic individualism, wedded to the practice of consumption, and hostile to the traditional constraints of cultural systems whenever these inhibit the workings of the marketplace. In this capitalist metaculture, cultural beliefs and practices are not traditions that constrain and guide behavior but commodities that may be deployed in order to create effects of pleasure, knowledge, profit, and power. Hence the much observed phenomenon of the postmodern subject, a person whose cultural identity is essentially and repeatedly decentered. But, as we have seen, the freedom of a person to choose or resist various cultural identities suffers painful constraints under regimes of discrimination, in part because these regimes are economic and not just cultural.

• • •

In discussing the role of ethnicity in the classroom, one might take the pun on "class" as a serious topic of investigation. We would do well to talk about taking class personally, especially today, when we are so accustomed to saying that "the personal is the pedagogical." To what degree does the classroom function as a place for reproducing or resisting class relationships of hierarchy, exploitation, and ethno-racial distinction? If the classroom works to organize the assignment of students to class positions, and thus to both economic and social ranks, how does introducing an analysis of race or ethnicity or gender affect this process? Are the volumes of controversy over the validity of these as identity categories made possible largely by evading the powerful class-based motivation for those categories? If people from African, Asian, Native American, or Latino communities now find a positive value in identifying with a race or ethnicity, may this not be a sign that previous avenues of upward social mobility have been closed — or remain closed despite earnest efforts to open them?

For most European ethnics from the seventeenth to the nineteenth centuries, the lure of assimilation was class driven. Upward mobility required the shedding of languages, customs, and beliefs that might interfere with the efficiency of the farm, shop, factory, or corporation. The process of becoming an American required leaving much of the baggage of the old country in the old country, or at least at home. What the economy wanted were workers, people who understood enough English to take — and later give — orders, and people who would embrace the essential principle of American culture: the principle that the marketplace determines all values, and that no one and no thing has value except in terms of the marketplace. Cultural identity in America, in its dominant form, is the identity of being a worker and a consumer in a capitalist marketplace. Ethnic or racial traits or practices will be preserved or destroyed insofar as they are judged conducive to profitable labor or susceptible to commodification. The celebration of diversity movement today seems inextricable, then, from the emergence of a consumer economy in which the marketing of ethnic commodities is a highly profitable way of opening new markets, creating new products, and fulfilling the need for incessant novelty.

From this vantage, the persistence of racism toward African Americans and other "racial minorities" may be attributed to capitalism's structural requirement that there must always be an immiserated underclass to supply cheap labor and provide a constant downward pressure on wages. As a means of preserving such a class, racism is relatively more efficient than ethnic prejudice, since ethnic traits tend to be less easy to discern and more ambiguous than the more easily spotted difference of skin color. Ethnic distinctions, both physical and cultural, have undoubtedly been used as instruments of class domination to be sure. Yet often in those cases we find the group — be they Jews or Japanese or Italians — frequently targeted as a *race*. When the Irish, the Swedes, the English, the Germans, or the Greeks cease to be seen as members of races and instead become known as ethnics, it is a sign that these categories have lost most of the ability they once had to produce class distinctions. The relative physical similarity of people from these lineages and their history of intermarriage in America makes them very inefficient agencies for marking and preserving class distinctions. So class analysis helps us understand how concepts of race and ethnicity are not synonymous and have functioned differently in American history.

This relation of ethnicity to class can be seen in the way the term "white" was invented to give these heterogeneous cultural groups a false sense of racial identity for economic purposes. "White" is a metaphor used to demarcate the members of the dominant economic class, especially in the United States, though with the extension of American market culture around the world, the value of whiteness as a class distinction has been exported and/or reinforced globally (whiteness, however, has functioned as a regulator of class privilege since the earliest days of European imperialism abroad). Once an ethnic group has enough clout in that dominant class, its members become whites. This has happened to the Germans, the Irish, the Poles, the Italians, the Jews, and now maybe even to the descendants of some Asian immigrants (at least as seen from the perspective of African Americans). The unique history and economic function of the term "white" in the United States and much of Northern Europe must be grasped if we are to understand the enduring marginalization of African Americans relative to other ethnic populations.

A number of class factors may be seen in the current debates over ethnic revival, multiculturalism, and Afrocentrism, to pick a few examples. Because the so-called "new immigrants" from Latin America and Asia are relatively susceptible to social surveillance on the basis of physical characteristics, members of these groups experience a degree of the racial discrimination long directed at African Americans. These groups constitute much of the new economic underclass in the United States. The constant temptation of whites to discriminate racially against people of these ethnic groups makes it less easy for them to assimilate than European ethnics, especially during a period of economic restructuring, when low-skill entry-level manufacturing jobs are disappearing. But, in light of the immigration statistics since 1960, the size of the resulting underclass is too large for the health of the U.S. economy, which requires a greater balance between economic classes and more upward mobility for individuals (though not at the expense of maintaining rigid class structures overall). Hence, the positive media coverage and corporate attention given to "diversity" indicates a reluctant recognition that at least some forms of racial discrimination are no longer profitable. In a market economy even racism can lose its value if it does not serve the bottom line.

One effect of discrimination is to reinforce the conviction among the oppressed that assimilation is impossible and undesirable, and so a celebration, preservation, and expansion of the distinct community's own cultural identity is promoted. One problem that immediately arises, however, again takes us back to economics. Ethnic communities are rarely economically self-sufficient, especially in our era. Usually they continue to be colonized landscapes, pools of cheap labor, or simply zones designated off-limits to investment. No amount of ethnic revival is likely to preserve a community in such a condition, since members of that community will most often have to leave the community — either physically or in terms of language, values, and cultural practices — to survive economically. Whenever immigrant groups, whether Polish or Korean or El Salvadoran, have created relatively autonomous *economic* zones, the preservation of the *cultural* identities of those communities has been far greater. The flourishing of organized crime in ethnic ghettos illustrates the paradoxes of these developments quite nicely: groups barred by discrimination from access to much in the way of legal upward mobility, from the Irish and Jews to the Vietnamese and African Americans, turn to organized crime as an available economic practice which also reinforces a cultural homogeneity. Thus, however important, no preservation of cultural traditions by schools or other institutions can have a decisive effect when a community remains in a condition of economic colonization. Multiculturalism cannot liberate oppressed classes, all puns intended.

By bringing a class analysis into the classroom, the teacher may be able to help delineate those experiences that bridge what may otherwise be seen as nonnegotiable differences between students (or between students and teachers). However vital and essential it is to recover, study, and encourage the separate cultural productions of different communities, such labor does not necessarily forge those alliances across borders without which the struggle against oppression may not succeed. Class analysis connects the histories of different ethnic and racial communities by illuminating the common structures of economic and social distinction that reinforce and reproduce the cultural meaning of ethnic or racial categories. This is why antiracism may be more important, in the long run, than multiculturalism, at least so far as confronting and crossing real social boundaries is concerned.

Solidarity between different communities is not likely to be produced by a focus on culture, since culture is seen as that which distinguishes, rather than connects, ethnic and social groups. What does connect such groups is the common way the dominant system positions them, whether as a "racial" group relatively prohibited from economic or social mobility or, similarly, as an "ethnic" group occupying an ambiguous position between the underclass and the middle class. Obviously, too great a focus on race or ethnicity undermines such class alliances and only serves the interests of the dominant class. Focusing on race and ethnicity also obscures the character of the antagonism between classes, papering over economic differences with either the celebration or the denunciation of cultural differences. In the setting of the classroom, students should be given an opportunity to use class analysis to cross the borders between identity categories, to explore common class experiences with students of very different racial or ethnic communities, or, perhaps more explosively, to confront students from the dominant class with an analysis that targets their economic privilege rather than their skin color.

Taking class personally into the classroom, as bell hooks recounts, involves the use of personal narrative to connect the authority of experience with the historical and theoretical issues under discussion. "Sharing experiences and confessional narratives in the classroom," writes hooks, "helps establish communal commitment to learning. These narrative moments usually are the space where the assumption that we share a common class background and perspective is disrupted." By bringing personal experience into the class dialogue, students and teachers can give the abstract concept of "difference" flesh-and-blood detail (as a good poet or novelist does when dramatizing the complexity of any concept). The exchange of these experiential narratives becomes, in turn, an experience itself as each participant is moved to recognize the hard facts of another's life. "Just the physical experience of hearing, of listening intently, to each particular voice strengthens our capacity to learn together" (186). Such conversations tend to work against the ingrained habit of thinking that the uniqueness of our personal experience gives us a superior accesss to the truth, for in these exchanges we hear of different truths that emerge from equally powerful stories. We often begin such dialogues presuming that, once we have offered our narratives from experience, others must agree with our point of view. Instead we discover that other points of view have the same claim to the authority of experience. This realization may make us question the narrowness of the experiences on which we have based our opinions.

Often we take our experiences of class or race or gender for granted, especially if social or educational arrangements ensure that we rarely hear stories from lives radically different from our own. The assignment of literary texts that represent a broad spectrum of experience can initiate this dialogue of stories, but the lessons may be even more deeply learned when accompanied by relevant narratives produced in and by the whole class, including the instructor. If the body of available instructors includes a range of individuals from many backgrounds and with diverse experiences to share, so much the better. Because the conversation inevitably points up the limits of the authority of experience, students learn the necessity of doing historical research, data analysis, close reading, theoretical argument, and other forms of inquiry that can help resolve the conflict between personal stories. The use of narratives, then, need not end in a relativistic standoff in which people cling to "where they are coming from." Precisely because the stories will differ, the class will have to reframe the tales with intellectual and scholarly materials that make the analysis of difference meaningful. As a group, a class can establish its own narrative of inquiry as a way of bridging individual stories and of connecting personal experience to the experience of groups, regions, classes, and nations.

Class analysis will and should inevitably engulf the teacher in its challenges. There is a rich, growing, and necessary literature (including the essays by Caughie and Johnson) on the contradictory effects that the subject position of the teacher has in the classroom (see also Awkward). Discussions of the identities of students and teachers, however, are vulnerable to degenerating into the stale charge ("You can't know what we've been through") that resonates through debates over multiculturalism. Such charges may be leveled by students at one another, by students at teachers, and by teachers at students, since the logic of identity politics allows any cultural group to claim an exclusive authority to know and express its experiences. This acrimony leads to an intellectual and political dead end. As an alternative, students might instead be helped to explore — through novels, poems, films, music, historical events, the study of material culture — how assertions for and against cultural identities may be unintentionally reinforcing class divisions (again, all puns intended). Readings that pinpoint how different cultural communities share certain historical experiences, erotic dreams, family struggles, and artistic longings can help fashion solidarity across lines that might otherwise divide. But to keep this approach from degenerating into "universal humanism," the connections among community stories have to be made *through* the differences, not by ignoring them.

In Hisaye Yamamoto's short story "Seventeen Syllables," for example, we read of the encounter between Japanese Americans and Mexican Americans in California's farm country just prior to World War II. The differences between these communities, and implicitly between these communities and the white community, are connected in a number of ways. The Hayashi family work a small tomato farm, where they have hired the "Mexican family" of Carrascos to assist with the harvest. Everyone helps with the picking in the sweltering sun and with the sorting in the heat of the sheds. The plots revolving around love affairs and generation gaps show individual persons struggling with their identities against the backdrop of conflicts within as well as between groups. The alliance or antagonism between groups, moreover, operates in the context of larger socioeconomic structures (such as the California agricultural labor system or the patriarchal regime of the Japanese husband). In this extraordinarily complex tale, Yamamoto dramatizes the common class position of the Japanese and Mexican working families, which she embodies in the teenage erotic attraction of Rosie Hayashi for Jesus Carrascos. The prelude to their one intimate moment takes place in the fields, where what Rosie "enjoyed most was racing him to see which could finish picking a double row first" (28).

The possibility of solidarity and love between them, however, is challenged by Rosie's mother, Tome, who has just won a prize for her writing of haiku. What appears to be aristocratic pretension on Tome's part (her disgruntled husband prefers the imagery of *Life* magazine) turns out to be a woman's protest against her fate in a patriarchal marriage. After her husband burns her prize, Tome tells Rosie the story of how she gave premature birth to her lover's stillborn son back in Japan. Theirs had been a secret romance because of her lower class position. She had come to America out of desperation, having arranged a wedding to a man she had never met. She warns Rosie against the fate that naive romanticism leads to, urging her shocked daughter, "Promise me you will never marry!" Apparently the lesson of the old country is that class distinctions cannot be transcended, and that marriage locks women into a status of economic and social disempowerment that only fitfully allows for self-expression.

The ethos Tome prescribes for her daughter derives from her ethnic experience, and so does not readily fit Rosie's idea of life. Rosie's cultural identity is derived from the marketplace of American commercial culture. She does not know enough Japanese to read her mother's poetry, but she can delight her Japanese American girlfriends with imitations of Fred Allen, Rudy Vallee, Shirley Temple, and the Four Inkspots. As her name symbolizes, Tome's daughter Rosie is as American as she is Japanese, which is to say that she has already assimilated the belief in the romance of the rose: hers is the ethos of individual choice, of freedom from the past, of rebirth through the love of Jesus: "Jesus, Jesus, she called silently, not certain whether she was invoking the help of the son of the Carrascos or of God, until there returned sweetly the memory of Jesus' hand, how it had touched her and where" (38). The border-crossing romance of Jesus and Rosie echoes that long tradition of tragic American tales of miscegenation, from the plantation novel to *Ramona* to *West Side Story*. Although Rosie makes the promise her mother demands, her heart is not in it, and her mother's "consoling hand" at story's end cannot wipe away the memory of Jesus's touch.

What connects all these hands is that they are the hands of tomato pickers and sorters. Tome had adopted a pen name to write haiku, renouncing the labor of the fields for the handiwork of writing. Significantly, her husband's rage is provoked when the arrival of the prize takes his wife momentarily away from the urgent business of sorting the fast-ripening crop. His act forces Tome back into her identity as wife and laborer, ending her brief exercise of agency and artistic expression. In turn, Rosie's flirtation with Jesus and her appropriation of American voices are, though she barely realizes it, crucial moments in the development of her own power to take hold of things and to act on her own desires. The bitterness of Rosie's parents comes, I think, from their respective feelings of diminishment, and their daily experience of how quickly the ripe fruit rots. This bitterness is Rosie's Japanese American heritage, but it is one that she turns from in seeking Jesus's kiss. Her challenge is to negotiate between the accounts of ethnicity and gender she learns at the hands of her parents, on the one hand, and the seductive possibilities of self-transformation offered by love and popular culture, on the other hand. Her way of life will be a series of choices framed by the rival demands of her cultural and personal identities. These, too, are plural, since her cultural identity ranges from Japanese poetry to American pop songs, and her personal identities include the positions of daughter, lover, worker, and woman.

"Seventeen Syllables" shows how the tensions between ethnos and ethos can inform multicultural American texts, and how issues of economics come into the plot when characters have to sort out the contest between personal and cultural identity. It is fascinating to explore with students whether the alliance of Rosie and Jesus is meant to symbolize a working-class insurgency or is mere American romanticism designed to distract the victimized from their plight. The story offers multiple points where the reader can identify with a variety of subject positions, and so diverse students will find themselves walking in a lot of surprising shoes. Although Rosie's predicament stands out as the one with which readers, especially younger students, will empathize, the power of her mother's story and the symbolic attraction of Jesus split our allegiances as well. It is difficult to know, then, how to interpret the meaning of this tale, made intentionally as elliptical as the haiku form that gives it its name. Is Tome's harsh injunction also a word against assimilation and hybridity, against the "life" her husband vainly seeks in magazines (like Myrtle in *The Great Gatsby*)? Does Tome think Jesus is (because of race and class) beneath her daughter, and if so, how can she so clearly repeat the very injustice once done to her? How will Rosie reconcile the tragic Old World warning of her mother with the New World's crooning of "On the Good Ship Lollipop"? And where are the white people in this story? Do they need to be present to influence the plot, or does the American story go on without them?

• • •

Although multiculturalism begins in identity politics — in the conflation of personal and cultural identity — it should not end there. Taking multiculturalism personally is a way to move in, through, and beyond identity politics while respecting the conditions that make those politics a recurrent necessity. We may want to challenge the centrality of "identity" itself in arguments about culture, for example, by considering the difference between "having" an identity and living by an ethos. Living by an ethos implies an important degree of agency, freedom, and responsibility in the way a person responds to the various claims of multiple and contradictory identities. While the notion of having an identity tends to reinforce deterministic scenarios, in which persons become prescribed categories, the notion of ethos envisions the future of persons as a series of meaningful choices. In this way the relationship between personal and cultural identity becomes more, rather than less, political, in the sense that by choosing to accept or refuse the claims of racial or national or sexual or class identities, a person acts politically and makes a difference in the future. But ethos also recalls the ancient sense of the way a character acts in response to "fate" or "fortune." To talk of agency and choice is not to return to a fantasy in which the individual can be or do just anything, and it is certainly not to forget the histories and material conditions that shape the context of any agent's choices. On the contrary, the notion of ethos demands that a person be aware of his or her fate and know well the historical circumstances that shape the moment in which a person must respond to *what is* with an action aimed at *what might become.*

Even if a first step toward ethical human relations may be to recognize and respect someone else's difference from me, that realization still tends to leave me in the privileged position: I have the luxury of deciding to be tolerant and liberal. The structure of superiority is left intact. The sense of my own settled and unquestioned identity is also left intact, while all the "Otherness" is projected onto someone else. Discourses about the "Other" tend to replay the original discrimination, in which nonwhites or nonmales or non-Westerners are the Others. If you are one of those Others, of course, you do not see yourself as the Other except insofar as you look at yourself from the dominant ideological point of view. The next step, then, and it is an ethical as well as a political step, is to see my own subjectivity from the Other's point of view. Especially for those of us accustomed to identifying with, or being treated as, the "norm," it is vital to undertake an active defamiliarization of one's own cultural identity and the way one has taken it personally. The exploration of Otherness and cultural identity should achieve a sense of *my own* strangeness, my own Otherness, including the story of how my assumed mode of being came into existence historically. I could have been someone other than I think I am. And maybe I am.

As for those long accustomed to suffering the imposition of a sense of Otherness as a judgment on their cultural identity, they continually struggle with that "double-consciousness" classically described by W. E. B. Du Bois: "It is a peculiar sensation, this double-consciousness, this sense of always looking at one's self through the eyes of others, of measuring one's soul by the tape of a world that looks on in amused contempt and pity" (364). Identity politics provides one way to reunify this consciousness, rejecting the values of the oppressor's gaze and affirming instead the measures of a group's own experiences, beliefs, and visions. There may be some form of "double-consciousness" for the dominant subject, too, for that subject also sees himself or herself through the eyes of the marginalized, the colonized, and the despised. But we look away from their gaze, or fear it, or reject the view of ourselves it expresses. While the dominated subject is cajoled, seduced, or coerced at times into identifying with the consciousness of the dominant, the reverse is not true for the dominant, and so their moments of identification with the marginalized usually follow the forms of pity, sympathy, or horror. Insofar as the dominated achieve a sense of self through identity politics, they too will experience the need to question the consequences of privileging their own point of view. Insofar as the dominant fail to find modes of understanding and empathy that force a reassessment of their way of life, they will deserve the contempt that the word "liberal" has gained in some quarters. A dialectic of dis-orientation characterizes the relationship between personal and cultural identity for both the dominant and the dominated. This dis-orientation is made more complex when we realize that we may occupy both positions at once depending on which of our social relations we are talking about. Dis-orientation, then, is both the alienated condition we strive to heal *and* a goal of self-critical thought.

I would thus propose a pedagogy of dis-orientation as a complement to recent calls to restructure the educational institution from the Other's point of view. I know that many of our students already feel dis-oriented, either by the lives they have led or by the things we teach. But I think we need to make these dis-orientations into explicit subjects of study in our classrooms, and into methods of analysis whose intellectual and ethical claims we theorize and practice. Cameron McCarthy cites Bob Connell's contention that we ought to "bring the uninstitutionalized experiences of marginalized minorities and working-class women and men 'to the center' of the organization and arrangement of the school curriculum." This is to suggest that "a political and ethical principle of positive social justice should inform the selection of knowledge in the school curriculum" (132). Personally, I take McCarthy's "ethical" as an injunction to dis-orientation, a call to subscribe to a principle larger than my own self-interested identity.

Taking multiculturalism personally will not, in the end, provide us with an identity, or resolve the hostilities between races, or defuse tribal warfare, or remedy those inequalities inherent in multinational capitalism. But the often surprising kinds of personal and cultural identification or empathy facilitated by the multicultural literature classroom produce antiessentialist affiliations. Students do make connections across the insulating boundaries we have taught them to respect, and they do find this adventure in dis-orientation challenging and exhilarating. Taking multiculturalism personally does not mean harmonious understanding or celebrations of ethnic diversity, however; more likely it involves bringing cultural and personal conflicts into the open and dis-orienting the fictions of tolerant pluralism. The classroom will need an ethical discourse for handling these conflicts, just as it will need a political analysis for understanding their material conditions and consequences.

Thus, politics can also be understood in terms of how the person negotiates the space between identity and community. A relentless critique of every student's and every teacher's bad faith is contemptuous of the ideal of community. Unlike critique, politics as a social enterprise requires that persons form communities based on a mutual recognition of common interests, which must be understood in part by testing discourses against persons and ideas against experiences. One thing that multiculturalism dis-orients is individualism, since multiculturalism continually ties persons back to the web of their interpersonal cultural identities and affiliations. In the dialectic of personal and cultural identity, an analysis of one's cultural identities may dis-orient the fictions of one's personal selfhood — and vice versa.

Still, I would resist the movement toward "depersonalization" among some advocates of oppositional pedagogy. According to Donald Morton, for example, "persons" must be "distinguished from their 'discourses'" so that those discourses can be effectively critiqued (82). This distinction removes the critique of discourses from the realm of the ethical, where relationships between persons require attitudes such as tolerance, respect, accountability, sympathy, justice, empathy, and humility. Most students will not readily perceive a distinction between the professor's contempt for their discourse and contempt for their person. I do not think we can remedy past injustice, which dismissed people's discourse because of their bodies, by returning to an ideal wherein discourses are evaluated without reference to the bodies that produce them. If multiculturalism has a central lesson, it is to teach us to respect this embodied character of cultural production.

Treating persons only as discourses would apply poststructuralist theory to pedagogy in a manner that is both theoretically reductive and strategically harmful. Depersonalizing critique and pedagogy would underestimate the emotional and idiosyncratic ties that individuals have to knowledge and power (see Worsham). An ethic of care for cultural differences in the classroom is superior, in my experience, to the pedagogy of confrontation and hostility that Morton advocates. As Patrocinio Schweickart argues, engendering critical discourse requires a good deal of listening to others rather than speaking at or for them. The connection of persons to discourses is an ethical one and cannot be reduced to ideology because discourse is where the person mediates between the various ideologies and social positions that claim allegiance or obedience. The person takes responsibility for negotiating the relationship between ideologies (or institutions) and the experience of the individual. An ethic is precisely a set of principles that is not coincident with the person but rather something he or she embodies only individually and imperfectly. The gap between personal and cultural identity creates the space where ethics must take place.

I believe that ethical imperatives inform political change, since concepts of justice and of rights include a moral dimension. Self-interest and the acquisition of (or resistance to) power cannot found a community or a political philosophy; the former cannot do justice to social relationships involving conflicting self-interests, and power without a concept of the good is merely instrumental and thus nihilistic. Social inequalities will not be alleviated without structural changes in the government and the economy, to be sure, but these cannot be motivated or justified without recourse to arguments about the evils of unbridled self-interest and the irresponsibility of the will-to-power. Demonstrating these points will involve careful historical argument about the particulars of a social legacy, as well as scrupulous theoretical debate about what constitutes the good, universally and in a given instance.

A focus on ethics can strengthen the process of creating mechanisms that do justice to the competing claims of different cultural groups (see Taylor). It can also make for affiliations between individuals who in their everyday lives often differ with one another, and within themselves. The importance of this ethical moment needs to be reasserted and restored in the current climate, where "the political" (often theorized vaguely if at all) reigns. Politics, I have argued, has come to be seen as either the submission to dogma or the expression of self-interest. So understood, politics tends to rigidify differences and prevent coalitions. If, however, we analyze how individual persons act as ethical agents in everyday negotiation with one another, the result could be a more complex and hopeful insight. In practice we always make choices among competing ideologies, and our self-interests are divided among contradictory aims. Often we find ourselves caught between universals and particulars in making these choices. Responsibility and accountability, as I have been developing these terms, refer to our ethical position as we negotiate our way through these networks of demands and affiliations. We seek to do justice to the various claims made upon us (and that we make upon ourselves), although we know that the justice we do achieve will be a practical rather than an ideal one. Engaging in good faith in the political process means acknowledging our involvement with others, and so resisting the isolationism bred by ideological absolutism or cynical self-concern.

The ethnic and the ethical will have to recognize each other in this territory of competing demands, a borderland that includes the classroom. To get beyond the accusations and scapegoating and namecalling, we need to acknowledge the mutual dependence of our ethical and political persons. Unless we can believe in our accountability to one another, and then act upon it, we may be in store for an endless course of self-righteousness and violence. If multiculturalism, in whatever guise, can help us fashion this kind of accountability across the borderlines, then it will have been a contribution well worth the controversies it provokes.

f o u r **The Discipline of the Syllabus**

n the first three chapters of this book I have argued that American literary studies is caught up in a struggle over representation which began as early as the Declaration of Independence and continues to this day in the controversies surrounding cultural identity, political correctness, and multiculturalism. What happens when this struggle enters the arena of pedagogy, where historical and theoretical speculation gives way to the more mundane tasks of choosing an anthology, picking required readings, designing paper topics, and managing classroom discussion? This is the question I began to address in Chapter 3, and which will be my primary focus throughout the rest of the book. While making specific recommendations about changing American literary studies, I also look back at its history. The need for change can be measured in part by understanding where the discipline has been, which in turn helps us imagine where we want to go.

Looked at from the standpoint of pedagogy, the debate over the canon comes down to a question of the reading list, of what can be assigned and how it is to be taught. Antagonists in the debate share the assumption that such decisions have consequences far beyond that of shaping the aesthetic taste of students. Lines of connection are drawn that link the syllabus to the canon and the canon to political positions. Before going further, I want to scrutinize the perhaps necessary but misleading tendency to equate a "canon" with a "hegemonic ideology." The first term refers to a literary text that some group of authorities elevates to a position of superior merit. The second term refers to a system of beliefs that some powerful class of people elevate to a position of dominance. Although a canonized text may be shown to express or uphold some hegemonic ideology, this is not always or simply so. Values and beliefs described as inherent to the text may actually be imposed on it by readers and critics who use the text as an instrument for expressing their own ideology. Often the effort to bestow canonical status represents a struggle against a reigning orthodoxy, as, for example, when T. S. Eliot canonized the Metaphysical poets as superior to the Romantics. Or one could cite the present success in canonizing any number of previously marginalized writers. Once we recognize that the canon changes, we see that authorities may canonize a text as a means of challenging dominant ideologies, not reinforcing them.

Analyses of canonization and ideology grow more complicated when we admit that no even modestly complex literary work expresses a single ideology. It is far more accurate to describe literary works as giving voice to or dramatizing conflicts among ideologies. Literature participates in the cultural work of evaluating the political, moral, social, aesthetic, and psychological character of competing ideologies. Given the fact that literary works do not embody merely one ideology, critics and teachers cannot persuasively claim that a work has been canonized or marginalized solely on the basis of its ideology, though this is not to say that this never happens. John Guillory's historical study of canon formation reminds us that canons are basically the creatures of schools and institutions, apart from which they have no substantial existence. This reminder in turn points us back to the distinction between the canonical and the popular.

A work may be popular and not canonical or vice versa, and indeed since the advent of modernism these two qualities have often been seen as mutually exclusive. One could make the argument that no effective or widespread system of canonicity existed for works of English and American literature before the twentieth century, since these were not widely taught subjects in colleges and universities (the case of secondary education is parallel but differently arrayed). In other words, without a syllabus there is no canon. Moreover, one might even contend that the notion of a literary canon is a recent invention designed to thwart the power of the popular or to replace the authority of the reading public with the authority of the professors. According to this view, the literary canon in English is about a hundred years old as a concept, though its specific contents have varied wildly even in that short space of time. What is clear is that the canon of the academic syllabus rarely resembles the *New York Times*'s best-seller list.

The identification of the canon with a hegemonic ideology, then, results in part from the perception that a specific class of professionals constructed the canon so as to relocate authority for literary evaluation to their campuses and away from book clubs, magazines, reading circles, and other nonacademic forums. In replacing the popular with the canonical, the professors also achieved a shift in ideology, at least insofar as the New Criticism in particular enshrined texts and modes of reading that had a conservative bent. The antipopular and elitist cast of much high modernism involved an active rejection of known works by women, minorities, and working-class writers at least as much as it involved a continued ignorance of certain classes of literature produced by marginalized groups. In a partially comic historical twist, some of the students of New Criticism professors went on to become literary journalists outside the academy, from where they have reacted with increasing hostility to the new generation of academics who are altering the canon and using formerly unauthorized methods of literary theory. The reformist professors, in turn, have drawn much of their energy from the enormous popularity among average readers of texts by women and minority writers and gay and lesbian authors. As the canonical and the popular begin to move back toward each other, the cry goes up that the standards are going down.

Critics disparaging political correctness assume that this new canon is nothing but a vehicle for the imposition of a political ideology. In making this crude accusation, they mirror the reformist charge that the previous canon was nothing but a machinery of political oppression, and they repeat the fallacy of assuming that a literary work expresses a single ideology that can be forced on unsuspecting readers. Neither Twain's *Huckleberry Finn* nor Kingston's *Woman Warrior* can be trusted to effect a predictable revolution in the beliefs of students, even if the instructor makes that dubious goal a priority of the syllabus. The canonical and the popular each stands for different ways that the struggle for representation plays out, especially as it concerns who has the authority to evaluate representation. A culture as variegated as that of the United States will contain both canonical and popular reading lists that serve different ideological ends, sometimes reinforcing and sometimes contesting one another. Insisting on a strict distinction between the canonical and the popular only confuses matters, as does demonizing any value judgment as nothing but the disguise of a will-to-power. The canon debate brings us back once more to questions about how a democratic society is to value and distribute knowledge. We should not be surprised, then, to find that magazine and media coverage of the culture wars regularly features juicy details from individual course syllabi. Agent of hegemony or revolution, the syllabus is an instrument whose history and functions we need to examine more closely.

What is the role of the syllabus in determining the shape of American literary and cultural studies? Perhaps this question seems a bit pedestrian compared to the highly sophisticated and complex theoretical debates over cultural identity, nationalism, canon formation, the definition of literature, the claims of criticism, and the future of higher education. As we have already seen, however, these topics are never very far from the practices of the classroom, which often have a hand in originating or transforming them. The outpouring of speeches, articles, and books on the culture wars has not released teachers from the practical decisions they must make, semester in and semester out, about what to teach and how to teach it.

Such decisions, of course, are not so much ideal solutions as compromises made with the conditions that limit the available choices. Many things constrain the freedom of teachers in setting the borders of the syllabus, not least of which are the borders that define a discipline's place in academic history, a department's place in a specific institution, a course's place in the curriculum, and the instructor's position within the educational hierarchy: Are we speaking of teachers in a public school or community college or research university? Is the instructor a T.A., an untenured faculty member, an adjunct instructor, or a full professor? In his book on the genealogy of American literature as an academic field, David Shumway argues that we have yet to pay enough attention to the question of discipline (all Foucauldian, sadomasochistic, and academic puns intended). Shumway points out (partly in dialogue with the position I will be advancing in Chapter 5) that there is little likelihood of any rapid "end" of American literary studies as long as we who are professors have so many disciplinary incentives to keep it going and so many investments in its reproduction (345–59). These include our fellowships and professorships, our required or elected courses, our book series, our journals, our conferences, and our professional associations. Who would want all that to end?

Readers can look to Shumway and his book for more discussion of what a postdisciplinary academy might look like. I want to examine the syllabus as a place where, despite the best of intentions, the crisis of the discipline continues to play itself out. In the first part of this chapter I discuss the theoretical problems posed by the concept and use of the academic syllabus, as well as efforts to critique the traditional syllabus in American literature. In the second part I look skeptically at recent efforts to provide alternatives to the tradition, efforts that I endorse even as I wonder how to escape their flaws and contradictions.

● ● ●

We are probably not very close either to the end of American or English literature or to the advent of a postdisciplinary knowledge. Surveys by the Modern Language Association seem to indicate strongly that few dramatic changes have occurred in the choice of texts assigned in college literature courses. Canonical figures such as

Hawthorne, Melville, Twain, and T. S. Eliot still reign.[1] Catalogue course descriptions, as prime disciplinary devices, seem to have ensured a certain inertia of the syllabus, though without a systematic comparison of differences between catalogue descriptions and actual syllabi, it is hard to judge the extent of change. Anecdotal evidence from both supporters and opponents of reform suggests that the changes are more extensive than the MLA wants to admit, though less profound than either radicals or reactionaries may think. Politics and bureaucracy dictate that official course descriptions change at a snail's pace, while the actual material assigned in class by an individual instructor may bear little resemblance to the traditional syllabus or to the section of the same course being taught down the hall.

In my experience, whatever reforms have taken hold in English studies at the curricular level have most often been advanced first by the individual syllabi of instructors, who use their academic freedom to alter the direction of the discipline in ways that often depart from the unchanged catalogue or the departmental statement of goals. Such incremental changes are much easier, politically, than the fractious task of redesigning the major. Indeed, it might be argued that revisions of the major should usually be preceded by a period of encouraged innovation at the level of the syllabus, so that the new curriculum can be built at least in part out of courses that have been tested by faculty who are capable of, and enthusiastic about, teaching them. Thus, the disparity between traditional catalogue descriptions and the reformed content of actual syllabi can be made part of the healthy and inevitable process by which departments continue to redesign their programs. But this will require that we go public about these disparities, debate them with our colleagues and administrators, and decide on a regular basis which innovations to institutionalize as the new orthodoxy (knowing well that in the fullness of time an even newer orthodoxy will replace it). Allowing the disparities to flourish with a wink and a cynical smile as we do now only reinforces

1. Judith Fetterley notes what may be a parallel development in the genre of literary history, where she detects little substantial progress in writing the history of nineteenth-century American women writers despite all the attention ostensibly given to them now. See her "Commentary."

outdated curricular models more respected in the breach than the observance.

General readers will recall that the syllabus is among the first sheets of paper that the teacher hands out at the beginning of the semester. On a smeary dittoed, mimeographed, or Xeroxed page, the syllabus sets out the plan for the semester: its goals, its topics, the required readings, the writing assignments, the criteria for grading, the teacher's office hours, and so on. Some of these syllabi are quite brief; others run to ten or more pages, with elaborate narratives and bibliographies. For teachers in the humanities, the syllabus is at the heart of the enterprise, and we sweat over ours like no other document. This explains in part the rage we feel when students lose the syllabus, for they little imagine the labor that went into it or the extraordinary importance that we attach to it. That importance stems from the fact that the syllabus is much more than a bureaucratic instrument of organization: like a little essay, it expresses the teacher's vision of the subject, including historical judgments, interpretations of meaning, and aesthetic evaluations. No wonder that the syllabus is among the first standard items posted by professors on the World Wide Web. In literary pedagogy syllabi differ radically from instructor to instructor, depending on the amount of freedom that instructor has to choose the textbook and determine the assignments. Generally that freedom is in proportion to the instructor's rank in the hierarchy, though often T.A.'s and adjunct faculty will have surprising flexibility since many tenured faculty care little what goes on over in the freshman and sophomore divisions.

A key instrument of any disciplinary formation, the syllabus expresses both the discipline of the instructor who formulates it and, in some measure, the discipline that formulates the instructor. Indeed, one can conclude, as I think John Guillory does in his illuminating study of canon formation, that even the most extreme changes in individual syllabi are rendered impotent by the disciplinary restraints of the educational system. According to this line of thought, what counts is the "hidden curriculum" of socialization, obedience, competition, class distinction, and training for the work force that is the "real" content of the class, no matter its purported topic. (And this would hold for the social and natural sciences as well as the humanities.) In addition to reproducing good citizens and good workers, the syllabus operates as a disciplinary instrument to reproduce the academic discipline in a number of ways. By commanding a place in the catalogue of courses, it maintains the space that the discipline occupies in the institution, curriculum, and department. Insofar as it legitimates the objects it studies, the syllabus reproduces the legitimation of the discipline to which it belongs, leading to an almost "catch-22" relationship between the legitimacy of the syllabus and the legitimacy of the discipline. For the students disciplined by the syllabus, the syllabus brings the discipline into being for them, outlining its borders and delimiting its contents and ends. The apparently natural claim of the assigned objects to a place on the syllabus, however, obscures the process of disciplinary construction that has put them there in the first place.

This last point deserves elaboration. A postdisciplinary approach to the syllabus involves letting students in on the secrets of the discipline, including its history, its local features, and its material and ideological constraints (local as well as global). The traditional syllabus tends to frame its materials of study as mere objects, that is, as events or texts that precede the syllabus, determine the syllabus, and in some way transcend the syllabus. They are the referent of the syllabus, the reality to which the syllabus points; or, the syllabus is a mirror held up to the world to be studied. "We are most of the time," writes Shumway, "convinced that American literature has as much an independent existence as a rock or a tree" (1).[2] What could be more natural than to find Shakespeare's *Hamlet* on an English Renaissance syllabus or Toni Morrison's *Beloved* on a Contemporary American Literature syllabus? What more inevitable than to study such objective events as the Age of Romanticism or the genre of the bildungsroman? Like the critical theory it often utilizes, the traditional syllabus relies on a mimetic theory of representation, as if the objects to be studied existed entirely apart from the disciplinary procedures that produced them as legitimate topics for investigation. One need not be a doctrinaire poststructuralist to question what exactly the syllabus represents and who had a hand in shaping it.

2. Shumway's "Introduction: The History of a Discipline" provides an excellent overview of how to approach disciplinarity in American literary studies (1–24).

It might be helpful to think of the syllabus as rhetoric. Rhetoric is the art of persuasion, and the rhetorician employs devices to move an audience to some particular point of view. The rhetorician enters a field of conflicts already shared by the audience, whose interests and desires must be skillfully addressed. But who is the audience for the syllabus? One's students, one's colleagues, the administration, the tax-paying public? Steven Mailloux usefully argues that contests over the canon as well as individual interpretations of literary texts can be approached as instances of rhetoric. Itself a rhetorical act within the larger conversation of the department and the discipline, the syllabus introduces students to the rhetorical history that includes debates over what literary texts to study and how to study them. Since rhetorical acts happen in history and are social by definition, this approach allows students to see the culture wars as a series of historically specific episodes rather than as a battle over timeless principles. Interpretations of literature have a messy history, featuring a cast of grand if flawed characters whose disagreements with one another are thoroughly part of their own culture's concerns. If the value or meaning of literary texts is presented with no reference to that history but instead as abstract or ideal truths, then students receive a misleading education in aesthetics and no education at all in how cultures actually develop. There is, writes Mailloux, "no escape from rhetoric and history into some transcendental realm from which the past can be heard speaking itself through a chronicler beyond all rhetoric" ("Rhetorical Hermeneutics in Theory" 17). And yet, too many syllabi masquerade as just such a chronicler. In assigning cultural objects, the traditional syllabus remains suspiciously silent about their social and institutional construction, about the choices the syllabus has made, the alternatives it has considered and abandoned, and the external pressures that have shaped it. These demystifying dirty secrets must themselves become a part of the syllabus.

In other words, we could draw a lesson from Russian Formalism and urge that there be a "baring of the device" in the pedagogy of the syllabus. Instructors could develop a host of techniques, approaches, and assignments that would help defamiliarize the syllabus and expose its rhetorical history. This should usually begin with the instructor candidly detailing why the department offers or requires the course, how this version of it differs from that taught by other instructors, what past incarnations of the course in other times and places have looked like, and what assumptions the instructor has made in putting the syllabus together. The World Wide Web now makes such an exercise fairly simple, since just typing in "American Literature Survey" or any other more specific topic in a standard search engine will quickly lead to syllabi of actual courses. Alternatively, students can begin at the Web site of the American Studies Crossroads Project, where clicking on "Curriculum" will lead to the "Electronic Archives for Teaching the American Literatures," which contains essays on pedagogy as well as bibliographies and syllabi. A teacher can demonstrate this search in class (if he or she is lucky enough to have the equipment) and bring up on the projection screen a series of alternate ways that the subject matter of the course could be (and is) being taught.

Another even wider resource is the World Lecture Hall site at the University of Texas, with links to syllabi and courses in dozens of disciplines. Students could write research papers on questions of canonicity, the culture wars, interpretive disagreement, or historical contextualization by finding and analyzing these materials. They might even then be asked to produce their own syllabi and to write justifying narratives for them. On the Web students can also find sites built by students and teachers in other courses and/or at other schools, colleges, and universities. A class might also choose a number of Internet discussion lists in American literature and related topics, and have students subscribe to one or two of their choices. The discussions on these can be exceptionally illuminating in showing how tenuous some of our choices and dogmas really are. Instructors could also go the more old-fashioned route by helping to put together a research collection at the library of previous syllabi from other instructors. These could be accompanied by holdings in past literary histories of the United States and textbooks marketed in the field.

In historicizing the course, the instructor can foreground how it belongs to a history of conflicts within the discipline, and how these conflicts might relate to conflicts in higher education and in society at large. Most teachers are already being pressured to make their pedagogical goals more explicit as part of the institutionalization of "assessment procedures." Baring the device of the syllabus would at once announce the goals of the course and put them into question, making for a critical and reflective relationship of the students to the goals of the course. Baring the device of the syllabus is yet another way to "teach the conflicts" while simultaneously engaging students in the intense study of assigned materials (see Graff, "Teach the Conflicts" and *Beyond the Culture Wars*). The effect is likely to be similar to that in courses on literary criticism, where the reading of essays about works of literature prompts students to go back to those works and read them even more closely. Once students are alerted to the different possibilities of interpretation, they have a sense of what is at stake and why differences in the meaning given to *Uncle Tom's Cabin* or *Iola Leroy* or the poetry of Wallace Stevens or the stories of Sherman Alexie matter so much. Although some critics complain that students should simply read the "works themselves," students know that actively researching the contexts for understanding the work enormously enriches their grasp of its significance and their capacity to make use of it in their own lives.

What would we discover in baring the devices of the syllabus in American literary studies, for example? In terms of history, students would learn, as Lawrence Levine and others have documented, that the canon debate has grossly misrepresented what actually happened in the history of our discipline. Classes and departments in *English* literature were not widespread in higher education before the end of the nineteenth century, and even then they often got in by modeling themselves on the deadly grammatical and philological pedantry of the curriculum in Latin and Greek which they sought to replace. The study of Chaucer, Shakespeare, and Milton as great literature was sternly resisted, since obviously these latecomers represented a minor strain when compared to Homer, Virgil, and Horace. Levine points out that in order to get the English into the canon, the same claims for universality, timeless merit, and cultural superiority had to be made for them that had been made for the classics, so that "while the contents of the canon may have changed, the *character* of the canon did not" (81). When serious efforts began after World War I to institutionalize American literature as a subject, the strategy would in many ways be the same: now the claims for Hawthorne, Melville, and Emerson would be made in the name of their classic status, their universal and timeless appeal, and their embodiment of the nation's exceptional cultural and political values. In 1941 F. O. Matthiessen would assert the continuity (and equality) between the Greco-Roman classics, the English classics, and the new American classics by calling his literary history of the antebellum United States *American Renaissance*.

While during the first four decades of the twentieth century the question of American literature occasioned a river of essays and books (quite often in the general interest quarterlies, magazines, and works published by mainstream publishers), the progress in the schools and colleges and universities was painfully slow. Here is Levine's summary of the years between the wars:

> In 1928 Ferner Nuhn found that in American colleges and universities Scandinavian literature was taught as often as American literature, Italian literature twice as often, Spanish and German literature three times as often, French literature four times as often, Latin and Greek literature five times as often, and English literature ten times as often. More undergraduate courses were devoted to two English poets, Chaucer and Milton, than were offered in all of American literature. Thirteen years later, Floyd Stovall surveyed seventy English departments and found that American literature constituted no more than 20 percent of the offerings. (84)

So much for the contention that a long-standing consensus about the greatness of America's masterpieces and their centrality in our curriculum has been irrationally attacked by the armies of the politically correct.

The academic establishment of what came to be recognized as the American canon did not gain wide force until after World War II, when it would serve the dual purposes of underwriting America's global mission and of educating the thousands of students (almost exclusively white men) now pouring in to higher education under the GI Bill and, later, during the boom time of college construction in the 1960s. Still, something like a canon in American letters had been in the making in books by Barret Wendell, Vernon Parrington, Van Wyck Brooks, and others, though the 1930s witnessed a brief interlude of diversity in some of the anthologies. These efforts at canonization built on debatable definitions of "literature" and "American," which revisionists now argue were inaccurate and pernicious (see Lauter, *Canons and Contexts*, esp. 22–47). Whether or not this is true, there seems little evidence that syllabi in the past actively worked to bring students into a debate over these terms or to a knowledge of how the discipline had become invested in them. Such a self-reflection would have gone against the grain of the American studies movement, which had always been obsessed with justifying the study of American literature (and, indeed, with asserting its very existence and value, as Shumway documents). Since the pedagogical model presumed that the aim of the course was to develop an appreciation of the best, most representatively American literary classics, such a baring and debating of the device was unlikely (if not un-American).

How fair is this portrait of the first generations of American literary critics and professors? "The value of the new American studies" of the 1990s, asserts David Levin, "does not depend on the accuracy with which the innovative scholars depict their predecessors" (526). Levin reminds us that scholarship before 1950 was more diverse and more historicist than we imagine, and that Stowe was taught regularly in courses at Harvard. He further documents syllabi at Harvard and Stanford in which students were asked to undertake studies in cultural rhetoric — analyses of the Salem witchcraft trials, the case of Sacco and Vanzetti, the controversy over Diego Rivera's mural at Rockefeller Center — that resemble the program advanced by Mailloux and instanced by his analysis of the ABM Treaty debate in *Rhetorical Power* (170–81). But Levin's exceptions still seem to highlight rather than disprove the rule. He does not uncover widespread assignment of black or women writers at Harvard or Stanford. Nor do his examples run counter to the claim that the aesthetic, mythic, and nationalist agendas of the 1950s and 1960s created an institutional canon more restrictive in scope than the literary histories of previous generations.

Witness the summa of the (old) new American studies scholarship, *Literary History of the United States*, edited by Robert Spiller and other luminaries (first published in 1946, it included a chapter by Matthiessen on modern poetry). In the words of the 1953 preface to the second edition, the "master plan" of their work is the "view of literature as the aesthetic expression of the general culture of a people in a given time and place. . . . Rejecting the theory that history of any kind is merely a chronological record of objective facts, [the editors] adopted an organic view of literature as the record of human experience and of its history as the portrait of a people, designed from the curves of its cultural cycles and the colors of its rich and unique life" (ix). These "colors" were, racially, almost exclusively white, and this experience predominantly male. When we look at the table of contents, we find a now predictable cast of characters: Edwards, Franklin, Cooper, Poe, Emerson, Thoreau, Hawthorne, Melville, Whitman, Howells, Twain, James, Adams, Dreiser, Robinson, and O'Neill are the authors meriting separate chapters (Dickinson shares a chapter with Sidney Lanier). Incredibly, the 138-page section on the "Crisis" (the words "civil war" do not appear in the table of contents) contains no discussion of African American literature, no history of the slave narrative, and no account of African American abolitionist writing, though Stowe and white abolitionism get many pages, and an entire chapter is devoted to "The Tradition of the Old South." Frederick Douglass does not appear in the index. Nor does Harriet Jacobs or Nella Larsen, though Hurston and Wright get passing mention. A nine-page section covers "The Indian Heritage." Emory Elliott's 1988 *Columbia Literary History of the United States* is an improvement, but its "diversity" appears mainly in individual sections devoted to racial and ethnic groups or women writers. The canonical white male figures still get their long individual chapters. Emily Dickinson and Gertrude Stein are the only women whose names appear in the table of contents, and no writers of color appear there by name at all. Levin's brief for our predecessors notwithstanding, then, there remains strong evidence that the syllabus in American literary studies deserves the criticism it has received.

Judging from the textbooks and critical studies of the modern period, syllabi in American literature developed during the first six decades of the twentieth century showed a dominant concern with the nationalism of "a people," with establishing the value of American civilization and the qualities it required. This curriculum might be called the "pedagogy of nationalism," insofar as the syllabus disciplined the students to become "citizens" in a "democracy" where literature expressed the spirit of the people. As Nina Baym and others have shown, this nationalism in literary pedagogy was part of a larger effort to socialize what was perceived to be a threatening influx of non–Anglo-Saxon immigrants in the latter nineteenth and early twentieth centuries. Aspirants to citizenship learned to leave the baggage of their cultural differences at Ellis Island or Angel Island; assimilation to a homogenized American culture descended from white New England roots was the rule. For those hoping to rise in the growing ranks of the academic literary profession, conformity to this nationalism was as important a stricture as conformity to other social, political, racial, and sexual norms. Thus, in the careers of the Jewish Lionel Trilling and the homosexual F. O. Matthiessen, for example, we can discern how the nationalist pressure to assimilate worked together with anti-Semitism and homophobia. Trilling would write his dissertation and first book on the archproponent of the Anglo-Western canon, Matthew Arnold; more resistant, Matthiessen — whose early books included studies of both Sarah Orne Jewett and T. S. Eliot — would still have to bury the overt expression of his deeply held and radical views on politics and sexuality, which are implicit but largely allegorical in his public writings (see Arac, Bergman, Cain *F. O. Matthiessen*). Our retrospective criticism of the conformist influence we find in their contributions to the American literature syllabus, then, has to be tempered by a recognition of the forces that disciplined and limited their psychology and their careers. When future generations look back on today's syllabi, we have to hope they will be as generous.

In 1929 Matthiessen had announced, "It is time for the history of American literature to be rewritten" (*Responsibilities* 181). While the "new historian must take into account every side of American culture," from movies and cartoons to the Ford and the radio, he "must remember that his real quarry is aesthetic values" (181–82).[3] A decade later *American Renaissance* gave the pedagogy of nationalism a

3. Perhaps Matthiessen is answering Arthur M. Schlesinger, Sr., whose article "Social History in American Literature" had appeared a few months earlier in the same periodical (the *Yale Review*). Schlesinger welcomes the new attention of literary historians to social history in language that would have many parallels in discussions of the New Historicism of the 1990s. Schlesinger asserts that "just as no self-respecting historical student" believes any longer in narratives of "great heroes, epical battles, and imposing institutions," the new literary historian must have "vastly more than an acquaintance with belletristic monuments, indeed nothing less than an inti-

monumental textbook still caught in this divide between the history of America's specific culture, on the one hand, and the timeless realm of aesthetic achievement, on the other. Matthiessen stated at the start that his canon would be made up of writers who exhibited "devotion to the possibilities of democracy" (ix). Yet, as Shumway concludes, the idea of "democracy" that "becomes in *American Renaissance* the essence of American civilization" is just that, an Idea — floating above the actual historical struggles of antebellum America. Shumway goes on to argue that in this kind of approach, "great works differed only in the positions they took toward perennial human(ist) concerns: innocence and experience, hope and tragedy, good and evil. Differences of region, class, race, or ethnicity could not be comprehended by this practice. 'Democracy' and 'humanity' stand for the irrelevance of these differences in American culture" (260).

Matthiessen's preface sought to portray his work as "opposite" to Vernon Louis Parrington's explicitly political and neo-Marxist reading of the "liberal tradition" in American literary history. Steeped in Eliot, the Elizabethans, and the New Criticism, Matthiessen asserted that his own work would strive to focus on "the writing itself," "to be preoccupied with form," and "to evaluate [authors] in accordance with the enduring requirements for great art" (ix, xi). Listing the many writers of the period he will exclude (including Whittier, Longfellow, T. S. Arthur, Fanny Fern, Maria Cummins, Susan Warner, Harriet Beecher Stowe, and E. D. E. N. Southworth, and never mentioning Frederick Douglass), Matthiessen remarks condescendingly that "such material offers a fertile field for the sociologist and for the historian of taste" (xi). This attitude had not prevented the younger Matthiessen from writing a book on Jewett which celebrated her love for Annie Fields; under the spell of Eliot, whose tortured repression of his own homoeroticism leads to an almost hysterical investment in the sublimating structures of the Anglican

---

mate knowledge of the writings, good, bad, and indifferent, in which the mass of men have found instruction, inspiration, amusement, and escape" (135–36). Schlesinger's critique of the "aesthete" and his call for a separation of literary criticism from literary history is met only halfway by Matthiessen, who wants to hold on to aesthetic idealism even as he hopes to democratize criticism.

Church and high culture, Matthiessen undertakes in *American Re-naissance* to continue the New Criticism's exploration of the linguistic "dissociation of sensibility" while hinting as best he can at the sexual roots of that dissociation.[4]

Thus, in his preface Matthiessen immediately adds that his volume of formalist close readings "is based on recurrent themes," the first being "the relation of the individual to society" (xiv). Soon we learn that "an artist's use of language is the most sensitive index to cultural history," and that Matthiessen's chosen few were writers who "felt that it was incumbent upon their generation to give fulfillment to the potentialities freed by the Revolution, to provide a culture commensurate with America's political opportunity," and to create "a literature for our democracy" (xv). At its origins the syllabus in the American Renaissance — and, by extension, many of the subsequent syllabi in American literature — harnessed aesthetic formalism to the theme of America's prophetic democratic mission, and so nationalized the New Criticism and made the academy safe for American literature. The vagueness here allowed readers to forget that Matthiessen's central (if obscured) referent was Whitman's *Democratic Vistas*, which reiterated the poet's belief that "the most substantial hope and safety of the future of these States" depends on the "intense and loving comradeship, the personal and passionate attachment of man to man" (981). Forgotten, too, were those many other writers who felt that their work also was devoted to the possibilities of democracy and language, though these possibilities were not for them by dictate of their gender or race or class or other marginalizing quality. Could Matthiessen not have known the claim of Langston Hughes, another of Whitman's heirs, that "I, too, sing America"?

If this narrowing of the American canon was indeed Matthiessen's legacy, as I think it largely was, he would be horrified by the uses to which it was put, given that for him "democracy" meant a socialist, egalitarian society in which the formerly marginalized would finally find their just place. As his correspondence to his lover Russell Cheney makes clear, Matthiessen's use of the term "democracy" comes

4. Mark Merlis has written a fascinating novel called *American Studies* which is in part a fictional interpretation of Matthiessen's life, with particular attention to the conflicts of sexuality, politics, and class.

by way of Whitman's argument that homosexuality is the vanguard movement of true egalitarianism. Matthiessen writes to Cheney in September 1924 that "I carried Walt Whitman in my pocket" while touring England (Hyde 26). More significantly, Matthiessen reads Whitman under the influence of Edward Carpenter, whose book on Whitman appeared in 1906. Carpenter's volume *The Intermediate Sex*, which Matthiessen reads in November 1924, gives him decisive help in understanding his relationship with Cheney and their joint struggle to understand their nature as homosexuals, "the idea that what we have is one of the divine gifts; that such as you and I are the advance guard of any hope for a spirit of brotherhood" (47). The vision that Matthiessen finds in Whitman and Carpenter provides the largely unspoken framework for the assembled canon of great authors in *American Renaissance*. Indeed, David Bergman argues that the book is a "covert celebration of the homosexual artist," that "Matthiessen erected in *American Renaissance* virtually a gay canon of American literature" based on the "belief that only through the acceptance of one's primordial homosexual feelings can an artist both penetrate to the deepest wellsprings of experience and fully express the democratic spirit" (94, 96–97). This belief, however, cannot be expressed explicitly or at length by Matthiessen, given the social, legal, and professional codes of homophobia in place at Harvard and around the nation in the 1940s. What comes through at the literal level of *American Renaissance*, then, is a contradictory emphasis on New Critical formalism *and* nationalist politics. The radical element joining them — Matthiessen's utopian belief in the power of gay egalitarianism — cannot speak its name, and so does not make it onto the syllabus in the decades to come. What does come through, as Shumway indicates, is the program of aesthetic humanism that enables a universalizing, ahistorical discourse at the expense of the particular differences in American lives. And along with that universalizing comes a pedagogy of "close reading" and thematic expostulation that pushes students away from detailed engagement with the actual historical events and struggles that form literature's context.

The spirit of nationalist pedagogy grew stronger during the period of the Cold War consensus, when xenophobia, homophobia, and other pathological anxieties about "Others" reached a fever pitch. Almost as if to mark the inauguration of that repressive era and to signal despair at the political and sexual purges to come, Matthiessen (still mourning Cheney's death five years earlier) committed suicide on April 1, 1950. That year also witnessed the publication of Lionel Trilling's book *The Liberal Imagination*, which would become the bible of that Cold War consensus as intellectuals and academics spurned the radicalism of the 1930s. Trilling launched his critique of liberalism in essays advocating the supreme value of authors such as Hawthorne and James, whose "complexity" and "tragic vision" were to be preferred to the supposedly more one-dimensional and "ideological" authors preferred by Parrington and the critics of the left-leaning 1930s. In what would become, alongside Matthiessen, the most influential theoretical description of the writer's relation to American culture, Trilling asserted:

> A culture is not a flow, nor even a confluence; the form of its existence is struggle, or at least debate — it is nothing if not a dialectic. And in any culture there are likely to be certain artists who contain a large part of the dialectic within themselves, their meaning and power lying in their contradictions; they contain within themselves, it may be said, the very essence of the culture, and the sign of this is that they do not submit to serve the ends of any one ideological group or tendency. (9)

Notice that Trilling's important sense of the dialectical nature of cultural struggles turns into an inner psychological debate within the minds of great geniuses (see my *America the Scrivener* chap. 8). The many diverse voices in this struggle fall silent before the spectacle of authors capable of absorbing them into their work, "containing" them and capturing the culture's essence. Debate appears to wither, in fact, when conflicting forces are reduced to a single "essence" that one author can embody. Thus, it isn't necessary to teach a broad spectrum of authors in order to represent the "struggle," "debate," and "dialectic" of culture. It suffices to find those few representative men who contain it within themselves. It is no accident, I would argue, that from the 1940s to the 1970s the number of authors represented in most American literature college textbooks declined drastically in comparison to textbooks and histories from the 1930s or even the 1890s. Trilling's theoretical model provided these syllabi with their rationale, since the few great writers could contain the history of the culture as a whole. And they could "contain" that history, supposedly, without becoming "ideological."

Trilling did not share Matthiessen's thematic interest in "democracy," or Matthiessen's commitment to Whitmanian adhesiveness between men. Having barely escaped an effort in the early 1930s to fire him at Columbia because he was a Freudian, a Marxist, and a Jew, Trilling learned the lesson of assimilation all too well. Liberation came from the power of the individual genius to transcend circumstances and politics; any man, even a Jew, could be the embodiment of an age or a nation if only his mind were "complex" enough. Whereas Trilling's father had been forced to emigrate from Poland after failing a test for the rabbinate, Trilling would become an almost Talmudic commentator on the moral dilemmas expressed by literary texts. For Trilling, Freud would emerge as the key theoretical figure, another Jew whose strong secularism did not prevent his fascination with the intellectual, philosophical, and literary legacy of Judaism. Almost as if to rewrite Arnold's essay "Hebraism and Hellenism," Trilling would implicitly argue that the tragic vision of Judaism, with its antiutopian irony and historical skepticism, was a superior wisdom to Protestant-inflected liberal schemes of social improvement. Thus, his religious roots and his adult political life combined to produce a neoconservative whose prescriptions for finding "tragic vision" would become the staple of literature syllabi throughout the 1950s and into the 1960s. Then Trilling tried briefly to mediate the student uprising at Columbia, only to retreat into increasingly harsh denunciations of the times.

These reminders of Matthiessen's and Trilling's influence on American literary pedagogy should suggest the kind of demystification that one can attempt in the process of teaching the primary texts. By juxtaposing, say, Henry Thoreau and Harriet Jacobs, one can reasonably ask whether either one fulfills Trilling's criteria, and what the effects have been of assuming that Thoreau "contained" all we needed to know about "civil disobedience" in antebellum America. Or we could ask whether *The Great Gatsby* adequately contains the contradictions of the Jazz Age, or whether we need also study the prose and poetry of the Harlem Renaissance (which is at most a kind of vast "Cotton Club" for the characters in Fitzgerald's novel). Or we might go even further and challenge the "great author" basis for syllabi, since it inevitably excludes important literary forms, figures, and historical developments. Simply elevating a few women authors or writers of color to the status of "great authors" may only perpetuate the old problems in new ways.

Granted, it takes time, in class and on the syllabus, to undertake such an activity of disciplinary or pedagogical self-reflection. Instructors who feel hard-pressed to cover the basic material or to get through all the student papers might object that such meta-pedagogical speculations and disciplinary histories are at best a luxury and at worst a frivolous waste of time. Of course, it is hard to appreciate an object while simultaneously analyzing and debating why you are studying it at all, and difficult to cover a set of objects while holding open the possibility that the borders of the set are themselves up for grabs. The coverage model dictates that precious space on the syllabus not be lost in digressive discussions of history, theory, or biography, much less of disciplinary regulations, professional formations, or institutional budgets.

Yet I would argue that a postdisciplinary classroom that integrated such issues and debates would in fact motivate students to read texts more intensely, since the texts would no longer be taken for granted. Their status would ultimately depend on the class's analysis of them and of their disciplinary placement and function. I dare say one would continue to appreciate texts studied in this way, though perhaps in contexts of evaluation that transgress the borders of traditional aesthetic humanism or literary nationalism. In the examples of Thoreau and Jacobs, or of Fitzgerald and the Harlem Renaissance, we might find ourselves getting closer to the dialectical contradictions that Trilling rightly saw as the engine of cultural history, though we can do so only by abandoning his belief that a few canonical authors can represent that history. Consider, for an alternative, Judith Fetterley and Marjorie Pryse's anthology *American Women Regionalists*, which eschews the great author model and proposes that we read a large number of authors as together constituting a significant and hitherto overlooked moment in American literary and social history, one that could never be adequately taught were we to seek just one canonical writer to contain it.

The syllabus that tries to contain cultural history through a few representative men may simply end up reproducing the social and political conflicts of a culture rather than making these conflicts available for analysis or change. Revisionists and critics of the canon claim that, when we bare the devices of traditional syllabi, we find that they reproduce inequalities and injustices of a political nature. They point out that the syllabi of nationalism constructed a vision of America which was overwhelmingly white and male, which marginalized women writers, and which gave little or no attention to historical issues such as slavery or the assault on Native American culture. The relative power and status of different cultural groups is reflected in the discipline, both at the institutional level of faculty hiring, departmental arrangements, and resource allocation, and at the pedagogical level of the classroom and the syllabus, where only certain groups and privileged interests have access or get represented. Trilling never published an essay dedicated to an American writer of color or to an American woman writer. Somehow he must have thought that they did not contain the "essence of the culture." Whatever its flaws, the movement toward multiculturalism in the syllabus recognizes the basic error of the pedagogy of nationalism, which was to assume that a nation had one culture. The disciplines of American literature and American studies often proceeded on the basis of this error, especially insofar as they became dedicated to finding the "exceptional" quality defining "the American experience." Multiculturalism, then, represents a move toward the "postdisciplinary" in that its syllabi reject the equation of nation with culture, and of that culture with a few singular minds.

• • •

If I were to stop here, I would leave the impression that the revisionists have liberated the syllabus from the bad old habits of the past and taken American literature into a brave new world of possibilities. The story, however, is not this simple, as the discipline of the syllabus has proven a stubbornly difficult one for the champions of reform. In response to the traditional syllabus, with its monolithic cast and its nationalist bent, revisionists have pursued two connected but distinct alternatives, though whether these have yet yielded a postdisciplinary effect remains debatable. I call these two alternatives the "equality of representation" syllabus and the "cultural work" syllabus (while admitting that in practice the two often overlap). The equality of representation syllabus takes the existence of relatively distinct cultural groups as its object and premise of study. It follows a vaguely democratic politics in assuming that each of these groups has a right to cultural representation, including representation on the syllabus. This form of democracy pedagogy implicitly or explicitly accepts the political mission of education, defined as the training of citizens equipped to participate in democratic decision making. Of course, in so doing it bears a suspicious resemblance to the democracy pedagogy carried out in the name of nationalism by previous generations of American studies professors, an irony that ought to be thematized in baring the device of revisionary syllabi. One form of this democracy pedagogy is multiculturalism, especially in its "celebration of diversity" mode.

Critics of the revisionists point out that the application of identity politics to the construction of the syllabus has many problems. It is not clear what the borders between cultural groups are, or which has a right to institutional representation. It is also not clear how authors or texts can be categorized, since all texts and authors belong to more than one cultural group. Do we include Frederick Douglass as an African American writer or as a representative of the ideology of masculine self-reliance? Do we put Edith Wharton on the syllabus as a representative of women writers, or do we leave her off (or even put her on) as a representative of upper-class white writers? Do we assign Audre Lorde to represent West Indian writers, black poets, lesbian activists, or artists of the erotic? Indeed, Lorde's own contention in *Zami: A New Spelling of My Name* that she lives in a very "house of differences" argues against the possibility of knowing what category she represents on a syllabus. Rather than assume that teachers can know what, in advance, they are representing by putting an author or work on their reading list, they need to bare the device of the assignment and work with their students to explore the many different things such a choice and such texts could represent. The questions I am raising here pertain as well to the construction of the anthologies out of which many syllabi are fashioned. Tables of contents for the newer anthologies demonstrate the dangers of incoherence: they group some writers and texts by race, some by gender, some by historical period, some by genre, and some by vague themes such as "self" or "vision." The table of contents of the *Heath Anthology*, even in its revised second edition, shows the inevitability of this incoherence, though the editor has done a heroic job to minimize it.

Deciding what groups to represent and justifying the reasons for those decisions remain stubborn problems, since these decisions are by definition institutional, pedagogical, or political rather than strictly formal or aesthetic. Once one has ostensibly abandoned the notion that texts are chosen on the basis of their superior aesthetic merit or their capacity to contain a whole culture, one is still left with choices and the justification of those choices. As critics of the revisionists point out, the decision to teach writing by women or ex-slaves or Asian immigrants still leaves the question which writers and texts to choose from within the group, and often these decisions are again made on the basis of assertions of representativeness or superior quality. This is where the "cultural work" thesis comes in.

The cultural work syllabus strives to solve these problems by resorting to historicism, but with limited success. According to the cultural work thesis, we should reconstruct literary history by studying the cultural work that texts have done — for the people who wrote them, published them, sold them, bought them, read them, borrowed them, or wrote about them. Prominent exponents of the cultural work model include Jane Tompkins in *Sensational Designs: The Cultural Work of American Fiction, 1790–1860*, Cathy Davidson in *Revolution and the Word: The Rise of the Novel in America*, Philip Fisher in *Hard Facts*, and Paul Lauter in *Canons and Contexts*. The cultural work thesis is attractive because it seems to end-run interminable debates about literary value — about which are the best timeless works. Now we study, well, not every text that was ever published, but at least everything influential. Obviously there is a disturbing tautology here, as the critic may produce the influence or cultural work that a text does by virtue of constructing its reception by reviewing it, writing articles and books about it, or by teaching it.

Measuring the cultural work done by a text is a bit tricky. Certainly one can try to document and interpret the sales, reception, use, and popularity of texts, contextualizing their cultural work both empirically and ideologically (though Davidson smartly shows how difficult this is to do with any great confidence). Yet one can also make a case for the overlooked and unread, as in arguments that a widely ignored book — such as *Moby Dick* or *Our Nig* — can nonetheless be a solid indicator of the contemporary cultural work done by the kind of representational ideologies it uses or expresses, such as those regarding race, industry, and religion. In other words, the cultural work of unpopular texts may belong to the political unconscious of a group or era or period. So understood, the cultural work of a text seems to slip back into the category of the "representative," and we assign it less because of the work it did than because it represents the cultural imaginary of its period or place. The hierarchy of texts created by cultural work methods appears more democratic than in the aesthetic model. It allows us to respect the audience that bought Susan Warner's *Wide, Wide World* and preferred *Ruth Hall* to *The Scarlet Letter*. It also prompts us to question the discipline that delegitimated the extraordinarily influential *Uncle Tom's Cabin* while simultaneously resuscitating *Moby Dick* decades after contemporary readers had apparently decided that it did no useful work for them.

But those of us who are designing syllabi soon run into the problem of what kind of cultural work we value, whether among the texts we assign or those we write about, and this decision is inseparable from our agonizing over what kind of cultural work our own performances as scholars, critics, and teachers are doing. Claims to "critical" or "radical" pedagogy are claims about the kind of cultural work done by professional educators and academic writers, who may at times confuse the cultural work of the texts and authors they study with the cultural work accomplished by the teacher's own syllabus, journal article, or critical essay. Even the best revisionists have trouble denying that the texts they choose to study are the texts that do the kind of cultural work that they, today, as politicized academics and citizens, want to see done. We may assign women writers and writers of color not only because we respect and want to teach the struggles they undertook, but also because we see such teaching as integral to our own struggles against racism and sex discrimination.

The avowedly political character of these choices casts doubt on the "representativeness" of what we study. Thus, Richard Ruland, in his review of the first edition of the *Heath Anthology*, pointed out that Lauter had included a section on abolitionist literature but no selections from the voluminous and influential canon of proslavery pamphlets, poems, and novels. Obviously these did not do the kind of cultural work that Lauter wanted to make the aim of syllabi that used the anthology. In his second edition, Lauter retitled the section "Literature of Slavery and Abolition," and included selections from proslavery authors.

But what is the principle behind this revision? Is it because white racist slaveholders, as a cultural group, have a right to representation, and so are included for the same reason that the anthology includes a section of writings from the Harlem Renaissance? Are we simply celebrating diversity, "affirming the differences" that make some of us owners of other people? Or are proslavery texts included, objectively, because of their influential place in American literary and cultural history, however we may despise the effects of that influence? If so, what are we representing or reproducing when we assign or study such texts? Can we know in advance the "cultural work" our efforts are supporting? Certainly we might retreat to saying that, objectively, the war of words over slavery cannot be understood without representing the many sides writers took. This is doubtless true, but it leaves unanswered the question why the war of words over slavery should hold a privileged position on the syllabus, since this appears to make a priori historical and political assertions the basis for the study of literary works. Why is such a decision better, say, than deciding to include proslavery novels because they are excellent representations of the development of the genre of the romantic and regional novel in America? I am not saying that either of these two positions is necessarily the correct one; but whichever rationale one adopts, students ought to be brought into the history and terms of the debate about what has been put on the syllabus or in the anthology, and why.

Personally, I welcome this particular revision in the *Heath*, since I believe it exposes the paradoxes, in theory and practice, of a narrowly conceived advocacy pedagogy — or any pedagogy in which the syllabus assigns works that represent the "right" political or social views. If antiracism is the cultural work you want this unit of your syllabus to do, you and your students are better served by analyzing expressions of racism alongside critiques of it. For some time now I have taught proslavery writings in a variety of courses, and found that they are often more useful instruments in the struggle against racism than are the sanctioned denunciations of discrimination. Students expect to read protests against bigotry and cruelty, since such positions are the dominant sentiments of liberal ideology. But they are literally incredulous when confronted with Thomas Jefferson on the subject of black inferiority, or with fictional texts that depict slaves as loving their station. Understanding how persons who are otherwise brilliant, kind, loving, wise, or just ordinary citizens could espouse such views and undertake such practices requires great analytic, imaginative, and historical work.

If antiracist pedagogy aims to uncover the residual racism that structures our own beliefs and practices, then it may best be served by studying esteemed texts or figures that give full voice to that racism, for then racism cannot be held at arm's length as some aberration of sick minds. Identifying with the resistance to oppression of David Walker or Harriet Jacobs may be relatively easy compared to confronting the possible links between the views that Jefferson or Poe or Stowe had of racial "Others" and the sentiments we feel in this same area. Recognizing ourselves in such texts can be a painful and transformative experience. Only if you retain a notion of pedagogy as transmission of truth or instruction in appreciation will you choose to teach just those works whose viewpoints you agree with, or refuse to assign texts whose messages you find oppressive. Of course, the very idea that a text has a single viewpoint or message which is the essence whereby one can judge the kind of cultural work it does, and which can thus be the test of its suitability for the syllabus, also must be challenged.

Mailloux proposes that the best way to approach the cultural work of the text is through "rhetorical hermeneutics," a method that examines the reception of the text as part and parcel of a culture's debates with itself. Somewhat indebted to the new pragmatism as well as the New Historicism, Mailloux would have us turn our concern from a search for the meaning of the work to an examination of how the rhetorical situation of the interpreters determines the meanings that they advocate. Or, to put it another way, our concern is with discerning why a particular interpretation is found persuasive, or with how a reader constructs a persuasive interpretation, especially in relation to the social or historical or political context that determines what audiences find believable and valuable. But the results of this method are ambiguous. Mailloux's examples include studies of the widespread fears about the damage novel reading may do, whether to the bad boys who imitate adventure plots or to the good girls led astray by romance narratives ("Cultural Rhetoric Studies"; "Rhetorical Hermeneutics as Reception Study"). This antiliterary rhetoric, we know, is as old as literature itself, even if it took its modern form during eighteenth-century debates over the new genre of the novel. But Mailloux and others usually present these expressions of novel-phobia in a tone of incredulity: they don't really believe that novels have these effects and mock the early reviewers for their naive fears. The selection of these particular incidents in the history of reception, moreover, betrays the contemporary critic's evaluative choices about what kinds of interpretive and social issues are worth studying. What this reception history tells us, then, is something about the ideology of past reviewers and present critics but little or nothing about the actual reading practices of individual persons or social groups.

In other words, Mailloux's accounts tell us something about the history of literary ideologies but very little about the history of the use of literature. If this is a fair judgment, then one must question what this "rhetorical pragmatism" accomplishes. By attending so much to the ideological conditions of reception, Mailloux's analysis tends to move away from the "cultural work" school insofar as he avoids analyzing the practical — or pragmatic — effects of texts on readers or communities. His own evidence suggests that boys may very well have shaped their behavior in imitation of dime novels, while girls may likewise have modeled their own domestic dreams on sentimental romance. Even if this is so, we cannot say in advance or in general that such uses of literature have a specific political or moral valence, that is, that such uses indicate the oppression or the liberation of individual readers. I imagine Mailloux would be uncomfortable with any crudely mimetic pragmatism in theorizing the uses of literature; but in the absence of a theoretical or historical account of the complex ways in which readers use texts, the reader of Mailloux's argument is left in the dark. Theoretical work in popular culture studies and in feminist theories of spectatorship, by contrast, indicate that there are ways of doing reception history that prove more concrete than Mailloux's hermeneutics.

Consider, for example, Mailloux's treatment of Louisa May Alcott in his essay "*Huckleberry Finn* and 'The Bad Boy Boom.'" His discussion of "affectionate discipline" in Alcott gets contextualized within a discussion of prisons and reformatories that, owing much to Foucault, gives a dark intimation of the oppression supposedly informing Alcott's carceral domesticity. The effort to get "beyond interpretation" through rhetorical historicism seems to me to be founded on an interpretation that reads domestic discipline as essentially oppressive. This rather standard way of devaluing women's fiction of the nineteenth century fails to consider the pragmatics of its production and reception, a pragmatics that other critics have described as containing far more liberating or subversive power than Mailloux's disciplinary discourse suggests. Likewise, we may feel less sorry for the disciplined bad boys when we consider Judith Fetterley's argument, in "Not in the Least American," that bad boy stories form the center of the American canon, to the exclusion of the stories of women, the elderly, and people of color. Her analysis of Rose Terry Cook's "Miss Beulah's Bonnet" may leave us wishing that more boys had gotten a sound whipping.

It is clear that many teachers in the discipline of American literature have adopted some version of the equal representation or cultural work syllabus (including me). The borders of these syllabi, however, need to be transgressed again by laying bare the devices of these courses as well, resisting the temptation to naturalize the selections or contents of antiracist, antisexist, anticlassist, or antinationalist syllabi. As part of a disciplinary apparatus, the syllabus can always revert to becoming an instrument of intimidation and domination, even when the cause is believed just. As Carl Herndl observers:

> A pedagogy which sets up a stark confrontation between the repressive ideology of the dominant discourse and the teacher's emancipatory ideology structures the classroom as an opposition between the teacher and the students. Not only does such an opposition ignore the struggles and the differences within discourse, even within the dominant professional discourse, it establishes a classroom politics that restricts the cooperation and dialogue so central to radical pedagogy. The more this opposition structures

the classroom, the less chance the students have of exploring their own discourse and cultural position. Ironically, students will become once again the objects of what Freire calls the banking model of education, the objects this time of the teacher's ideological enlightenment. (359)

There is a tension between the liberatory pretensions of such syllabi and their use as instruments of a discipline, a tension I think we need to highlight and discuss before uncritically adopting advocacy pedagogy as a substitute for the disreputable formalism of the past.

In working to bare the devices of our syllabi, then, we discover that defamiliarization and critique are not enough. Even though it is vital to denaturalize and historicize the syllabus, such a radical pedagogy remains a pedagogy, remains part of the discipline, and so requires in turn that its own devices be challenged and historicized. Here I think we are up against the double bind inherent in the discipline of the syllabus: any syllabus that attempts to transcend its disciplinary function as an instrument for propagating a party line quickly turns into an instrument for teaching students the discipline of critique. How to avoid turning critique into a new party line is the challenge of a postdisciplinary pedagogy. And that challenge needs to be on the syllabus for the course of our (un)disciplinary futures.

Given that we must still make and justify assignments, I think that some combination of the equality of representation syllabi and the cultural work syllabi should be designed as the bulk of the curriculum in English studies, allowing some room for the syllabi based on more traditional claims of aesthetic or literary merit. The lines between these types are difficult to draw in practice, and no one wants to volunteer to police them. Happily in many cases our courses might be designed to foreground actively the conflict among these principles of course design, as I have suggested in recurrently framing aesthetically validated texts such as *Moby Dick* in contrast to texts that did cultural work (*Uncle Tom's Cabin*) or that represent an important historical population (*Incidents in the Life of a Slave Girl*). With students we might explore how it affects our reading to present Jacobs in terms of representing her race rather than as standing for artistic accomplishment or individual genius. And if this now recovered text had no opportunity to do cultural work in its own time, how do we measure the cultural work it does for us, or for the academic institutions that now make room for it? Or we might turn that question around and ask about the effect on Melville of *not* reading him as representative of a gender or a race or a class.

Reading James Baldwin's denunciation of Stowe, a class might explore why the novel did no valuable cultural work for Baldwin, and thus raise the issue of the relativity of cultural work. That might lead to reading Jane Tompkins's essay on *Uncle Tom's Cabin* in her *Sensational Designs*, which once more argues for Stowe's importance. Break the students into groups and ask each to workshop a comparison of these two readings of Stowe. It will not take long before students begin to wonder to what extent gender played a role in Baldwin's judgment that "*Uncle Tom's Cabin* is a very bad novel, having, in its self-righteous, virtuous sentimentality, much in common with *Little Women*" (14). Baldwin goes on to denounce "sentimentality" in terms even harsher than the earlier white male modernists had used to distance themselves from the literature of nineteenth-century women. The cultural work done by the rhetoric of interpretations, then, becomes an issue in reading Baldwin and Tompkins. One cannot help but feel that Baldwin's fierce attack on sentiment derives from its particular role in representing (or misrepresenting) race, while Tompkins's equally strong defense of sentiment derives from its particular role in empowering (or disempowering) women. The boom in the scholarship on sentiment in American literature shows critics taking the opportunity to combine cultural work and representativeness, as they explore how men and women, whites and blacks, different classes and groups, participated in this cultural form — even Herman Melville, who in *Pierre* joined the rhetorical culture wars over literature and sentimentality.

On the one hand, the equality of representation syllabi will facilitate the vital task of developing courses in previously undertaught literatures, figures, and forms. Here I again take the position that investing in the separate and independent study of particular traditions is essential. Establishing a range of such courses as permanent parts of the curriculum helps justify the allocation of faculty, teaching assignments, and enrollments to them, and so constitutes a healthy kind of curricular affirmative action. On the other hand, the cultural work syllabi will usually evolve out of traditional historical survey and period courses, which will be refined and revised as the cultural work thesis replaces the aesthetic thesis of "masterworks" and "great authors" which drives many of these syllabi. These courses will continue to be historicist in character, as the cultural work thesis draws analytic attention to the text's production and reception within a clearly delineated historical context. Yet the application of New Historicist principles will also ensure that what counts as history in such courses, as well as what kinds of texts are read and studied, will be fundamentally altered. One could then add to these principles Mailloux's ideas about rhetorical hermeneutics in order to frame rigorous studies of the interpretive conflicts at work in the various stages of a work's reception, from its first publication to the latest round of debates at the MLA convention. Ultimately, these renovated survey courses will have to be made accountable to the equality of representation approaches, so that a diversity of cultural workers is studied and comparative analyses of their writings are made possible. This brings us back around to a kind of cosmopolitanism or worldliness in the curriculum (about which I will have more to say in the next chapter).

These alterations in the syllabi and the curriculum will not themselves produce much in the way of coherence for the literature curriculum as a whole if they are not framed by well-designed courses in the history and principles of literary criticism, preferably required during the sophomore or junior years. I would take this moment to add that students also need exacting and sophisticated courses in rhetoric and composition, another area of the curriculum where the attacks of the culture wars have misrepresented a rigorous and innovative discipline. The syllabi for the literature courses should teach the conflicts between various schools, movements, and critical vocabularies, enabling the students to begin the process of testing different critical methods on specific literary works. Students should spend considerable time in "case book" units, reading a range of essays and articles that present diverse interpretations of the same literary work or critical problem. Students who have an initial training in the different critical approaches, in turn, will be well prepared to join their instructors in baring the devices of the syllabi in upper-division English studies courses. There will never be an end to the controversies that recurrently throw English studies into crisis, but we can assign these disputes a more productive and self-conscious role in the discipline of the syllabus.

five The End of "American" Literature

t was a long and hard fight that established, by the middle of the twentieth century, the legitimacy of courses in American literature and (a little later) American studies. Now the angry quarrels brought on (yet again) by the question "What is an American?" have made the use of the very term "American" troublesome, for it no longer seems to provide a stable ground or point of clear origin for organizing the discipline. The patriotic nationalism and proselytizing spirit that once helped excite enthusiasm for putting the "American" into the curriculum do not have the same hold in the academy, or among public intellectuals, that they once had. Worldliness cautions against building up another imperial narrative of America's unique cultural virtues or manifest political destiny. Even "victory" in the Cold War has left the United States unsure of its mission and vulnerable to seeking out enemies within to replace the antagonist abroad. A pedagogy of disorientation has set in, whether intended or not, that may prompt us to speak of the "disuniting of American literature." When one looks at what is actually occurring in the classrooms, however, dismay gives way to excitement as we witness so much curricular innovation based on such a wealth of scholarly discoveries.

Whether you visit the college textbook store or surf the syllabi on the World Wide Web, you will find that American literature courses today cover a wider range of writers, explore a vaster expanse of sophisticated topics, and require more rigorous student papers than at any time in the past. At first this flowering seems paradoxical. Given the undoing of the consensus about our national character, one could argue that it is time to stop teaching "American" literature. The lessons of critical theory, classroom practice, and contemporary history have inspired not simply a revision of the curriculum and pedagogy of "American" literature courses, but a forceful uprooting of the conceptual model defining the field itself.[1] On the one hand, this uprooting is cause for celebrating the reforms that have taken hold at numerous institutions and in recent critical studies and anthologies now too numerous to mention.[2] On the other hand, it can be pointed out that many of these reforms have been merely pluralist in character (JanMohamed and Lloyd make a good case against pluralism, while Ravitch upholds it). They add a few new texts or authors without dismantling the prejudicial framework that has traditionally prescribed the kinds of works studied in "American" litera-

1. See, among many others, Baker, *Three American Literatures*; Baym, *Woman's Fiction*; Bercovitch, "America as Canon," "Problem of Ideology"; Elliot, "New Literary History" and "Politics of Literary History"; Fetterley, "Not in the Least American"; Fetterley and Pryse; Gates, "Master's Pieces"; Kolodny; Lauter, *Canons*; Tompkins. For a recent powerful discussion of directions for the future, see Carolyn Porter, "What We Know That We Don't Know."

2. Special credit must be given, however, to Paul Lauter and the editorial team that produced the monumental *Heath Anthology of American Literature* which went farther than any previous textbook in upsetting the pedagogical premises of the discipline. For its equivalent in the discipline of American history, see Takaki, *A Different Mirror*.

ture courses and the issues raised in "American" literary scholarship. That scholarship and the classes in which it is taught thus often continue to depend on, and reproduce, those damaging aspects of our nationalist ideology which form (to paraphrase Malcolm X) the nightmare side of "the American Dream" (Cone 1).

Nonetheless, if the discipline of "American" literature can be defined as the teaching of those few great artists who best express the true meaning of America and of America's exceptional mission in the world, then it may be accurate to say that the discipline has ended, for many of its teachers have stopped working by this model. These instructors have not stopped teaching the poems, stories, plays, autobiographies, and essays written in the United States. On the contrary, they are teaching more of them than ever before, often assigning writers and genres unknown to their dissertation directors. Students are responding to this change in the discipline's ends with great enthusiasm, often expressing disbelief when told that Fern or Sui Sin Far or Hurston was not always in the canon, or that students in the past did not study slave narratives, *corridos*, work songs, Indian trickster myths, or blues lyrics in previous versions of the survey course. They are incredulous when they learn that the artistic superiority of Melville and James and Eliot was confidently asserted by prior generations of scholars who often had never read much if any of the literature by women or minorities which they nonetheless dismissed as unworthy of study. Today's students are being equipped with the cultural literacy necessary for democratic citizenship in America, as well as enjoying some of the finest experiences of aesthetic pleasure and intellectual stimulation available. They are also gaining remarkable expertise in the theory of literary history and in understanding how a nation's narrative of its cultural past influences so many of its policies and institutions in the present. These students regularly disagree with one another, and with their instructors, as one would expect when the pedagogical ethic is to put diversity on the table and solicit different accounts of the American. The results are not always pretty; but such classrooms can be laboratories for learning to work together across borders, to ground empathy in historical knowledge, and to practice the making of community out of a respect for group as well as individual experience.

• • •

What is emerging through the labors of countless teachers and students is a multicultural and dialogical model for the study of writing in the United States. By dialogical I mean a pedagogy that is comparative, that puts books into dialogue with one another, making each responsible to the others rather than presenting each as an isolate masterpiece to be revered. The dialogue extends to that between students and books, as "process" pedagogy and computers prompt us to engage in more interactive relationships with what we study, rather than continuing a model in which students passively receive the wisdom of the talking head at the lectern. Response-ability in learning translates into the student's taking up the challenge to respond actively to the reading, whether in the form of a journal, an oral presentation, an on-line discussion, a Web page, or the more traditional essay of research and interpretation. This emphasis on dialogue in learning coincides with an emphasis on how the texts, in their own time and place, were themselves the products of active dialogues between real protagonists, who designed their works to alter the feelings and actions of those who read them.

Writing in the United States is misrepresented when it is characterized as the production of a few autonomous works of art by lonely geniuses who had no interest in society or politics or the land or sex or race or the other issues about which human beings care so passionately. By the phrase "writing in the United States" I mean to include both the study of writing produced in the United States and the way that "we" in the United States study writing. This second meaning allows me some wiggle room, as it makes way for the study in the US of texts produced in the "borderlands," not on native grounds but in the hemispheric geography that is nonetheless part and parcel of our (literary) history. Not everyone writing in the US is an American, and not all of them write in English. The way we study writing in the US may have to include texts produced beyond its borders but in active dialogue with the US, or involve following the sources of texts back into cultural geographies far from our shores. (For those of us located in the United States, the problem is precisely whether we are an "US," especially at a time when the rhetoric is full of dividing lines between us and them. Thus, my decision to use the unpunctuated abbreviation — US — for the remainder of this chapter signals an effort to recall the specific heterogeneity of our cultural history and the difficulty of speaking for, or about, it in a univocal voice.)

What models can we find for imagining the spirit and principles of such a project? One major resource for me is the poetry and prose of Adrienne Rich, whose 1971 essay "Writing as Re-Vision" helped launch contemporary feminist criticism (*On Lies* 33–50). Since then Rich has gone on to envision the way race and nation affect the production and reception of literature. Her work strives not to colonize or marginalize the Other, but to read, think, and feel the differences that our bodily locations — in history, in geography, in ethnicity, in gender, in sexual orientation — can make. Rich's "politics of location" begins, however, not with the continent or nation "but with the geography closest in — the body." She would "pick up again the long struggle against lofty and privileged abstraction.... Even to begin with the body I have to say that from the outset that body had more than one identity [female, white, Jewish, middle-class, southern, North American, etc.].... Two thoughts: there is no liberation that only knows how to say 'I'; there is no collective movement that speaks for each of us all the way through.... And so even ordinary pronouns become a political problem.... Once again, Who is *we*? " (*Blood* 212–13, 215, 224, 231).

Rich is herself the Other as well as the privileged one; hers is both a stubbornly individual voice of freedom and a vocal desire for community. Her mapping of the located body graphically resists the abstract liberal humanism which, for all its accomplishments, continued to force the Other to assimilate to the values and interests of an idiosyncratic yet predominant Western self. Her revisionist mirror exposes the complacency in which that self regarded its image as unitary, normative, and universal. Rich's argument resembles those made by postmodern anthropologists and ethnographers such as James Clifford, who writes: "Once cultures are no longer prefigured visually — as objects, theaters, texts, — it becomes possible to think of a cultural poetics that is an interplay of voices, of positioned utterances" (Clifford and Marcus, "Introduction" 12). For Rich and Clifford, multiculturalism is a dialogue among (and within) socially constructed bodies and historically experienced subject positions. This dialogue, then, forms the basis for what I have called the dialogical model for approaching "American" literature, a dialogue of different responses and new response-abilities. In and out of the classroom, students of writing in the United States can become like Clifford's "indigenous ethnographers," self-conscious of both the positions they write from and the positions they describe.

Given the ethico-political self-consciousness of Rich and the sensitivity to positioned utterance of Clifford, I feel anxious about my place in this writing, in this profession, in this country. I am proud of what my colleagues have accomplished, but I also want to heed the warning of Guillermo Gomez-Peña not to "confuse true collaboration with political paternalism, cultural vampirism, voyeurism, economic opportunism, and demagogic multiculturalism" (133). I have to question the politics of the "we" here, in my own writing, and in my own teaching. In part this "we" refers to a set of dominant groups I participate in — European American, male, middle-class, heterosexual, US citizen, educated, institutionalized by a discipline, and so on — and I speak to those same groups about our need to question the basis of our own privileges. Real dangers (leading to "demagogic multiculturalism") lie in imagining that social harms and ideological errors are always someone else's doing and someone else's responsibility. Before "we" get too busy celebrating our position at the forefront of the liberation of the culture, we (and I think this includes, at some point, all of us) need to recognize that *we* are often the problem. It is our racism, our sexual prejudices, our class anxieties, our empowered desires that we have to confront and resist. The unconscious character of these biases means that we cannot be complacent or comfortable just because we have consciously articulated our positions and privileges (as in this chapter). Such avowals can easily turn into bad faith as we congratulate ourselves for our self-flagellating perspicacity or imagine that we have transcended our social contradictions simply by naming them. These routines can be nothing more than a defensive reasserting of our authority. They are just as mistaken as the cultivation of guilt, which rarely leads to much more than denial and defensiveness in this arena.

I was made particularly aware of these difficulties when I presented an early version of this chapter before an audience of whom half were African American scholars. I felt painfully the difficulty of the "we" in my talk, and the strain to find a voice that could articulate a dialogue among positions. Some who might read the present chapter do not belong to many of the privileged groups I have mentioned. Their — your — relation to the pronoun "we" will have its own mappings, as will your relation to the "American." In imagining this dialogue among us, I think of the pronouns as moving from the dimension of the representative to the horizon of the possible. "I" and "you" and "we" and "us" may then operate performatively, in utopian fashion, as they do in the texts of Walt Whitman and of Rich — as invocations to the possibility of community. "What is it then between us?" asks Whitman. "What is the count of the scores or hundreds of years between us? . . . I too had received identity by my body" (130). To play ungrammatically on Rich's question, we might say that the motto for American criticism can only be: "Once again: Who is US?"

The US represented by our educational institutions, textbooks, anthologies, curriculums, and faculty rosters has never been representative of our social reality. Rather, it mirrors, in each age, the authorized image of cultural identity in the US. In the service of this imaginary "America," the complexion of cultural history in the US has been misrepresented so as effectively to underwrite the power and values of privileged classes and individuals. The "we" of the utopian "American Dream" had a power to liberate, to encourage resistance to the past, but it also had a power to censor, tyrannize, and destroy those who became the objects of the fantasy (women, slaves, immigrants, racial minorities, et al.) rather than the subjects doing the dreaming. Whoever "we" may be, we should act now on the recurrent observation that literary judgments have always already had a political dimension; our responsibility for justice in cultural education requires more self-criticism in this regard than we have yet shown. Although literary judgments are never simply or exclusively political, neither can the practices of book reviewing, publication, teaching, research, and interpretation escape having political meanings, influences, and effects. There is no choosing between aesthetics and politics, no occupying one position to the exclusion of the other.

Engaging in this dialogue of positions involves making explicit, and sometimes altering, the values at work in our schools and scholarship (see Giroux, "Liberal Arts Education"). The movement toward multicultural literacy reflects more than a dedication to intellectual honesty and historical accuracy; it expresses a conviction that the legacy of American nationalism needs to be reevaluated, whether in the direction of asserting the viability of a multicultural nationalism or in the direction of abandoning nationalism altogether. It also means revisiting the discussion of what the purposes of education in a democracy should be. A commitment to multicultural education belongs to our historical moment in that we are witness to a renewed interest (albeit often only rhetorical) in democracy, one that leads us to ask how a democratic culture might be fashioned as part of a democratic polity. One place to begin is by looking at how the "politics of knowledge" joins forces with the "politics of location" to map those who are exploitable, those who are expendable, and those who have the privilege to discriminate between the two.

As the foregoing chapters of this volume have shown, multiculturalism is various and has its own dangers. Diane Ravitch argues that a proper multiculturalism teaches respect for the diversity of America's "common culture" (and so is pluralistic), while a dangerous multiculturalism advocates conflicting ethnocentrisms and implies that "no common culture is possible or desirable" (and so is particularistic) (340). Constructing the choice as one between a common culture and chaotic ethnic rivalries, however, will not suffice. As we have seen, appeals to the common and the universal have all too often been made at the expense of particular peoples. Any recourse to a notion of a national culture risks reimposing a biased set of principles or historical narratives, and Ravitch is conspicuously silent on what the content of that common culture may be. She may well be mistaking a common political arrangement for a common set of cultural beliefs, mistaking a widely held belief in democracy and entrepreneurial capitalism for a widely shared commonality of convictions about religion, sex, nature, food, violence, sports, clothes, music, and art. (I think we have the former but not the latter.) Ravitch is right, though, to warn that replacing Eurocentrism with a series of ethnocentrisms would only multiply the original problem. Rather, multicultural study should put people into a dialogue with the Other — with the subjects that have historically formed the boundaries of their cultural experiences. Essentialism does not have to be the result of affirmative action, especially if one understands the latter as an affirmation of the Other and not of one's self. Ravitch's notion of common culture is actually another version of the idea of a civic religion, which appears as a subject for discussion in a number of liberal responses to multiculturalism (see Gitlin; Hollinger; Lind). From a civic perspective, Americanness is not a substance or an essence but a political ethos: as a way of life, it is a process of social existence predicated on the espoused, if not always realized, principles of cultural democracy, political rights, community responsibility, social justice, equality of opportunity, and individual freedom. When these principles are subordinated to totalizing ideologies seeking to invent or impose a particular commonality of religion or race, art or philosophy, then the actual multicultural life of Americans suffers in a manner that is in no one's best interests.[3]

These issues are relevant because the institutional history of American literary studies is closely tied to the history of American nationalism. The urgency to invent an American nation and urgency to invent a uniquely American literature were historically coincident. So long as we use "American" as an adjective, we may be reinforcing the illusion that there is a transcendental core of values and experiences that is essentially "American." This illusion of the "American" in turn fosters the delusion that literary or cultural studies may be properly shaped by selecting objects and authors according to how well they express this essence. This metaphysical approach to artistic nationalism has shaped American literary theory ever since the first attempts to invent a uniquely American literature in the 1820s, and has persisted through every theory that has used arguments for American exceptionalism. Insofar as women, African and Asian and

3. The debate over the meaning of a "pluralistic" multiculturalism took a distinctive turn at the University of California at Berkeley during the development of the "American Cultures" breadth requirement. Berkeley rejected the route of achieving diversity through separate courses in separate cultural traditions. Students can meet the requirement only with approved courses that examine, in a comparative fashion, the cultural experiences in the United States of indigeneous peoples, African Americans, European Americans, Asian Americans, and Latinos. Unlike the "happy tolerance" models of other multicultural pluralisms, the Berkeley program tends to make students aware of the differences between cultures, rather than offering them a facile exercise in "celebrating diversity."

Native Americans, Latinos and Latinas, gays and lesbians, and others make an appearance in such accounts, it is usually in terms of their also being made into exemplars for traditional values and schemes. Their "assimilation" or "acculturation" into American literature comes at the cost of their cultural heritage and obscures their real antagonism and historical difference in relation to the privileged classes.

For example, the authorized stories that portray assimilation as a universally available process of citizenship (and perhaps even redemption) overlook the history of how race and ethnicity have functioned to keep a lid on the melting pot. As Victor Villanueva argues, the difference between the immigrant and the minority person of color is a case in point. This difference falls outside the sanctioned stories of our common culture:

> None tells our story. Us: those who are not immigrants but long-time citizens and residents who never quite assimilate. . . . The immigrant seeks to take on the culture of the majority. And the majority, given certain preconditions, not the least of which is displaying the language and dialect of the majority, accepts the immigrant. The minority, even when accepting the culture of the majority, is never wholly accepted. . . . I think of those who try to calm others by saying that it takes two generations for ghetto dwellers to move on. This has been the pattern for immigrants. But what then do we do with the African American or the Latino, especially the Mexican-American, on American soil, in American society, far longer than two generations? What happens to them — to *us*— those of us who are of color, those of us normally labeled "minority"? (xvi, 23–24)

According to Villanueva, what distinguishes the "immigrant" from the "minority" is the history of violent colonization and subjugation aimed at people of color. Race — like gender — becomes the basis for a caste system that obstructs any sizable assimilation into the dominant culture. Just as women discover a "glass ceiling" in the workplace, people of color discover a white border preventing them from blending into the mainstream.

As Michael Lind demonstrates convincingly, we need to look back at the idea of the "melting pot" and see that it was fashioned in particular reference to developing a "pan-European" American racial

identity. This would replace the more restricted Anglo-Saxon identity still dominant at the dawn of the twentieth century, when New
Englanders and southerners fought a rear-guard action against the
new immigrants from Southern Europe. Randolph Bourne gave voice
to this relatively progressive notion in an essay that has become part
of the multicultural canon: "The failure of the melting-pot, far from
closing the great American democratic experiment, means that it has
only just begun. Whatever American nationalism turns out to be, we
see already that it will have a color richer and more exciting than our
ideal has hitherto encompassed. In a world which has dreamed of
internationalism, we find that we have all unawares been building
up the first international nation" (93). Students who are assigned
Bourne's essay eventually notice that he never mentions Americans
of African or Hispanic or Asian descent, though these have certainly
given America "a color richer and more exciting than our ideal has
hitherto encompassed." The internationalism here represents an ethnic (rather than racial) pluralism of Euro-American cultural groups
free from the burden of assimilating to Anglo-Saxon hegemony.
Neither the original melting pot nor Bourne's "trans-national" vision was ever intended to accommodate a more diverse racial stew
(Hollinger 93–97; Levine 105–20; Lind 234–45).

American literary pedagogy played its part in the effort to keep
Anglo-Saxonism at the heart of Americanness. From 1882 to 1912
(and beyond), observes Nina Baym, "textbook writers made literary
works and authors display the virtues and achievements of an Anglo-
Saxon United States founded by New England Puritans" ("Early
Histories" 459). This narrative served the purpose of "Americaniz-
ing" and assimilating the growing industrial and immigrant classes
arriving from Southern Europe, an alarming number of whom were
Catholics and Jews: "Paradoxically, the non-Anglo-Saxons could become American only to the extent of their agreement that only those
of Anglo-Saxon lineage were really Americans" (463). At the level of
class, the ambitions and disappointments of exploited workers could
be mediated by an education in transcendentalism: "What more
likely to deflect the (usually foreign-born) poor from their desire
to have a substantial piece of the country's settled wealth than expo-
sure to an idealism from whose lofty perspective the materialist
struggle would seem unworthy?" (462). Literary and cultural histories

reflected the Anglo-Saxon bias, and so fabricated a symbolic consensus about the American Dream that papered over real social contradictions and racial conflicts (see Graff, *Professing*, 130–32, 209–25). As a social practice, then, institutions of pedagogy manufactured consenting subject positions among European immigrants, spreading the American Dream of assimilation even as the 1882 Chinese Exclusion Act, the resistance to women's suffrage, the ongoing expropriation of Indian lands, the Jim Crow laws, and the epidemic of lynching made apparent who would be allowed to share the dream.

As the institutionalization of American literary studies continued, its ends evolved from the propagation of the Anglo-Saxon Puritan tradition to the construction of a "democratic" literary tradition whose complexion would match that of the new pan-European culture. Again, the universalizing discourse of this stress on democracy (from Parrington and Brooks through Trilling) had an implicit ethnic component and was bounded by an unspoken racial line. Though dissenters were always around, and subcultural literary traditions continued to flourish, it was not until the 1960s and after that a frontal assault on the melting-pot canon took place. What had happened from the 1890s to the 1950s was a drastic reduction in the scope of accounts of American literary history. Many of the writers resurrected after 1970 had been importantly featured in anthologies and histories prior to 1920. The twin forces of aestheticism and American exceptionalism acted to reduce the canon to exemplars of aesthetic greatness who expressed the American essence.

• • •

In rejecting the models of American literary study based on white ethnic particularism, idealized notions of democracy, and faulty criteria of artistic excellence, contemporary multiculturalism opens the classroom and the library research desk to the full spectrum of writing in the United States. If we combine the imperatives to broaden the range of people represented and to consider the cultural work done by writing, we end up sketching the definition of the field of US writing. It includes acts of writing committed within and during the colonization, establishment, and ongoing production of the US, including those writings that resist and critique its identification with nationalism (some of which may have been produced in Canada or Cuba or Mexico, but nonetheless have a part in the story). Granted, organizing courses on the basis of national entities inevitably reproduces certain biases and fallacies, and we need to protect against these by including specific theoretical questions and methodological devices in the curriculum.[4]

Other rubrics besides "Writing in the United States" have been proposed which also work well. Paul Lauter calls one of his chapters in *Canons and Contexts* "The Literatures of America — A Comparative Discipline," an approach which states that in America there is a multiplicity of literary traditions, and each deserves independent study, though ultimately within a comparative framework. This approach has influenced another interesting variant, the "Literatures of the Americas" rubric, which takes multiplicity one step further by stating that there is a multiplicity of Americas, and not all of them are in the United States. "Literatures of the Americas" thus envisions a wider hemispheric perspective with an intercultural as well as multicultural curriculum. The question here is put succinctly by the title of a volume edited by Gustavo Pérez Firmat: *Do the Americas Have a Common Literature?* Renaming our field "Comparative American Literature" or "Comparative Literatures of the Americas" might also accomplish much, though at the risk of implying that there is an American literature that is not comparative. These approaches would also raise the question whether fluency in Spanish or Chinese or one of the Indian languages should be a requirement for the degree. In parallel fashion, we could remake the discipline of "American Studies" to establish courses and programs in North or pan-American studies that would integrate the cultural history of the US with those of Canada, Mexico, the countries of Latin and South America, and

4. In her introduction to *Cultures of United States Imperialism*, Amy Kaplan warns that "the new pluralistic model of diversity runs the risk of being bound by the old paradigm of unity if it concentrates its gaze only narrowly on the internal lineaments of American culture and leaves national borders intact instead of interrogating their formation. That is, American nationality can still be taken for granted as a monolithic and self-contained whole, no matter how diverse and conflicted, if it remains implicitly defined by its internal social relations, and not in political struggles for power with other cultures and nations, struggles which make America's conceptual and geographic borders fluid, contested, and historically changing" (15).

the Caribbean, though to do so would present the danger of repeating the history of colonial imperialism at the level of academic study.

In discussing the essay on which this chapter was based, Carolyn Porter remarked that my notion of studying "Writing in the United States" had brought nationalism back in just when its end was in sight. She advocates transforming the discipline into a hemisphere-wide enterprise in literary and cultural studies. Her exciting ideas about how Caribbean, Chicano, and Latin American literatures can help decenter the "Americanist field-imaginary" deserve close attention. Aside from the obvious practical question whether texts written in Spanish should be subject to analysis by English professors, there are dangers in thinking that we can go beyond a critique of nationalism in cultural studies and just do away with organizing our work on a national basis. It is clear that much can be gained from structuring our theories, classes, books, and articles on principles or issues that cross national borders and contest the effects of these boundaries. After all, the borders between the nations of the Americas are less the origins of our history than the products of it (witness the US takeover of the Mexican Southwest and California).

At the same time, we should recognize that calling for an end to the study of a national American literature means calling for an end to the study of a national Mexican or Canadian or Colombian literature as well. Do "we" in the United States want to prescribe such an abandonment of local and regional cultural traditions? Do we have that right? Would this call for postnationalism return us to the widely discussed observation that the criticisms of identity politics arise just at the moment when those whose identities have been marginalized demand recognition? What happens to the analysis of other cultural categories, such as gender, when the model clearly seems to focus on the priorities of international class or race struggle? (Feminism seems as absent from Porter's vision as it was from those of Lind and Hollinger.) Here again, we have to be careful to balance the global and the local, the particular and the universal. To some extent I think we can distinguish between idealistic approaches to cultural nationalism, on the one hand, and historically self-critical accounts on the other. However we may wish to dispute their ideologies and behaviors and borders, nation-states are fundamental elements of modern cultural life which require separate study, if only to provide a better understanding of what they do not encompass or what they may give way to in the future. There are many ideas afloat about what will come at the end of nationalism, but it is not clear that we are there yet (or that that's where we want to arrive). Putting an end to the worst effects of nationalism will necessarily involve analyzing the separate historical formations of literary culture in the US and other nations, even if our ultimate goal is to open the borders among them.

A focus on "Writing in the United States," then, would both analyze the specific cultural history of a nation and chart the fluidity of its borders. While exploring issues about representation, cultural work, and aesthetics that come up in many literature courses, this discipline would also face the added burden of putting the validity of nationalism on the syllabus for discussion (since the nation is right there in the catalogue and course title). This instability of the principle of nationalism is not simply theoretical, since our peoples and writers have been flowing back and forth over our changing borders since before the colonial adventure began. Keeping these borders closed makes little sense when one is studying the histories, say, of Hispanic or African American or American Indian literature. This crossing of the borderlands, as José Saldivar and others argue, becomes the paradoxical center of Mexican American and Chicano literature, for example, which has been violating lines of nationality and of language since the 1500s (see Paul Jay, *Contingency Blues* 142–79; Gomez-Peña; Rosaldo; Saldivar). How does one categorize a work such as Rudolfo Anaya's *Bless Me, Ultima* or Arturo Islas's *Rain God*, which cross so many of these linguistic and cultural divides? What "Americanist" pedagogy could do justice to the traditions, historical representations, and contexts of utterance in *Black Elk Speaks* or James Welch's *Fools Crow*? Can the borders between Hispanic, American Indian, and Anglo-American literature be drawn without recalling the political treacheries that imposed a series of violated borders on indigenous peoples and settlers from Mexico, borders that were shifted whenever white economic interest dictated, so that Latino and Indian cultures come to be an "outside" within the "inside" of the US?

Within the boundaries of the US, the borders between cultural groups do not form impassable walls, though they often take oppressive shape. Historically these zones are an area of constant passage back and forth, as each culture borrows, imitates, exploits, subjugates, subverts, mimics, ignores, or celebrates the others. The myth of assimilation (which is often acculturation) homogenizes this process by representing it as the progressive acquiescence of every other group to a dominant culture. Writers who analyze this myth often depict the experience instead under the metaphor of "passing"— as in having to "pass" for white, for gentile, for straight, for American. The "object of oppression," writes Cherríe Moraga, "is not only someone outside of my skin, but the someone inside my skin" (30). Thus there are borders within, as well as between, our subject positions. This "double consciousness" (to recall the phrasing of W. E. B. Du Bois) affects every group and individual, though with particular differences that writing or film or music can well express.

Language is a primary vehicle for passing, a way of performing one's way into a cultural identity or out of one. This is true for the writer as well as the ordinary speaker, since writers confront a dominant literary language in which certain styles and forms and conventions may be expected, even though these originate in a culture alien to the writer's own experience or subject matter. Students as well as critics can study how the development of aesthetic forms participates in the rituals and contradictions of passing, and thus how establishing one's identity as a writer gets caught up with the legacies of one's cultural identity. As we highlight the politics of linguistic assimilation — of the consequences for non–English-speaking people who must learn to speak and write the master's tongue — we can exploit the pun in the phrase "Writing in the United States." "Writing" here designates not simply a static set of objects but the activity of verbal expression, what a speaker or writer experiences when she or he attempts to write within the boundaries of the US (see Baker, *Journey* 1–52; Gates, *Figures* 3–58).

In her eloquent chapter "Language: Teaching New Worlds/New Words," bell hooks meditates on Adrienne Rich's line "This is the oppressor's language yet I need it to talk to you" (from "The Burning of Paper Instead of Children") and Gloria Anzaldúa's assertion

"So, if you want to really hurt me, talk badly about my language." In it hooks evokes the trauma of enslaved Africans stripped of their speech, "compelled to witness their language rendered meaningless" as they were forced to pick up English as best they could (168). Yet hooks also imagines them "realizing that this language would need to be possessed, taken, claimed as a space of resistance. I imagine that the moment they realized the oppressor's language, seized and spoken by the tongues of the colonized, could be a space of bonding was joyous. For in that recognition was the understanding that intimacy could be restored, that a culture of resistance could be formed that would make recovery from the trauma of enslavement possible" (169). Black vernacular, by this account, is a speaking/writing in dialogue with the dominant, capable of expert artistry and joyous intimacy as well as resistance. Spurred by this model, we can ask about the historically specific relationship to English of Native American or Hispanic or Asian American speakers and writers, conceiving this relation as far more complex than simply the total loss of authenticity or the complete assimilation to a new literacy. The literal bilingualism practiced by Anzaldúa in a text such as *Borderlands/La Frontera* stands also for the crossing of language practices in English-only texts that nonetheless borrow from, or are in dialogue with, the expressive traditions of other cultures (be they Yiddish or Yoruba, Elizabethan or El Salvadoran, Chinese or Choctaw).

This broadened understanding of "writing" includes the historical conditions in which people write and the institutions that control the production of writing, for these are integral to understanding writing's cultural work, aesthetic forms, and distributions of representation. "Writing in the United States," then, involves questions of literacy, of the access to writing and representation. If we replace the term "literature" with "writing," moreover, we can resist the cultural biases built into the former term and institutionalized by academic departments that have built their curricula around the privileged genres developed in modern Europe. Of course, much of the verbal production of representation takes an oral rather than a literally written form, and I would not want to be understood as excluding non-print media. Rather, I use "writing" in the extended sense as referring to systems of representation, or what the theorists call "textuality." So understood, writing or textuality can encompass songs, creation tales, oral performance, and other previously marginalized media as well as canonical forms produced by marginalized people. For example, we can look at how women writers in the nineteenth century took up the European discourse on sentiment to develop in "domestic fiction" a powerful assertion of the value of women's lives. Or we can consider the way contemporary American Indian writers graft the techniques of postmodern narration onto traditional tribal forms of storytelling. Or we can study the blending of African and European elements in the growth of jazz, as well as study the material conditions of the people who expressed their sense of life through its improvisations, its call and response, and its production outside the dominant economy.

Historically, "Writing in the United States" would begin with Indian expressive traditions and include those narratives produced by the first European explorers and colonizers, Spanish and French as well as English.[5] This would effectively decenter histories of American literature, which have always placed their origins in the Anglo-Saxon culture of Puritan New England (see Reising 49–91). That culture was a culture of the Book— of the Bible —which confronted an oral culture among the Indians. The cultural and literary politics of this confrontation require consideration, as does the problematic of translation it dictates. The survival of American Indian discourse henceforth began to depend on its translation into written form, often through the mediation of whites, or on the translation of Indian experience into white expression in the public speeches and documents produced by tribal leaders in defense of their lands and rights. The literary history of the US includes the story of how the assault against indigenous tribal cultures was essential to the literary and political invention of "America," as the struggle for culture coincided with the struggle for land. The boundaries of "Writing in the United States" could thus be drawn geographically and historically, not linguistically, through attention to the demographics of cultural populations, as we witness the dialogical interaction of succeeding gener-

5. Since first advocating this curriculum in the late 1980s, I have watched with interest as most major college anthologies of American literature have gone this route, notably those published by Heath, Harper, and Prentice Hall.

ations of arrivals from Europe, Africa, Asia, Mexico, and Latin America. "Writing in the United States" could then be placed within the history of colonialism and imperialism, as well as nationalism, better providing a foundation for comprehending the current political and social dilemmas facing the US as it reconceives itself as a multicultural society in a multicultural world.

The problem of nationalism within literary studies has been built into the organization of higher education. For about a century we have had departments of English, French, German, Spanish, Portuguese, Italian, and so forth. These were originally conceived as the modern heirs to the tradition of classical philology. They centered on the study of language, with literature read as an illustration of the history of linguistic development. This philology, like the New Criticism that replaced it, was never entirely a formalism, for it inevitably reproduced the cultural values of the canonical texts it studied (just consider the political, ideological, and evaluative prejudgments inherent in naming a department "Classics"). Many language faculty advocated more cultural study in the curriculum, until a basic ambiguity haunted these departments: were they designed to teach the history of a language or the history of a nation? (Graff, *Professing* 55–120). The question, as in the case of English, became vexed when languages crossed national borders and historical periods. If we want to teach literature written in English today, this will mean teaching many texts written in Africa and Asia as well as in Great Britain, Canada, and the US.

When the *interpretation* of literary texts, as opposed to their philological description or use for national historical celebration, becomes the center of professional literary studies, then the very rationale for language-based departments begins to crumble, though we have not yet faced this fact or imagined real alternatives. "English" is a misleading name for departments offering courses in psychoanalysis, postcolonialism, film theory, feminism, Native American autobiography, lesbian fiction, and Chicano poetry. "Indeed," says Annette Kolodny, "no longer can we hold to the linguistic insularity implied by the Americanist's presence in departments of *English*" (293). I would side with Kolodny against William Spengemann, who concludes that because "American" does not designate a language, we ought to abandon efforts to conceive an American literary history and instead return to the study of texts written in English, specifically those great texts that have markedly changed the language itself (as if the only texts that had changed English were those originally written in English). Spengemann tumbles into tautology and circular reasoning when he advocates a canon based on the linguistic practices of modernism: according to him, only those past texts that belong to modernism's history get into the canon, and modernism is the origin of the canon because past experiments in literary language lead to it.

Even though I have expressed reservations about a wholesale incorporation of non-English cultural production into the disciplinary machine of an imperial English department, this does not translate into an English-only curriculum for approaching writing in the United States. The exclusion of texts not written in English or of authors drawing heavily on non-European sources limits the canon with pernicious results, as Porter and others have argued. One cannot even adequately interpret works in American English without some knowledge of the various cultures surrounding and informing them. Most writing produced in this country after the eighteenth century, moreover, borrows words, characters, events, forms, ideas, and concepts from the languages of African, Hispanic, Jewish, Native, and Asian Americans. At the same time, speakers and writers from these different cultures adapt the English language to create hybrid forms and texts. For analyzing writers such as Frederick Douglass, Isaac Singer, or Leslie Silko, a background in Chaucer or Restoration drama or Imagist poetry may be less helpful than, say, studying the traditions and vocabulary of religious representation in the author's cultural group or of the ancestral language the author draws upon. One could argue that the study of US writing cannot be adequately pursued within the boundaries of the English department, for this comparative project ultimately subverts the very premises of that academic organization — as, indeed, the multicultural demographics of the US subverts Eurocentric premises about the nation and its "common culture." Even if we maintain the academic premises of "English," we ought to study it as a hybrid language of hybrid peoples and so approach it as a discipline that ideally requires a multilingual perspective.

Although I believe in a historical approach to writing, I recognize that historicism will suffer the same transgressing of boundaries as those approaches that impose artificial limits on language or geography. US history cannot be represented a priori as a totality, a unity, or a grand story whose plot and hero we already know. A chief model for modern literary nationalism is that historiography which represents the nation as a collective self, a figurative mind or spirit which is realizing its great soul through the unfolding progress of the national community's history. Not surprisingly, this fiction has often been compared to the bildungsroman, and we are familiar with the claims it makes on us, from *The Autobiography of Benjamin Franklin* through Manifest Destiny, to *The Great Gatsby*, and the career of Ronald Reagan. The metaphorical self used to figure such national histories, of course, turns out to wear the idealized face of a very real class or group of individuals — what we now in the West reductively call white (male) patriarchy. The spiritual story of the nation's quest to realize its dream is in some cases fabricated through the exploitation, repression, and even genocide of those subjects deemed peripheral to the tale.

Of course, undoing the canon doesn't just mean adding on previously excluded figures; it requires a disturbance of the internal security of the classics themselves. Reworkings of the syllabus must be transformative and not just additive: the new texts will alter our readings of the traditional ones, and the canonical texts will have to answer to previously silenced voices. This is why defenses of the academy which stress that Shakespeare and Melville and Faulkner still occupy a predominant place in the curriculum are wrongheaded, and for two reasons. First, they defend academics against charges of political correctness by inaccurately asserting that not much has really changed, though this is done in the spirit of defending an opening of the canon. Second, they overlook the fact that when canonical authors are taught today, they are taught through different critical lenses and placed in different interpretive contexts than before. I may still teach *Moby Dick*, though I approach it now as a novel that explores the racial and class contradictions of Jacksonian America rather than as an aesthetic experiment that should be formally linked to the modernism of Joyce. Even more to the point, I might, as the conservative critics fear, decide that I do not have room for *Moby Dick* in my course "Antebellum American Fiction," since Melville's novel was a minor episode in light of the cultural importance at the time of texts such as *Uncle Tom's Cabin* or *The Wide Wide World*, which thousands of readers eagerly bought and debated, while Melville's abstruse story of a whaling voyage sat forlornly on dusty shelves with other poor sellers such as Thoreau's *Walden*.

In gay and lesbian studies, to take another example, cultural revision extends beyond including avowedly same-sex–oriented writers in the curriculum, as if adding a queer figure alongside the "normal" writers will do. What is at stake is precisely the norming of the "normal." Gay and lesbian studies challenge the way "normal" heterosexuality invents and reproduces itself. How long can we go on teaching courses on thematic topics related to "love" and "sexuality" while assigning only the literature of heterosexuality, or, even more to the point, while overlooking how that literature contains anxieties about its "Other"? Just as feminism is (also) about men, gay and lesbian studies is about everybody's sexual orientation. In literary studies it extends to questioning the sexual economies of ambiguous and (supposedly) straight texts, to the ways they police their desires. According to Eve Sedgwick, since "the problematics of homo/heterosexual definition, in an intensely homophobic culture, are seen to be precisely internal to the central nexuses of that culture," teasing out these contradictions in classic texts reveals the subversiveness and repression integral to them, so that "this canon must always be treated as a loaded one" (148). Because patriarchy reproduces itself through "the stimulation and glamorization of the energies of male-male desire" (150), argues Sedgwick, homosocial male bonding must also incessantly deny, defer to, or silence the erotic satisfaction of this desire, forming the double bind characteristic of much male writing. Thus, she remaps the territory of Leslie Fiedler by exposing the ties that bind homophobia and misogyny. The mask of identity worn by the straight man covers a split subject, from Hawthorne and Melville to James, Eliot, Fitzgerald, Hemingway, Mailer, and beyond.

The literary history of the US ought to be represented not by "*the* American" and "*his* dream," but in terms of how various cultural groups and their forms have worked with, or against, one another during the nation's ongoing construction. As Elizabeth Meese explains, once we abandon notions of literature's intrinsic value and look instead at the contingencies of writing's use values, we may stop thinking in terms of canons altogether. The "history of literature," she writes, "if it seems necessary to create such a thing, might then be a description of the uses to which texts have been put" and of the value writings have had for their subjects (33). (See also the discussion of canons and literary value by Barbara Herrnstein Smith.) Such a history would have many protagonists, wearing many faces, speaking many languages, recalling divergent histories, desiring different futures. Syllabi and critical studies could be focused on contestation rather than unity, putting to work in this area the principle Gerald Graff has dubbed "teaching the conflicts." Instead of selecting a set of books and authors that express a previously agreed-upon list of characteristics that are "uniquely American," we could assemble texts that openly conflict with one another's assumptions, terms, narratives, and metaphors. These conflicts, moreover, should unsettle national generalities by reference to the specific pedagogical locality — to the state, region, city, area, and social group of the students, the professor, and the institution.

• • •

My own involvement in changing the canon, though precipitated by the Civil Rights movement of the 1960s, received its professional impetus from my being hired — fresh from an education in California and New York — to teach the American literature survey course at the University of Alabama in 1980. I felt strongly the responsibility to develop a multicultural curriculum, with special attention to black writers and issues of race. The politics of my pedagogical location, however, taught me a tough but simple lesson: these students from Montgomery and Tuskegee and Selma and Birmingham knew a lot more about racism — consciously and unconsciously — than I did. The readings they produced of texts and authors I thought I knew well challenged my complacent interpretations, as did the connections we began to draw between canonical and noncanonical texts. Our first paper, for example, focused on the comparison of Franklin's *Autobiography* with the *Narrative of the Life of Frederick Douglass*, and the semester ended with a paper analyzing treatments of region, dialect, gender, and race in novels by William Faulkner and Alice Walker. In the conflicts between such texts we found surprises, complexities, inspirations, and conundrums. For instance, Franklin's optimistic assertion that the individual can rise from poverty and obscurity to fame and power appeared both denied and confirmed by Douglass's escape from slavery and ascent to international celebrity. It was intriguing that both men saw the achievement of literacy as the key to freedom, and both made their careers through the material production of books and newspapers. Could both be assimilated to the "American Dream," or were both texts in fact potent exposés of that dream's failures?

These questions prompted us to examine how the inescapable differences between Franklin and Douglass could be better understood by locating their writings and careers in terms of their historical bodies. Although both came from poor families, race put their bodies in quite distinct relationships to the legal system and state power, beginning with the considerable difference between white indentured servitude and Negro slavery. Franklin's rise came through his genius for manipulating the legal systems of discourse; Douglass's literacy was literally a crime, and his very claim to "manhood" a violation of the dictates of the state, even as it reproduced patriarchal myths of masculinity (see Leverenz). Individual achievement could be the road to freedom for Franklin, whereas for Douglass even escape to the North meant only that he now had to watch for the fugitive slave bounty hunters. Ultimately Douglass's freedom had to be purchased, his status as property acknowledged by the sale. No amount of personal greatness on Douglass's part could alter the *system* that defined him as chattel, the same system that granted Franklin privileges not shared by the enslaved Africans of his time.

The ideology of individual accomplishment (the up-by-the-bootstraps story) that Franklin has been used to promote shows up as hollow in Douglass's case, betraying even Douglass's own complicity in this empowering narrative of the American Dream. In fact, both Franklin and Douglass were expert rhetoricians who constructed self-representations to further their social and political ends (on Franklin, see Breitwieser). When juxtaposing their texts we cannot simply see one as inauthentic and the other as real, for both men knowingly deployed the rhetoric of heroic individualism despite understanding its drastic limitations. Each saw writing in the United States as a rhetorical rather than primarily mimetic art; that is, whether in Franklin's adoption of the conduct book genre or Douglass's adaptation of the antislavery pamphlet, each man pursued his sociopolitical ends through a purposive aesthetic artistry that was inseparable from his desire to change history. In the theoretical language of the 1990s, they saw writing as a practical activity that did cultural work.

Their autobiographies offer, to use Fredric Jameson's formula, both the delusive ideology and the desired utopia of individual freedom. Trained more in utopian visions, however, than in critiques of ideology, and steeped in the discourse of racism, the majority of my white students wanted to read both Franklin and Douglass as presenting allegories of how the individual could triumph no matter the laws or powers of the state. Yet it is that belief, I think, that allows the legal powers of the state to go unchallenged, obscures the systematic tyrannies of the so-called "private" sphere, and thus tends to let people continue complacently in the myth of their radical autonomy. Eventually Franklin's work on behalf of the Revolution demonstrated his own understanding that freedom comes only through the structural reorganization of the political world that defines us as "subjects," and not as the result of some individual romantic quest for autonomy. In the end, perhaps the two revolutionary ex-servants were still in dialogue with each other.

For many of my black students, who were attending a recently integrated bastion of white academic racism, these materials created an uneasy situation. They did not desire to be drawn into open hostility with their white classmates, and they were sensitive to the bad effects of being located in one's historical body. Many were tired of being the token black or being asked to speak for "their people" on every occasion rather than for themselves. Their pride in Douglass was muted by their puzzlement over how to express their feeling in an oppressive context, which included me — a white instructor. Ultimately, we had to make these and other local tensions the subject of classroom discussion, to teach these conflicts to one another by openly questioning the relation of reading to race and of race to individual achievement. Many students began to open up, telling personal stories of their experience of racial and class difference; at that point I watched my position as the liberal champion crumble away into irrelevance, revealed as the dangerous delusion it can be. I was just another white American, one who had grown up in Los Angeles but had never heard of Watts until he watched black rioters burn it down from the cool comfort of his boyhood backyard pool. Racism to me had always been someone else's problem; now I began to feel my own participation in its history. I could criticize racism, but I would never be black (just as I could criticize sexism or homophobia yet never know them quite as women or gays and lesbians did).

At that time I also began teaching a unit on Jewish American literature. I had to spend hours in the library researching the history of American Judaism and the details of its culture, despite the fact that my own father was a Jew and my great-grandfather an Orthodox rabbi. I was myself, I realized, the divided subject of assimilation — "split at the root," in Adrienne Rich's phrase (*Blood* 100–123). I learned that Jewish American literature provides a useful vantage point for multicultural study, since the Jew both belongs to the hegemony of European cultural tradition *and* has been the excluded Other within the body of that culture. Jewish American writers, critics, and intellectuals have been very successful in securing recognition in the US, but they have also made the pathos and incompleteness of their assimilation a constant subject of address. The complexity of these realities is captured brilliantly in Tillie Olsen's *Tell Me a Riddle*, where the contrast between Jewish American and Mexican American assimilation unfolds a multicultural fable of the politics of recollected identities.

Teaching Olsen's story had a remarkable effect on me. As part of a multicultural syllabus, it puts the Jew into the curriculum alongside other Others, raising tough issues such as, Are Jews a race or a religion or a culture or a nation? How do the relations among these four terms change when we turn to the African American or the American Indian or the Irish American Catholic? As a tale of immigration, *Tell Me a Riddle* asks to be compared to other classics in the genre of the American Dream. Yet Eva's voice is that of an elderly, dying, embittered Jewish radical who remembers with increasing fervor the revolutionary passions of the old country. For her, the Americanization of her Coca-Cola–drinking grandchildren represents a failure of her dream. The strong feminist component of the narrative includes Eva's memories of a martyred childhood friend and the developing solidarity with her social worker granddaughter, who refuses to betray a Mexican American family out of respect for their cultural rights. The highly experimental modernist style of the text proved extremely difficult for my students, though at first it seemed to me readily assimilated to the tradition of Woolf and Joyce. In its form the story challenged us to go beyond thinking of modernism as an apolitical aestheticism unconnected to political or ethnic or gender issues, and it rebutted the charge that multicultural literature was less accomplished, daring, or avant-garde than the modernist classics.

Personally, I found Olsen's story illuminated the history of my own socialist grandfather and helped explain my own confused legacy when it came to cultural identity. As a literature teacher, I found the story connected well with stories of immigration and migration written by authors of other ethno-racial backgrounds, such as Sui Sin Far's "In the Land of the Free," Nicolosha Mohr's "The English Lesson," Mary Gordon's "Eileen," Bharati Mukherjee's "A Wife's Story," Helena Viaramontes's "Cariboo Café," and Anzia Yezierska's "Soap and Water," all of which tell of the difference that gender makes to the immigrant's dream. The innovations of Olsen's style can be interestingly compared to that of texts such as Toni Morrison's *Beloved* and Louise Erdrich's *Love Medicine*. I was struck by how contemporary multicultural literature achieved its complexity by combining modernist techniques from the literary history of English with formal devices, symbols, motifs, and narrative conventions that were rooted in other cultural sources. The hybridity I felt within my own cultural character found a match in the hybridity of the texts we were reading, and both kinds of miscegenation demanded new frameworks of interpretation. As I discovered my own diversity anew, my students discovered, to their surprise, the long history of Jews and Judaism in the American South, going back through commerce and politics to before the Civil War. My youthful ignorance of black Americans and complacent ambivalence toward Jews was reversed in my students' ignorance of things Jewish and their presumption that race was a black-white thing.

The autobiographical narrative of my argument about the ends of pedagogy may seem gratuitous, but it isn't. By bringing the writing home in this way, to our locations in the US, teachers and students can begin to feel and analyze the friction between ideological myths and particular histories. Anyone who has tried to teach feminism, for example, will testify to how the personal becomes the pedagogical, for the teacher as well as the students. Such pedagogical dialogues can be confusing, passionate, humiliating, and transformative, demanding that everyone learn better to interpret what Teresa De Lauretis calls "the semiotics of experience" (158–86). If we are to face honestly the rich diversity of life in the US, we will have to stop masquerading behind assumed poses of abstraction and generality, even if we continue — with Whitman and Rich — to use the pronoun "we" for utopian purposes. As a teacher I cannot speak on behalf of a united cultural vision or tradition, and I do not want to borrow authority from an ideology that gives me power at the cost of truth.

Historically, I belong to a class and generation raised in the knowledge of one tradition and brought by theory, history, and experience to seek a knowledge of others. My bookshelves are filling with texts and authors never mentioned to me in school. It will take years to begin to absorb them and to know how to speak or write about them with confidence. Of course, I could go on writing about Hawthorne or James or Eliot, but that, I think, would be less interesting than meeting the challenge to undertake what Annette Kolodny describes as a "heroic rereading" of those uncanonized works "with which we are least familiar, and especially so when they challenge current notions of art and artifice." Armed with the criticism and scholarship of the past twenty years, Kolodny urges, revisionists should "immerse themselves in the texts that were never taught in graduate school — *to the exclusion of the works with which they had previously been taught to feel comfortable and competent*" (302). I am not sure how long Kolodny's prescribed "exclusion" is supposed to last. I myself fell off the wagon when I wrote another piece on Eliot, albeit this time to contextualize his work through gender and popular culture studies.[6] I take it that the point here is a mundane one — that it takes a lot of time to catch up on so much reading, so that we had better be prepared to set aside the old favorites for a good long time if we are

6. See Gregory Jay, "Postmodernism in *The Waste Land*."

serious about the enterprise of reform. Still, my own preference for a comparativist approach means coming back recurrently to works once considered canonical — not because of that, but because I now see where in literary and cultural history they can fit, or where in the syllabus they produce interesting learning experiences.

• • •

What happens when teachers of American literature take up Kolodny's challenge to immerse themselves in texts and traditions about which they know little or nothing? At worst it can result in a kind of literary tourism or academic colonialism, as dilettantes skip superficially from the territories of Chippewa mythology to the Virgin of Guadeloupe to the joys of Yiddish with an enthusiasm that is in inverse proportion to their knowledge. Ethics comes back in with a vengeance, along with professional standards, as we come to apply in these new areas the same principles of depth and rigor that measured, say, one's knowledge of medieval Christianity or the American Adam or the pleasures of iambic pentameter. Faced with the daunting challenge of multicultural literacy, we forget how little we once knew, and how arbitrary our expertise may often be. This is not a problem for many of our students, who know as little about Hawthorne and Calvinism as about Sui Sin Far and the Chinese Exclusion Act.

If we get very far along in this reeducation, discovering just how much the literatures of the Americas actually contains, we may well feel like abandoning the notion of the American literature survey class altogether, since no one- or two-semester course can possibly live up to the implied claim of historical or representative coverage. Coherence in such courses is usually bought at the cost of reductive scenarios resting on dubious premises. Institutional imperatives, however, suggest that walking away from the survey course is not a realistic solution for the majority of faculty, who have to work with the requirements. Besides, as one does get immersed in the wealth of the newly available or formerly overlooked works, it now appears that the renovated survey course can be an exciting vehicle for introducing students to the incredible diversity of writing in the United States and the important light it can shed on our nation's cultural and social history.[7] As for overarching themes, one can begin with the question "What is an American?" and then work through close readings of texts chosen for the radically different answers they provide. The result is more of a rainbow coalition than a melting pot. Facile pluralism might be avoided through demonstrations of the real conflicts between texts and cultures as we witness how different, and difficult, the process of becoming an American has been for enslaved Africans, immigrant Irish, Jews in flight from the pogroms, Chinese excluded by law from citizenship, Japanese interned in camps, or Chicanos who are perceived as "foreigners" despite generations in this country. A comparative reading of texts that give voice to these disparate journeys pushes us to examine each in its particularity and historical specificity before we simply lump them together under broad thematic correspondences. There is not one universal tale of "arrival" or "rebirth" or "assimilation" that easily melts into one the varied literary efforts at cultural representation made by writers in the United States.

In sum, I advocate courses in which the materials are chosen for the ways in which they *actively interfere* with one another. In opposition to thematic arrangements that emphasize similarities and so privilege dominant models of American normality, I want to explore the active interference and dissonance among writers in the US, how in their texts they challenge one another's experiences, languages, and values. In this way a pedagogy of conflicts respects the power of writing to expand the horizon of the student's cultural literacy in order to encompass peoples he or she has scarcely acknowledged as real. By also putting on the table our methods of selection — whether by the criteria of aesthetic excellence, equality of representation, or cultural work — we can produce yet more interference between texts as each unsettles the claims of the other, or the claims that the categorization has made.

The socially constructed ignorance of teachers and students will be a formidable obstacle to multicultural literacy, for the knowledges it requires have been largely excluded from the mainstream classroom,

7. For samples of such syllabi, see Alberti; Lauter, *Reconstructing American Literature*, and the materials gathered in the Teaching American Literature on-line archives at http://www.georgetown.edu/crossroads.

dissertation, and published critical study until quite recently. Teachers have enough trouble trying to supply their students with information on the literary forms, historical contexts, and cultural values shaping *The Scarlet Letter* or *The Red Badge of Courage* or *The Waste Land*. Think of the remedial work for everyone when we assign David Walker's *Appeal*, Catharine Sedgwick's *Hope Leslie*, William Wells Brown's *Clotel*, Whitman's *Calamus*, Charlotte Perkins Gilman's *Herland*, Jacob Riis's *How the Other Half Lives*, Agnes Smedley's *Daughter of Earth*, the poetry and prose of Langston Hughes, the *corridos* of the Southwest, N. Scott Momaday's *House Made of Dawn*, Audre Lorde's *Zami*, or Cynthia Ozick's *The Shawl*. It's enough to make the average revisionist despair. Fortunately the profession has begun to respond with new pedagogical assistants in the form of anthologies, essay collections, and critical studies that bring us up to speed as fast as possible. On the historical side, we can crib from Howard Zinn's *People's History of the United States* or Ronald Takaki's *A Different Mirror: A History of Multicultural America* as we replace our yellowed lecture notes with unfamiliar tales.

In terms of method, this reeducation sharpens our ability to discern the various ways a text can participate in (or even produce) its context; in terms of pedagogy, this search for new knowledges makes the literature classroom part of a general project of historical recollection, analysis, and criticism; in terms of politics, it confronts the institution, the teacher, and the student with the imperative to appreciate and/or deconstruct the achievements of distinct cultural groups, which cannot be whitewashed with humanistic clichés about *the* universality of art, *the* eternal truths of the soul, or *the* human condition. In sum, a multicultural pedagogy initiates a cultural revision, so that everyone involved comes not only to understand another person's point of view, but also to see her or his own culture from the outsider's perspective. This decentering of cultural chauvinism can only be healthy in the long run, especially if it leads us to stop thinking of ourselves as subjects — heroes or heroines — of only one story.

From the standpoint of literary theory, this approach treats written works as active agents in the sociopolitical process, and thus owes much to the cultural work school. This need not mean, as numerous critics have shown, abandoning attention to the formal properties of writing. On the contrary, it strengthens that focus by locating the historical and material specificity of those forms and by charting how they take effect, are appropriated, or are transformed in concrete contexts. This *does* mean that purely formalist generic categories such as "the novel" or "the elegy" or "tragedy" must be called back from the hazy pedagogy of a naive aestheticism. Theorists from Virginia Woolf and Kenneth Burke to Fredric Jameson and Houston Baker and beyond have shown us the various ways that forms of writing become socially symbolic actions. Styles are linguistic and material practices that negotiate between documentation and fabrication, or history and fiction. In other words, a renovated *rhetorical* criticism can frame the written work as a historical utterance, as addressed both to the cultural traditions it draws upon and to the audiences it assumes or even transforms (see Mailloux, *Rhetorical Power*). Forms such as the slave narrative (produced for abolitionists) or the American-Indian autobiography (as told to an ethnographer) provide rich opportunities for deconstructing our categories and concepts of literary authorship and production. Likewise, the question of audience is reshaped by feminist and gay and lesbian criticism, transforming how we approach the stylistic difficulties of an Emily Dickinson or a Gertrude Stein, since rather than seeing these as purely aesthetic experiments, we might rather decode them as ways of circumventing conventional modes of expression that do not allow for what these writers have to say.

It is clear that a multicultural reconception of "Writing in the United States" will lead us to change drastically or eventually abandon the conventional historical narratives, period designations, and major themes and authors previously dominating accounts of "American literature." "Colonial" American writing, as I have already suggested, looks quite different from the standpoint of postcolonial politics and theory today. Our interpretations of writing in the period from 1500 to 1800 is being utterly recast as Hispanic and Indian and non-Puritan English texts are allowed their just representation. What are the effects of designating Columbus's *Journal* or the *Narrative of Alvar Núñez Cabeza de Vaca* as the origins of US literature, rather than Bradford's *Of Plymouth Plantation*? What happens when we put the creation myths contained in Cherokee, Winnebago, or Zuni traditions alongside the creation myths of Judaism and

Christianity, and consider the struggles of these value systems for control of US land and US cultural history? Taking seriously the challenge of increasing the representation of people previously left out of the accounts has the effect of forcing a reevaluation of the narratives we use to encompass and explain periods of literary history.

To take another example, the already shopworn idea of the "American Renaissance," probably the most famous and persistent of our period myths, ought to be replaced by one that does not reinforce the idea that all culture — even all Western culture — has its authorized origins in Greco-Roman civilization. The period 1812–65 would better be called that of "America During the Wars," since the final colonial war and the wars to take the property of the American Indians and Mexican Americans and to keep enslaved the bodies of African Americans dominated the sociopolitical scene and heavily determined its literary output, including that of canonical figures such as Cooper, Hawthorne, Melville, Emerson, and Thoreau. Such a designation for this period would bring back the historical context along with the verbal productions of those marginalized groups or cultures that were busy representing themselves in a rich array of spoken and written discourses. The transformation of this period has already begun through emphasis on Indian and African American texts and on the writing of women in these years, many of whom were actively engaged in these political struggles. Even if one were resolutely committed to the enduring superiority of Hawthorne, how can one understand *The Scarlet Letter* if one has never read Sedgwick, Parton, Warner, Stowe, Southworth, or others of "that damned mob of scribbling women" Hawthorne denounced and yet to whom his work is so indebted?

Rethinking our literary history in terms of cultural work, the struggle for representation, and the social construction of aesthetic values will bring us to question other key organizing terms in literary theory, such as "regionalism," whose biases and limitations we may not have recognized.[8] In their introduction to *American Women*

8. Even in so excellent a textbook as *American Literature: A Prentice Hall Anthology*, edited by Emory Elliott and others, local color and regionalism are conflated, with a decided bias toward sketches of male experience. The introductory essay, "Late 19th-Century Fiction," tries to defend "the cameo-

Regionalists, 1850–1910, Judith Fetterley and Marjorie Pryse offer their observation that "white men did not write the same kinds of regional texts that some white women or some members of minority groups did" (xi). They see regionalism as doing a particular kind of cultural work in resistance to dominant political and literary norms. "Region" becomes a name for the place inhabited by people whose social existence and subjectivity have been relegated to the margins of cultural geography. Writing in the US, regionalists give voice to lives that rarely appear on authorized itineraries:

> In the regional text, the narrator does not distance herself from the inhabitants of the region, as is the case in "local color" fiction; indeed, she frequently appears to be an inhabitant herself. The regionalist narrator empowers the voice of regional characters, viewing them as agents of their own lives, rather than undermining them with the ironic perspective characteristic of "local color" writing. And the narrator's stance of careful listening fosters an empathic connection between the reader of the work and the lives the work depicts. (xvii)

The protagonists of these fictions are usually not only women but older women, precisely the kinds of subjects who rarely appear in male writing without heavy doses of pity or ridicule. As infamously immortalized in the criticism of D. H. Lawrence and Leslie Fiedler, "classic" American literature has been seen as a field of boys' books, of tales out of school starring rebellious male adolescent loners whose every melancholy and lust deserves our most serious attention. To this narrative of the American subject, Fetterley and Pryse counterpose stories such as Rose Terry Cook's "Miss Beulah's

---

like achievement of the best regional fiction" by observing that the comparison of a sonata to a symphony does not signal a value judgment. The paragraphs that discuss Freeman, Woolson, and Jewett emphasize their "unpretentious distinction" and make no observations about the possible artistic or social subversiveness of their work. In the inset box on the facing page, headed "Regionalism," the textbook presents Bret Harte's "Luck of Roaring Camp" and other tales of the (male) Old West as the essence of the genre.

Bonnet."[9] Published four years after Twain's *Adventures of Tom Sawyer* but four years before *Huckleberry Finn*, Cook's story tells of Miss Beulah's problems with young Jack, "a veritable little pickle" with a "mind for mischief." Jack gets the notion to hide Miss Beulah's bonnet under a seat cushion, employing his little sister Janey for the task. In due course the bonnet is crushed by the weight of a visit from Mrs. Blake, the minister's wife. To make a short story shorter, it is Miss Beulah rather than Jack who eventually triumphs, and she does so in a manner that vindicates her in her quarrel with the town's patriarchy (grown-up versions of Jack). Unlike *Huckleberry Finn*, the story does not end with a boy lighting out for the "Territory" to avoid becoming "sivilized" by old women. Denounced by Miss Beulah as a lying rascal, Jack is "sent off in disgrace" halfway through the sketch. Cook pointedly refuses to "draw a moral here," saving her pedagogical lesson for the conclusion in which Miss Beulah outwits the community: "If there is any moral to this story . . . it lies in the fact that Mrs. Blake never again sat down in a chair without first lifting the cushion," as readers will not again sit down to boys' stories without first checking for what they hide (137).

Like "regionalism," "modernism" is a term that will never be the same. "Modernism" as the period of Eliot, Pound, Stevens, Williams, Hemingway, and Faulkner has been shattered by questions about the gender and race limitations of this historical construct, prompting renewed attention to Stein, H.D., Moore, and Barnes and a reconsideration of the Harlem Renaissance. F. Scott Fitzgerald bragged that *he* had given the "Jazz Age" its name, yet the black culture and musicians who invented the jazz world of the 1920s are mere bystanders in his fiction.[10] In the future, teachers can put Fitzgerald's *Great Gatsby* on the syllabus with Toni Morrison's *Jazz* and let the two texts tell their very different stories of that era and its meaning (stories that would be enhanced by playing some of the

9. My commentary on the significance of Cook's story derives from Fetterley's essay "Not in the Least American."

10. See Ellison's "Little Man at Chehaw Station" (*Territory* 3–38) and Mitchell Breitwieser's sensational essay "*The Great Gatsby*: Grief, Jazz and the Eye-Witness."

music and songs from the period as well). Students might then turn to *The Mambo Kings Sing Songs of Love*, in which Oscar Hijuelos dramatizes the Cuban connection so vital to the musical history of America since the 1920s, a history too often told in black and white without a Latin beat. Given that *Mambo Kings* also tries, with uneven success, to challenge the dominance of the "macho" in Cuban American culture, comparison of gender problems in that novel with those in *Gatsby* and *Jazz* could produce fascinating intellectual improvisations.

Take, finally, the currently fashionable tag "postmodern," originally used in literary studies to categorize the self-reflexive fiction of white men (Barth, Coover, Barthelme, Vonnegut, Pynchon) who struggled with the legacy of their modernist fathers. In the popular formulation of Jean-François Lyotard, postmodernism names a period without "metanarratives," a sort of extended epistemological and semiotic version of what we used to call the death of God. From his location in Paris, however, Lyotard sees this as the crisis of peculiarly disembodied, abstract, and metaphysical concepts, whereas these metanarratives belong to the ideological apparatus of identifiable institutional and historical groups. As Edward Said points out in his critique of Lyotard, the (supposed) breakdown of the metanarratives of "emancipation" and "enlightenment" cannot be comprehended as solely an internal event of Western civilization. The collapse of Western metaphysical metanarratives, especially those of what is called "the Subject," are (not coincidentally) contemporary with the struggle of non-European populations and countries for historical self-determination — for the freedom to be agents rather than subjects.

According to Said, Lyotard "*separates* Western postmodernism from the non-European world, and from the consequences of European modernism — and modernization — in the colonized world." Moreover, the crisis of legitimacy characterizing Western modernism involved "the disturbing appearance in Europe of various Others, whose provenance was the imperial domain. In the works of Eliot, Conrad, Mann, Proust, Woolf, Pound, Lawrence, Joyce, Forster, alterity and difference are systematically associated with strangers, who, whether women, natives, or sexual eccentrics, erupt into vision, there to challenge and resist settled metropolitan histories, forms, modes of thought" ("Representing" 222–23). Once one puts the color back into postmodernism, if you will, then the period's inseparability from (post)colonialism appears crucial. And this is not simply a matter of discerning the origins of modernism's traumatized consciousness in the West's confrontation with its Others or even of deconstructing the representations of those Others passed off by dominant discourses. Postcolonialism means recognizing, or at least trying to find a way to read, the texts produced by dominated peoples, and acknowledging their participation in narratives of resistance. The literary and cultural works of the marginalized during the nineteenth and twentieth centuries, then, suddenly appear as part of the ongoing development of a postmodern literature, insofar as they contradict the metanarratives of Western modernism. One could argue that, among "Americans" writing in English, a different canon of postmoderns could be compiled from the explosion of texts by contemporary African American, Asian American, and American Indian writers (see Vizenor).

Themes, like periods, derive from and are determined by a previously canonized set of texts and authors. The classic themes of American literature — the Virgin Land, the Frontier West, the Individual's Conflict with Society, the City versus the Country, Innocence versus Experience, Europe versus America, Dream versus Reality, and so on — make scant sense when applied to many previously overlooked texts and traditions, including those produced by women. Thematic criticism can be especially discriminatory, since themes are by definition repeated elements of a totality or metanarrative centered on a historically limited point of view, though thematic criticism regularly universalizes that perspective and so transforms an angle of insight into an oppressive ideological fabrication. The cartoon simplicity of these themes serves as a mask for this ideological pretension: it presents a partial experience in the form of an eternal verity, thus at once obstructing any analysis of the historical construction of that perception or any analysis of viewpoints that do not conform to the theme or that lose their difference and cultural truth when they are made to conform to the theme.

To supplement or replace periods and themes as points for organizing classes and critical studies, I would offer rather a list of *problematics* whose analysis would put texts from different cultures within the US into dialogue with one another. These problematics are structures of history in which issues of cultural work, representation, and aesthetics play key roles. Unlike a theme, a problematic does not designate a moment in the history of the consciousness of a privileged and unitary subject. Rather, a problematic indicates an event in culture made up simultaneously of material conditions and conceptual forms that direct the possibilities of representation. A problematic acts as one of the determinants of a representation, though it does not operate as an origin. A problematic indicates how and where the struggle for representation *takes place*. True to its connotation, a problematic indicates something troubling, something whose pieces do not quite fit, something requiring aesthetic treatment and analytic interpretation. A theme, says the *Random House Unabridged Dictionary*, is "a unifying or dominant idea, motif, etc., as in a work of art . . . a principal melodic subject in a musical composition," or "a short melodic subject from which variations are developed."

A theme, to play off the musical analogy, implies a similar tune played variously by different instruments, while a problematic implies a meeting of contradictory orchestrations. Each of us could construct a list of problematics conditioning US writing, but for illustrative purposes I would argue for the following: (1) origins, (2) power, (3) civilization, (4) tradition, (5) assimilation, (6) translation, (7) bodies, (8) literacy, and (9) borders. Although these problematics have indeed been addressed by some writers, and thus may appear to be themes, I want to resist reducing them to intentionalities or structures of consciousness. Having touched on most already, I wish to end by saying something more about origins and power, with a final return to the question of where in the world American literature belongs.

· · ·

One reiterated note in deconstructive and poststructuralist criticism concerned *origins*: origins were not original, not stable, and not the dependable centers we once took them for. Examinations of philosophical texts as well as poems and novels showed how often they sought to fix an origin, to return to an imagined starting place, to right the balance of things by identifying their origins. Origins have a power to govern, to dictate legitimacies, and to authorize interpretations (think of how fundamentalism works in the interpretation of the Bible or the Constitution as originating documents). This skepticism toward origins was initially resisted by advocates of marginalized groups, who rightly insisted on the need to affirm and recollect the difference of *their* beginnings. Because of the historic devastation of dominated (sub)cultures by privileged classes, much writing by women and persons of color tries to recover origins and traditions rather than to deconstruct or rebel against them. But, as Michael Fischer argues, ethnicity (and the same goes, in different ways, for other cultural identity categories) is less an essence than a constantly traversed borderland of differences, "something reinvented and reinterpreted in each generation by each individual. . . . Ethnicity is not something that is simply passed on from generation to generation, taught and learned; it is something dynamic, often unsuccessfully repressed or avoided" (195; see also Sollers). This process of recollection does not entail a simple nostalgia or the dream of re-creating a lost world: more painfully and complexly, it involves a risky translation of recovered fragments into imagined futures by way of often hostile presents.

"The constituency of 'the ethnic,'" writes R. Radhakrishnan, "occupies quite literally a 'pre-post'-erous space where it has to actualize, enfranchise, and empower its own 'identity' and coextensively engage in the deconstruction of the very logic of 'identity' and its binary and exclusionary politics" (199). What should be resisted are myths of origin that function in totalitarian fashion; what should be solicited are myths of beginning that delineate the historical and cultural specifics of a group's experiences and interactions (see Said, *Beginnings*). In multicultural studies we examine multiple sites of origin and multiple claims to foundational perspectives. Rather than adjudicate between these claims in a timeless philosophical tribunal, the student of culture ought to analyze the historical development of the conditions for these narratives and the consequences of their interactions. As I have stressed throughout, however, this is quite different from imagining that race or gender or class does not make a difference, or does not function as an originating distinction that cultures seize upon to shape the possibilities and meanings of our lives.

Cultural power may come from rediscoveries of origins, or from establishing as origins events, people, or feelings that once were considered inconsequential, or dead ends.

But if origins are socially constructed cultural agents, then the powers they exercise are open for negotiation and contestation. There is nothing natural or automatic about the distribution of power, no universal or fixed link between particular origins and particular ends. In the act of retelling the origins of America, or of positing some factor of ethnicity or religion or sexuality as the origin of one's self, different narratives become possible, and with them different powers of accountability. Multicultural studies cannot evade the question of power, since power is both a prime subject for analysis and a constitutive element of the situation of the analysis: the student and the professor are empowered in relation to the object of study, and this disciplinary power usually has its affiliations with distributions of power along lines of gender, region, class, age, race, and so on. While texts may be studied as expressions of struggles for power, and while we may reflect self-consciously on how scholarship participates in the institutions of power, we should not forget the cautions offered by various critical theories regarding the fallacies of reference and mimesis. We cannot assume that the text, no matter how seemingly powerful, refers to a truth outside itself that thus silences our questions; the origins of its truths still await our discernment and judgment. Likewise, the powers of a text are certainly not confined to its correspondence to an objectively verifiable reality. Our task includes understanding how texts *take power*—how they gain power through the modes of their production and reception.

The canonical status of a text is often justified by reference to its superior "power," and its endurance ascribed to the timeless claim it makes on readers. Multiculturalism challenges this received wisdom by examining the particular contexts that shape the power of aesthetics and the aesthetics of power. In *What Is Found There* Rich writes:

> A poem can't free us from the struggle for existence, but it can uncover desires and appetites buried under the accumulating emergencies of our lives, the fabricated wants and needs we have had urged on us, have accepted as our own. It's not a philosophical blueprint; it's an instrument for embodied experience. But we

seek that experience, or recognize it when it is offered to us, because it reminds us in some way of our need. After that rearousal of desire, the task of acting on that truth, or making love, or meeting other needs, is ours. (12–13)

Once one recognizes that the power of a text to move a reader is a culturally produced effect—that literary "taste" is not natural but taught, and taught in a way that reproduces values that go beyond aesthetics—then the issue of power becomes of vital pedagogical concern. Yet no teacher or text can ensure that the student will receive the letter as it is prescribed. No pedagogy or text, no matter how carefully it addresses the truth or the audience, can predetermine exactly the effect it has on everyone, for everyone's subjectivity is plural. Moreover, texts are not clear messages or simple unities but occasions when a mediation of conflicts is symbolically enacted. Perhaps more than other genres, works of imaginative writing are experiences, not messages. When the text ends, our own work begins.

Teachers have the responsibility to empower previously marginalized works and readers, and to teach in a way that risks surprising and painful changes in the interpretive habits, expectations, and values of our students—and of ourselves. If we acknowledge that the aesthetic power of a text is a function of the distribution of material and cultural power in society, our pedagogy cannot help but become politically embroiled. As I have argued in previous chapters, we will find ourselves presented with ethical challenges as we consider how this entanglement relates to our values, our desired way of life, our accountability to others. In teaching students to value other cultures and other worldviews—and to decenter their own presumption of normalcy—we necessarily draw them with us into conflicts. These include conflicts with the dominant culture which has produced and sustained our desires and identities and which has the power to enforce its precepts as law. But that culture also contains a wealth of resources that can be subversively appropriated toward ends their originators scarcely imagined. We as readers and writers of "American" literature may become agents of change, not just subjects of discourse; we may draw or take power from all sorts of canons and traditions, and turn their lessons in unexpected directions. If we do so, we had better be certain what good we wish to do, and for what ends.

What conclusions, however tentative, can we reach about "politi-cization" and the American literature syllabus? The questions raised about the limitations of identity politics and essentialism have a par-allel in questions about the use of the classroom as a site for advo-cacy. Does politics in the classroom mean that the teacher and the syllabus simply advocate a single point of view, a particular interpre-tation of the world, respecting no other and leaving it to the student to sort out the truth after class? Or can politicization mean bringing the process of dialogue and community building into the classroom? How can we design an ethos for the syllabus that will get us past the errors we think we find in the schoolrooms of yesteryear? Steven Mailloux contends that placing "rhetoric" at the heart of our curric-ula will encourage both historicism and self-consciousness; more-over, it might reinvigorate modern philology and textual scholarship by involving them in the process of cultural critique. This bringing together of cultural studies and rhetorical studies might even help heal the rift between the discipline of composition and that of liter-ary studies, as each rediscovers some of its foundations in the other. A "cultural rhetoric studies," Mailloux writes, "would move the cen-ter of attention toward the topics and perspectives of new forms of socio-political investigations of culture" ("Rhetorical Hermeneutics as Reception Study" 52). Mailloux is careful to assert that this recen-tering will not necessarily displace aesthetics, literature, and literari-ness from the syllabus; rather, his program "historicizes the literary [by] showing how a text works rhetorically *when it is categorized as lit-erary* within particular episodes of the cultural conversation" (52). In my formulation Mailloux would have us stress the cultural work and political effects that occur when decisions are made about whether to categorize a text as "literary" or evaluate it according to "aesthetic" criteria. Teaching students the history of such episodes of categori-cal dispute does produce a healthy skepticism about the timelessness of these categories and the claims to nonpolitical principles of the in-stitutions or groups doing the categorizing.

Yet, if we are going to be consistent, we will have to historicize the present urge to historicism and be self-conscious about our own ef-forts to go (once again) beyond formalism. The critique of literari-ness through rhetorical hermeneutics tends, like cultural work the-ory, toward functionalism. Literature is seen as one more instrument of something outside of itself, and students may be given the false impression that analyzing the literary work is best done by reading anything and everything except the work itself. The emphasis on demystification that pervades cultural studies from the 1960s to the 1990s suggests that class discussions of the function of literariness will soon turn into discussions about class, about how aesthetic claims mask the naked will-to-power of cultural and economic and racial elites. Although such a lesson now appears essential (if not central) to our pedagogy, we may underestimate the liberating power that comes when literary or aesthetic techniques match wits with dominant ideologies.

It is an institutional irony that the triumph of cultural studies in the English department may very well undermine its mission and its enrollments (though admittedly this antidisciplinary effect may be just what some doctors would like to order). While many students are attracted to the new syllabi of cultural critique, many of them become confused or resentful when they find that the aim of pedagogy appears to be incessant disbelief instead of that "suspension of disbelief" once championed as the condition of literary experience. If literary works are simply the masquerades of power, or arbitrary vehicles for engaging social struggles that are more important and true than the texts themselves, then the study of literature inevitably loses much of its rationale and allure. Why not, finally, major in political science or anthropology or even history? In arguing for the proposition that there is no such thing as literariness, we end up arguing for the end of the literature department as well. Replacing it with a department of "Rhetorical Cultural Studies" will not, I think, strike many people as a practical or attractive alternative. To colleagues outside of literature, the proposal smacks of imperialism, suggesting once again that English professors think they are experts on everything from medieval sexual practices to the Anti-Ballistic Missile Treaty. One danger of cultural studies is its endless syllabus; everyone feels entitled to pronounce expertly on almost everything and to study nothing in very much depth. When my students read Mailloux's account of the ABM Treaty dispute, they dismissed the pretension that the essay was an exercise in rhetorical historicism rather than a brief for one political position (which they overwhelmingly thought it was).

Since the history of curricular reform tends to be dialectical, it should be no surprise to discover a new return to questions of appreciation, aesthetic form, and imagination even as we solidify our efforts toward equality of representation and historical self-consciousness. Already it has been noted that courses dealing with women writers and previously marginalized texts follow a strikingly different agenda from that of cultural studies courses treating hegemonic figures. In these latter courses the methods are largely those of demystification and disbelief. In the newer courses we discover the return of an older pedagogy of appreciation, belief, and even celebration. When, out of consistency, the deconstructive methods of cultural studies do get applied to such emergent literatures, we often hear protests that these methods are inappropriate, colonizing, and even oppressive (even as others think that applying high theory to marginalized texts is a sign of respect for their equal powers). It should go without saying that we cannot construct syllabi that "critique" the ideologies of Franklin, Melville, and Faulkner while also constructing syllabi that celebrate Hannah Foster, Frances Harper, and N. Scott Momaday (at least not without doing a lot of explaining). Our students will rightly stop enrolling if they get the message that we do not believe in the works that we study, or that we think of art as just one more form of sophisticated advertisement for tyranny. We should not have to choose, after all, between the syllabus of critique and the syllabus of naïveté, or think that the suspension of disbelief entails becoming a mindless dupe of oppression. Our pedagogy will have to continue to have multiple ends if it is going to have any future.

For models I find myself again looking to Edward Said's incomparable lesson book *Culture and Imperialism*. In it, Said writes, he hopes to show that a "comparative literature of imperialism" need not be a one-sided story:

> I shall try to formulate an alternative both to a politics of blame and to the even more destructive politics of confrontation and hostility. A more interesting type of secular interpretation can emerge, altogether more rewarding than the denunciation of the past, the expressions of regret for its having ended, or — even more wasteful because violent and far too easy and attractive —

the hostility between Western and non-Western cultures that leads to crises. The world is too small and interdependent to let these passively happen. (18–19)

Inspired by Freire as well as Fanon, Said advocates a pedagogy of liberation that, in being secular, refuses the teleology of an older Marxism and finds inadequate the new curricula of identity politics and nationalism, whether pre- or postcolonial. In our own moment of rhetorical strife and hermeneutic suspicion, this call for a pedagogy of liberatory worldliness deserves a higher enrollment. The end of American literature may come in the realization of its worldliness — of the many worlds that compose it, and of the greater world that surrounds it. American literature as part of world literature, accountable to every voice and every story: perhaps an ideal end, but one well worth the imagining.

works cited

Adams, Abigail, and John Adams. *The Book of Abigail and John: Selected Letters of the Adams Family, 1762–1784*. Ed. L. H. Butterfield, Marc Friedlaender, and Mary-Jo Kline. Cambridge: Harvard University Press, 1975.

Alberti, John, ed. *The Canon in the Classroom: The Pedagogical Implications of Canon Revision in American Literature*. New York: Garland, 1995.

Anzaldúa, Gloria. *Borderlands/La Frontera: The New Mestiza*. San Francisco: Spinsters/Aunt Lute, 1987.

Aptheker, Herbert, ed. *From the Colonial Times through the Civil War*. Vol. 1 of *A Documentary History of the Negro People in the United States*. New York: Citadel Press, 1951.

Arac, Jonathan. "F. O. Matthiessen: Authorizing an American Renaissance." In *The American Renaissance Reconsidered*. Ed. Walter Benn Michaels and Donald E. Pease. Baltimore: Johns Hopkins University Press, 1985. 90–112.

Aufderheide, Patricia, ed. *Beyond P.C.: Toward a Politics of Understanding*. St. Paul, Minn.: Graywolf Press, 1992.

Awkward, Michael. *Negotiating Difference: Race, Gender, and the Politics of Positionality*. Chicago: University of Chicago Press, 1995.

Baker, Houston A., Jr. *The Journey Back: Issues in Black Literature and Criticism*. Chicago: University of Chicago Press, 1980.

———, ed. *Three American Literatures*. New York: Modern Language Association, 1982.

Baldwin, James. "Everybody's Protest Novel." In *Notes of a Native Son*. Boston: Beacon Press, 1955. 13–22.

Banks, James A., and James Lynch, eds. *Multicultural Education in Western Societies*. New York: Holt, 1986.

Bardes, Barbara, and Suzanne Gossett. *Declarations of Independence: Women and Political Power in Nineteenth-Century American Fiction*. New Brunswick, N.J.: Rutgers University Press, 1990.

Baym, Nina. "Early Histories of American Literature: A Chapter in the History of New England." *American Literary History* 1.3 (1989): 459–88. Rpt. in Baym, *Feminism and American Literary History*. New Brunswick, N.J.: Rutgers University Press, 1992. 81–101.

———. *Woman's Fiction: A Guide to Novels by and about Women in America, 1820–1870*. Ithaca: Cornell University Press, 1978.

Bercovitch, Sacvan. "America as Canon and Context: Literary History in a Time of Dissensus." *American Literature* 58.1 (1986): 99–108.

———. "The Problem of Ideology in American Literary History." *Critical Inquiry* 12.4 (1986): 631–53.

Bergman, David. "F. O. Matthiessen: The Critic as Homosexual." In *Gaiety Transfigured: Gay Self-Representation in American Literature.* Madison: University of Wisconsin Press, 1991. 85–102.

Berlant, Lauren. "The Female Woman: Fanny Fern and the Form of Sentiment." *American Literary History* 3.3 (1991): 429–54.

Bérubé, Michael. *Public Access: Literary Theory and American Cultural Politics.* New York: Verso, 1994.

Bérubé, Michael, and Cary Nelson, eds. *Higher Education under Fire: Politics, Economics, and the Crisis of the Humanities.* New York: Routledge, 1995.

Blassingame, John W., ed. *The Frederick Douglass Papers.* Series 1. *Speeches, Debates, and Interviews.* New Haven: Yale University Press, 1982.

Bourne, Randolph. "Trans-National America." *Atlantic Monthly* 118 (July 1916): 86–97.

Breitwieser, Mitchell. *Cotton Mather and Benjamin Franklin: The Price of Representative Personality.* Cambridge: Cambridge University Press, 1984.

———. "*The Great Gatsby*: Grief, Jazz, and the Eye-Witness." *Arizona Quarterly* 47.3 (1991): 17–70.

Brown, William Wells. *Clotel, or The President's Daughter* (1853). Ed. William Edward Farrison. New York: Carol Publishing Group, 1989. Reprinted in William L. Andrews, ed. *Three Classic African-American Novels.* New York: Mentor, 1990.

Buhle, Mari Jo, and Paul Buhle, eds. *The Concise History of Woman Suffrage: Selections from the Classic Work of Stanton, Anthony, Gage, and Harper.* Urbana: University of Illinois Press, 1978.

Cain, William E. *F. O. Matthiessen and the Politics of Criticism.* Madison: University of Wisconsin Press, 1988.

———. *Reconceptualizing American Literary/Cultural Studies: Rhetoric, History, and Politics in the Humanities.* New York: Garland, 1996.

Calloway-Thomas, Carolyn, and John Louis Lucaites, eds. *Martin Luther King, Jr., and the Sermonic Power of Public Discourse.* Tuscaloosa: University of Alabama Press, 1993.

Carafiol, Peter C. *The American Ideal: Literary History as a Worldly Activity.* New York: Oxford University Press, 1991.

Carby, Hazel. "The Multicultural Wars." In Dent 187–99.

Caughie, Pamela. "*Passing* and Pedagogy." *College English* 54.7 (1992): 775–93.

Chevigny, Bell Gale. *The Woman and the Myth: Margaret Fuller's Life and Writings.* New York: Feminist Press, 1976.

Chicago Cultural Studies Group. "Critical Multiculturalism." *Critical Inquiry* 18 (1992): 530–55.

Christian, Barbara. "The Race for Theory." *Feminist Studies* 14.1 (1988): 67–79.

Clifford, James, and George E. Marcus, eds. *Writing Culture: The Poetics and Politics of Ethnography*. Berkeley: University of California Press, 1986.

Cone, James H. *Martin & Malcolm & America: A Dream or a Nightmare?* Maryknoll, N.Y.: Orbis Books, 1991.

Davidson, Cathy. *Revolution and the Word: The Rise of the Novel in America*. New York: Oxford University Press, 1986.

De Lauretis, Teresa. *Alice Doesn't: Feminism, Semiotics, Cinema*. Bloomington: Indiana University Press, 1984.

Dent, Gina, ed. *Black Popular Culture*. Seattle: Bay Press, 1992.

Derrida, Jacques. "Declarations of Independence." *New Political Science* 15 (1986): 7–15.

———. "The Ends of Man." In *Margins of Philosophy* (1972). Trans. Alan Bass. Chicago: University of Chicago Press, 1982. 109–36.

Diamond, Sara. "The Funding of the NAS." In Aufderheide 89–96. Originally published in *Z Magazine* (February 1991).

Du Bois, W. E. B. *The Souls of Black Folk*. In *Writings*. Ed. Nathan Huggins. New York: Library of America, 1986. 357–547.

Elliot, Emory. "New Literary History: Past and Present." *American Literature* 57.4 (1985): 611–25.

———. "The Politics of Literary History." *American Literature* 59.2 (1987): 268–76.

Elliott, Emory, ed. *American Literature: A Prentice Hall Anthology*. Englewood Cliffs, N.J.: Prentice Hall, 1991.

———. *The Columbia History of the American Novel*. New York: Columbia University Press, 1991.

———. *Columbia Literary History of the United States*. New York: Columbia University Press, 1988.

Elliott, Mary. "Coming Out in the Classroom: Returning to the Hard Place." *College English* 58.6 (1996): 693–708.

Ellison, Ralph. *Going into the Territory*. New York: Random House, 1987.

———. *Invisible Man*. New York: Vintage, 1952.

———. *Shadow and Act*. New York: Random House, 1964.

Epstein, Barbara. "'Political Correctness' and Collective Powerlessness." *Socialist Review* 91.3–4 (1991): 13–35.

Erickson, Peter. "What Multiculturalism Means." *Transition* 55 (1992): 105–14.

Escoffier, Jeffrey. "The Limits of Multiculturalism." *Socialist Review* 91.3–4 (1991): 61–73.

Fern, Fanny [Sara Payson Willis Parton]. *Ruth Hall and Other Writings*. New Brunswick, N.J.: Rutgers University Press, 1986.

Fetterley, Judith. "Commentary: Nineteenth-Century American Women

Writers and the Politics of Recovery." *American Literary History* 6.3
(1994): 600–611.

———. "'Not in the Least American': Ninteenth-Century Literary
Regionalism." *College English* 56.8 (1994): 877–896.

Fetterley, Judith, ed. *Provisions: A Reader from 19ᵗʰ Century American
Women.* Bloomington: Indiana University Press, 1985.

Fetterley, Judith, and Marjorie Pryse, eds. *American Women Regionalists,
1850–1910.* New York: W. W. Norton, 1992.

Fischer, Michael M. J. "Ethnicity and the Post-Modern Arts of Memory."
In Clifford and Marcus 194–233.

Fisher, Philip. *Hard Facts: Setting and Form in the American Novel.* New
York: Oxford University Press, 1987.

Fliegelman, Jay. *Declaring Independence: Jefferson, Natural Language, and the
Culture of Performance.* Stanford: Stanford University Press, 1993.

Foner, Philip S., ed. *We, the Other People: Alternative Declarations of
Independence by Labor Groups, Farmers, Woman's Rights Advocates, Socialists,
and Blacks, 1829–1975.* Urbana: University of Illinois Press, 1975.

Gates, Henry Louis, Jr. *Figures in Black: Words, Signs, and the "Racial" Self.*
New York: Oxford University Press, 1987.

———. *Loose Canons: Notes on the Culture Wars.* New York: Oxford
University Press, 1992.

———. "The Master's Pieces: On Canon Formation and the African-
American Tradition." *South Atlantic Quarterly* 89.1 (1990): 89–112.

Geyer, Michael. "Multiculturalism and the Politics of General Education."
Critical Inquiry 19 (1993): 499–53.

Gitlin, Todd. *The Twilight of Common Dreams: Why America Is Wracked by
Culture Wars.* New York: Henry Holt, 1995.

Giroux, Henry A. "Liberal Arts Education and the Struggle for Public Life:
Dreaming about Democracy." *South Atlantic Quarterly* 89.1 (1990):
113–38.

———. "Post-Colonial Ruptures and Democratic Possibilities:
Multiculturalism as Anti-Racist Pedagogy." *Cultural Critique* 21 (1992):
5–40.

Gomez-Peña, Guillermo. "Documented/Undocumented." In *The Graywolf
Annual Five: Multicultural Literacy.* Ed. Rick Simonson and Scott Walker.
St. Paul, Minn.: Graywolf Press, 1988. 127–34.

Gordon, Avery F., and Christopher Newfield, eds. *Mapping
Multiculturalism.* Minneapolis: University of Minnesota Press, 1996.

Graff, Gerald. *Beyond the Culture Wars: How Teaching the Conflicts Can
Revitalize American Education.* New York: W. W. Norton, 1992.

———. *Professing Literature: An Institutional History.* Chicago: University of
Chicago Press, 1987.

———. "Teach the Conflicts." *South Atlantic Quarterly* 89.1 (1990): 51–68.

Graff, Gerald, and Gregory Jay. "A Critique of Critical Pedagogy." In
   Bérubé and Nelson 201–13.
Guillory, John. *Cultural Capital: The Problem of Literary Canon Formation.*
   Chicago: University of Chicago Press, 1993.
Gutmann, Amy. *Democratic Education.* Princeton: Princeton University
   Press, 1987.
Herndl, Carl G. "Teaching Discourse and Reproducing Culture: A
   Critique of Research and Pedagogy in Professional and Non-Academic
   Writing." *College Composition and Communication* 44.3 (1993): 349–63.
Hollinger, David A. *Postethnic America: Beyond Multiculturalism.* New York:
   Basic Books, 1995.
hooks, bell. *Teaching to Transgress: Education as the Practice of Freedom.* New
   York: Routledge, 1994.
Hyde, Louis, ed. *Rat and the Devil: Journal Letters of F. O. Matthiessen and
   Russell Cheney.* Hamden, Conn.: Archon Books, 1978.
Independence Day. From the screenplay and novelization by Dean Devlin,
   Roland Emmerich, and Stephen Molstad. Adapted by Dionne McNeff.
   New York: Harper Collins, 1996.
James, Alan, and Robert Jeffcoate, eds. *The School in the Multicultural Society.*
   New York: Harper, 1981.
JanMohamed, Abdul R., and David Lloyd. "Introduction." Special issue,
   "The Nature and Context of Minority Discourse," vol. 1. *Cultural
   Critique* 6 (1987): 5–12.
Jay, Gregory S. *America the Scrivener: Deconstruction and the Subject of
   Literary History.* Ithaca: Cornell University Press, 1990.
———. "The First Round of the Culture Wars." *Chronicle of Higher
   Education,* February 26, 1992. B1–B2.
——— "Postmodernism in *The Waste Land*: Women, Mass Culture, and
   Others." In *Rereading the New: A Backward Glance at Modernism.* Ed.
   Kevin J. H. Dettmar. Ann Arbor: University of Michigan Press, 1992.
   221–46.
Jay, Paul. "Bridging the Gap: The Position of Politics in Deconstruction."
   Cultural Critique 22 (1992): 47–74.
———. *Contingency Blues: The Search for Foundations in American Criticism.*
   Madison: University of Wisconsin Press, 1997.
Jeffords, Susan. *The Remasculinization of America : Gender and the Vietnam
   War.* Bloomington: Indiana University Press, 1989.
Johnson, Cheryl. "Participatory Rhetoric and the Teacher as Racial/
   Gendered Subject." *College English* 56.4 (1994): 409–19.
Kanpol, Barry, and Peter McLaren, eds. *Critical Multiculturalism:
   Uncommon Voices in a Common Struggle.* Westport, Conn.: Bergin and
   Garvey, 1995.

Kaplan, Amy, and Donald E. Pease, eds. *Cultures of United States Imperialism*. Durham: Duke University Press, 1993.

King, Martin Luther, Jr. "I Have a Dream." *Negro History Bulletin* 21 (May 1968): 16–17.

———. *I Have a Dream*. San Francisco: Harper Collins, 1963, 1993.

Kolodny, Annette. "The Integrity of Memory: Creating a New Literary History of the United States." *American Literature* 57.2 (1985): 291–307.

Kors, Alan. "In Loco Parentis: Necessity or Antiquity?" *Academic Questions* 4 (Summer 1991): 60–63.

Lauter, Paul. "Afterword." In Alberti 313–27.

———. *Canons and Contexts*. New York: Oxford University Press, 1991.

Lauter, Paul, ed. *The Heath Anthology of American Literature*. 2d ed. 2 vols. Lexington, Mass.: D. C. Heath, 1994.

———, ed. *Reconstructing American Literature: Courses, Syllabi, Issues*. Old Westbury, N.Y.: Feminist Press, 1983.

Leverenz, David. *Manhood and the American Renaissance*. Ithaca: Cornell University Press, 1989.

Levin, David. "American Historicism Old and New." *American Literary History* 6.3 (1994): 527–38.

Levine, Lawrence. *The Opening of the American Mind: Canons, Culture, and History*. Boston: Beacon Press, 1996.

Lind, Michael. *The Next American Nation: The New Nationalism and the Fourth American Revolution*. New York: Free Press, 1995.

Lipsitz, George. "The Possessive Investment in Whiteness: Racialized Social Democracy and the 'White' Problem in American Studies." *American Quarterly* 47.3 (1995): 369–87.

Lorde, Audre. *Zami: A New Spelling of My Name*. Freedom, Calif.: Crossing Press, 1982.

Lubiano, Wahneema. "Black Ladies, Welfare Queens, and State Minstrels: Ideological War by Narrative Means." In *Race-ing Justice, En-gendering Power: Essays on Anita Hill, Clarence Thomas, and the Social Construction of Reality*. Ed. Toni Morrison. New York: Pantheon, 1992. 323–63.

Mailloux, Steven. "Cultural Rhetoric Studies: Eating Books in Nineteenth-Century America." In Cain, *Reconceptualizing American Literary/Cultural Studies* 21–33.

———. "Rhetorical Hermeneutics as Reception Study: *Huckleberry Finn* and 'The Bad Boy Boom.'" In Cain, *Reconceptualizing American Literary/Cultural Studies* 35–56.

———. "Rhetorical Hermeneutics in Theory." In Cain, *Reconceptualizing American Literary/Cultural Studies* 3–20.

———. *Rhetorical Power*. Ithaca: Cornell University Press, 1989.

Marable, Manning. "Race, Identity, and Political Culture." In Dent 292–302.

Marshall, Paule. "The Making of a Writer: From the Poets in the Kitchen." In *Reena and Other Stories*. Old Westbury, N.Y.: Feminist Press, 1983. 1–13.

Matthiessen, F. O. *American Renaissance: Art and Expression in the Age of Emerson and Whitman*. New York: Oxford University Press, 1941.

———. *Responsibilities of the Critic*. Ed. John Rackliffe. New York: Oxford University Press, 1952.

McCarthy, Cameron. *Race and Curriculum: Social Inequality and the Theories and Politics of Difference in Contemporary Research on Schooling*. London: Falmer, 1990.

McCarthy, Cameron, and Warren Crichlow, eds. *Race, Identity, and Representation in Education*. New York: Routledge, 1993.

McFeely, William S. *Frederick Douglass*. New York: Norton, 1991.

Meese, Elizabeth. *(Ex)Tensions: Refiguring Feminist Criticism*. Urbana: University of Illinois Press, 1990.

Merlis, Mark. *American Studies*. Boston: Houghton Mifflin, 1994.

Messer-Davidow, Ellen. "Manufacturing the Attack on Liberalized Higher Education." *Social Text* 36 (1993): 40–80.

———. "The Right Moves: Conservatism and Higher Education." In *Literature, Language, and Politics*. Ed. Betty Jean Craige. Athens: University of Georgia Press, 1988. 54–83.

Mitchell, W. J. T. "Postcolonial Culture, Postimperial Criticism." *Transition* 56 (1992): 11–19.

Moraga, Cherríe. "La Guera." In *This Bridge Called My Back: Writings by Radical Women of Color*. Ed. Cherríe Moraga and Gloria Anzaldúa. New York: Kitchen Table Press, 1983. 27–34.

Morrison, Toni. *Playing in the Dark: Whiteness and the Literary Imagination*. New York: Random House, 1992.

Morton, Donald. "On 'Hostile Pedagogy,' 'Supportive' Pedagogy, and 'Political Correctness.'" *Journal of Urban and Cultural Studies* 2.2 (1992): 79–94.

Morton, Donald, and Mas'ud Zavarzadeh, eds. *Theory/Pedagogy/Politics: Texts for Change*. Urbana: University of Illinois Press, 1991.

Newfield, Christopher. "What Was Political Correctness? Race, the Right, and Managerial Democracy in the Humanities." *Critical Inquiry* 19.2 (1993): 308–36.

Newfield, Christopher, and Ronald Strickland, eds. *After Political Correctness: The Humanities and Society in the 1990s*. Boulder, Colo.: Westview Press, 1995.

O'Connell, Barry, ed. *On Our Own Ground: The Complete Writings of William Apess, A Pequot*. Amherst: University of Massachusetts Press, 1992.

Omi, Michael, and Howard Winant. "On the Theoretical Concept of Race." In McCarthy and Crichlow 3–10.

Pease, Donald E. *Visionary Compacts : American Renaissance Writings in Cultural Context*. Madison: University of Wisconsin Press, 1987.

Pérez Firmat, Gustavo. *Do the Americas Have a Common Literature?* Durham: Duke University Press, 1990.

Pinar, William F. "Notes on Understanding Curriculum as a Racial Text." In McCarthy and Crichlow 60–69.

Porter, Carolyn. "What We Know That We Don't Know: Remapping American Literary History." *American Literary History* 6.3 (1994): 467–526.

Radhakrishnan, R. "Ethnic Identity and Post-Structuralist Différance." *Cultural Critique* 6 (1987): 199–220.

"Rare in the Ivy League: Women on the Faculty." *New York Times*. January 24, 1993. 1, 11.

Ravitch, Diane. "Multiculturalism: E Pluribus Plures." *American Scholar* 59 (Summer 1990): 337–54.

Reising, Russell. *The Unusable Past: Theory and the Study of American Literature*. New York: Methuen, 1986.

Rich, Adrienne. *Blood, Bread, and Poetry: Selected Prose, 1979–1985*. New York: W. W. Norton, 1986.

———. *On Lies, Secrets, and Silence*. New York: W. W. Norton, 1979.

———. *What Is Found There: Notebooks on Poetry and Politics*. New York: W. W. Norton, 1993.

Rieff, David. "Multiculturalism's Silent Partner." *Harper's Magazine* 287 (August 1993): 62–72.

Roediger, David. *Towards the Abolition of Whiteness*. New York: Verso, 1994.

Roman, Leslie G. "White Is a Color! White Defensiveness, Postmodernism, and Anti-Racist Pedagogy." In McCarthy and Crichlow 71–88.

Rosaldo, Renato. "Politics, Patriarchs, and Laughter." *Cultural Critique* 6 (1987): 65–86.

Ruland, Richard. "Art and a Better America." *American Literary History* 3.2 (1991): 337–59.

Said, Edward W. *Beginnings: Intention and Method*. New York: Basic Books, 1975.

———. *Culture and Imperialism*. New York: Alfred A. Knopf, 1993.

———. "The Politics of Knowledge." *Raritan* 11.1 (1991): 17–31.

———. "Representing the Colonized: Anthropology's Interlocutors." *Critical Inquiry* 15 (1989): 205–25.

Saldivar, José David. *The Dialectics of Our America: Genealogy, Cultural Critique, and Literary History*. Durham: Duke University Press, 1991.

Schlesinger, Arthur M., Sr. "Social History in American Literature." *Yale Review* 18 (1929): 135–47.

Schlesinger, Arthur M., Jr. *The Disuniting of America: Reflections on a Multicultural Society.* New York: W. W. Norton, 1992.

Schweickart, Patrocinio. "Engendering Critical Discourse." In *The Current in Criticism: Essays on the Present and Future of Literary Theory.* Ed. Clayton Koelb and Virgil Lokke. West Lafayette, Ind.: Purdue University Press, 1987. 295–317.

Sedgwick, Eve Kosofsky. "Pedagogy in the Context of an Antihomophobic Project." *South Atlantic Quarterly* 89.1 (1990): 139–56.

Shumway, David. *Creating American Civilization: A Genealogy of American Literature as an Academic Discipline.* Minneapolis: University of Minnesota Press, 1994.

Sleeter, Christine E. "White Teachers Construct Race." In McCarthy and Crichlow 157–71.

Smith, Barbara Herrnstein. *Contingencies of Value: Alternative Perspectives for Critical Theory.* Cambridge: Harvard University Press, 1988.

Sollors, Werner. "A Critique of Pure Pluralism." In *Reconstructing American Literary History.* Ed. Sacvan Bercovitch. Cambridge: Harvard University Press, 1986. 250–79.

Spencer, Jon Michael. "Trends of Opposition to Multiculturalism." *Black Scholar* 23.2 (1993): 2–5.

Spengemann, William. "American Things/Literary Things: The Problem of American Literary History." *American Literature* 57.3 (1985): 456–81.

Spiller, Robert E., et al. *Literary History of the United States.* 3d ed., revised. London: Macmillan, 1963.

Takaki, Ronald. *A Different Mirror: A History of Multicultural America.* Boston: Little, Brown, 1993.

Taylor, Charles. *Multiculturalism and "The Politics of Recognition."* With commentary by Amy Gutmann, ed., et al. Princeton: Princeton University Press, 1992.

Teachers for a Democratic Culture. "Statement of Principles." In Aufderheide 67–70.

Tise, Larry E. *Proslavery: A History of the Defense of Slavery in America, 1701–1840.* Athens: University of Georgia Press, 1987.

Tompkins, Jane. *Sensational Designs: The Cultural Work of American Fiction, 1790–1860.* New York: Oxford University Press, 1985.

Trilling, Lionel. *The Liberal Imagination* (1950). New York: Oxford University Press, 1981.

TuSmith, Bonnie. *All My Relatives: Community in Contemporary Ethnic American Literatures.* Ann Arbor: University of Michigan Press, 1993.

Villanueva, Victor. *Bootstraps: From an American Academic of Color.* Urbana, Ill.: National Council of Teachers of English, 1993.

Vizenor, Gerald. "A Postmodern Introduction." In *Narrative Chance: Postmodern Discourse on Native American Indian Literatures*. Albuquerque: University of New Mexico Press, 1989. 3–16.

Walker, David. *David Walker's Appeal, in Four Articles, Together with a Preamble, to the Coloured Citizens of the World, But in Particular, and Very Expressly, to Those of the United States of America* (1829). Ed. Charles M. Wiltse. New York: Hill and Wang, 1965.

Wallace, Michele. "Multiculturalism and Oppositionality." In McCarthy and Crichlow 251–61.

Watts, Jerry Gafio. *Heroism and the Black Intellectual: Ralph Ellison, Politics, and the Afro-American Intellectual Life*. Chapel Hill: University of North Carolina Press, 1994.

West, Cornel. "The New Cultural Politics of Difference." In *Out There : Marginalization and Contemporary Cultures*. Ed. Russell Ferguson et al. Cambridge: MIT Press, 1990. 19–36.

———. *Race Matters*. Boston: Beacon Press, 1993.

Whitman, Walt. *Complete Poetry and Collected Prose*. Ed. Justin Kaplan. New York: Library of America, 1982.

Wills, Garry. *Inventing America: Jefferson's Declaration of Independence*. New York: Random House, 1978.

———. *Lincoln at Gettysburg: The Words That Remade America*. New York: Simon and Schuster, 1992.

Wilson, John K. *The Myth of Political Correctness: The Conservative Attack on Higher Education*. Durham: Duke University Press, 1995.

Wonham, Henry B., ed. *Criticism and the Color Line: Desegregating American Literary Studies*. Rutgers, N.J.: Rutgers University Press, 1996.

Worsham, Lynn. "Emotion and Pedagogic Violence." *Discourse* 15.2 (1992–93): 119–48.

Yamamoto, Hisaye. "*Seventeen Syllables*." Ed. and with an introduction by King-Kok Cheung. New Brunswick, N.J.: Rutgers University Press, 1994.

Young, Iris Marion. *Justice and the Politics of Difference*. Princeton: Princeton University Press, 1990.

index

American Enterprise Institute,
44–45
American Indians (as term), 50n.
See also Native Americans
American literature: boundaries
of, 2, 13, 172, 180–83, 187;
breakdown of consensus about,
1–2, 6–7, 169–70; "culture
wars" over, 1–5, 210–13; origins
of, as academic field, 76, 146–56,
177, 187; purposes of studying, 2,
4–5, 9; role of syllabus in, 13,
136–68; themes vs. problematics
in, 205–6. *See also* academia;
anthologies; canon; critical
theory; curricula; pedagogy;
texts; United States: writing in
*American Literature: A Prentice Hall
Anthology* (ed. Elliott et al.),
186n, 201n
American Renaissance (Matthiessen),
147, 150–53
American Studies (Merlis), 152n
American Studies Crossroads
Project (Web site), 145, 198n
American Women Regionalists (ed.
Fetterley and Pryse), 156, 201–2
Anaya, Rudolfo, 183
anthologies: early literary, 147–49,
154, 156; multicultural, 4, 6,
158–61, 186n, 199, 201n. *See
also* texts
Anti-Ballistic Missile Treaty, 148,
211
antiracist movements, 24–26, 106,
125, 161–62. *See also*
multiculturalism
Anzaldúa, Gloria, 4, 184–85
Apess, William, 54, 85, 91
*Appeal to the Coloured Citizens of the
World* (Walker), 82, 199
Aristotle, 20

Arnold, Matthew, 150, 155
Arthur, T. S., 151
Asian Americans, 71, 123
assimilation, 155, 194; as
acculturation, 150, 184–85;
American literature's role in,
149–50, 179–80; as casting off
of cultural identity, 115–16,
122, 150, 178; difficulties of,
for certain groups, 71, 119,
178–80; economy's effects on,
67–73, 124; and race, 122–24; in
"Seventeen Syllables," 128–30
audience, 6–9, 45–46, 200
*The Autobiography of Benjamin
Franklin*, 189, 191–93
Awkward, Michael, 108n, 126

Baker, Houston, 4, 97, 200
Baldwin, James, 166
Baraka, Amiri, 98
Bardes, Barbara, 86, 89n
Barnes, Djuna, 203
Barth, John, 204
Barthelme, Donald, 204
Baudrillard, Jean, 28
Baym, Nina, 149, 179
Beecher, Catharine, 85
Bellow, Saul, 5
Beloved (Morrison), 143, 195
Bennett, William, 47
Bergman, David, 153
Berlant, Lauren, 88
Bernstein, Richard, 3
Bérubé, Michael, 3, 45
Beyond the Culture Wars (Graff), 3
Bible, 207
bildungsroman genre, 189
Bishop, Elizabeth, 5
Black Elk Speaks, 183
black power movement (Black
Nationalist movement), 3, 92,

Crèvecoeur, Michel, 5, 113
critical theory, 6, 10, 11, 13–14, 42, 199–200. *See also specific critical theories*
cultural identity: analyses of one's own, 115–21; authorized versions of American, 175; differences within, 105, 109–11; discovery of one's, 18–19; ethics of, 74–75; and individuals, 61, 104, 110–11, 133; limitations of, 124; reinvention of, 207–8. *See also* identity politics; "passing"
"cultural literacy," 1, 5
culture: American, 24, 121, 122, 128, 129, 176–77; as contested term, 21, 25; seeking of identities through, 27, 115–21. *See also* cultural identity; "culture wars"
Culture and Imperialism (Said), 212–13
Cultures of United States Imperialism (Kaplan and Pease), 34, 181n
"culture wars": historical context of, 10, 28–30, 61–75; language in, 21–22; left-right splits in, 35; opponents of multicultural trends in, 2–3. *See also* difference; identity politics; multiculturalism; "political correctness" debate
Cummins, Maria, 151
curricula: based on identity politics, 52, 69–71, 73; case for reform of, 3–4, 8, 32; "hidden," 142; marginalized people's anger at standard, 19, 65; opposition to new, 2–3; role of politics in shaping, 65–73; selection of texts for, 5. *See also* academia; American literature; anthologies; canon; syllabus; texts

Daughter of Earth (Smedley), 199
Davidson, Cathy, 159
Declaration of Independence (U.S.), 10, 11, 59, 60–61, 75–83
"Declaration of Independence of the Producing from the Non-Producing Class" (1844), 80–81
"Declaration of Rights of the Trades' Union of Boston and Vicinity" (1834), 80
Declaration of Sentiments (Seneca Falls Women's Rights Convention), 86, 90n
Declarations of Independence (Bardes and Gossett), 86, 89n
Declaring Independence (Fliegelman), 78
deconstruction, 6, 14, 30, 206
De Lauretis, Teresa, 196
democracy: authorizing documents for, 76, 207; and education, 48–51, 176, 180; Matthiessen's conception of, 151–53, 155; and panethnicity, 26–27; and representation, 38, 43, 48–55, 62, 158
Democratic Vistas (Whitman), 152
"depersonalization," 132–34
Derrida, Jacques, 77
determinism, 12, 42, 76, 93, 105–6, 130. *See also* agency
diacritics magazine, 114
dialogical (defined), 172, 174
Dickinson, Emily, 149, 200
Dictatorship of Virtue (Bernstein), 3
difference: aesthetics a way to avoid acknowledging, 153; classroom debates about, 36, 130–31; as commodity, 37, 115, 121, 122, 174, 197; cultural politics of, 3, 204–5; "teaching the conflicts"

as way of discussing, 8, 14,
53–55, 64–65, 74, 100–102,
114–15, 118, 125–27, 131–32,
146, 161–62, 171, 197–206
*A Different Mirror: A History of
Multicultural America* (Takaki),
24, 70n, 170n, 199
Disuniting of America (Schlesinger), 3
*Do the Americas Have a Common
Literature?* (Pérez Firmat), 181
"double-consciousness," 131, 184
Douglass, Frederick, 19, 86, 87,
101, 158, 188; antislavery views
of, 82, 83–84; autobiography of,
191–93; as influence on King,
93–96, 97n, 100; literary neglect
of, 90n, 149, 151
Dred Scott case, 67, 100
Dreiser, Theodore, 149
D'Souza, Dinesh, 3
Du Bois, W. E. B., 131, 184
Dunbar, Paul Laurence, 19

education. *See* academia; pedagogy
Edwards, Jonathan, 149
"Eileen" (Gordon), 195
Eliot, T. S., 92; canon creation by,
137; as canonical author, 5, 141,
171, 196, 203, 204; Matthiessen's
work on, 150–52; sexual
orientation of, 151–52, 190
Elliott, Emory, 4, 149, 201n
Ellison, Ralph, 11, 59, 91–93,
97–100
Emancipation Proclamation, 94
Emerson, Ralph Waldo, 146, 149
The End of American History (Noble),
15
"The End of 'American' Literature"
(Jay), 15–16
"The English Lesson" (Mohr),
195

English literature, 146–47. *See also*
American literature
Enlightenment traditions, 10–11,
28–29, 39, 41–42, 59–61, 72,
76–77, 106, 162
Epstein, Barbara, 39
Erdrich, Louise, 195
Escoffier, Jeffrey, 38–39
essentialism. *See* identity politics
ethics, 11; defined, 111; of
multicultural pedagogy, 9, 11–12,
17, 61, 99–101, 112, 125–27,
130–35, 171, 197, 209, 213. *See
also* accountability
ethnicity: and aesthetic approaches
to literature, 151; assimilation
rates according to, 71–72; as
contested term, 21, 23, 59;
differences within, 25, 105,
109–11; and organized crime,
124; and "panethnicities," 25–27,
111; and race, 23, 119–20,
122–23; reinvention of, 207–8;
in "Seventeen Syllables," 127–29.
See also assimilation
ethos, 111, 130

Fanon, Frantz, 213
Faulkner, William, 189, 191, 203
Fern, Fanny (Sara Parton), 87–89,
96, 101, 152, 160, 171, 201
Fetterley, Judith, 4, 141n, 156, 164,
202, 203n
Fiedler, Leslie, 190, 202
Fields, Annie, 151
Fischer, Michael, 207–8
Fisher, Philip, 159
Fitzgerald, F. Scott, 54, 155, 156,
189, 190, 203–4
Fliegelman, Jay, 78, 79
"Flight to the Bahamas" (Jordan),
115

Hull, Gloria, 4
Hurston, Zora Neale, 19, 149, 171

identity politics (essentialism): authority in, 126–27; comparative approaches to, 20–22, 54–56, 70n, 172–75, 180–91; curricula based on, 52, 69–71, 73; defined, 10, 48; economic motivations for, 67–73; and Ellison, 92–93; individual vs. group in, 42–43, 103–12; limitations of, 20, 39, 52, 55, 73–74, 105–21, 129, 158–59; and panethnicities, 25–27; and self-representation, 38–39, 43; separatism linked to, 3, 18–22, 50–51, 54–56, 73–74, 100. *See also* class; cultural identity; ethnicity; gender; multiculturalism; race; sexual orientation
ideology: "hegemonic," 137, 138; lack of single, in literary texts, 137, 139, 162, 173, 209
"I Have a Dream" speech (King), 11, 93–98, 101
Illiberal Education (D'Souza), 3
imperialism: in American history, 34, 75, 169; globalization as, 64; nationalism vs., 20–21, 34; resistance to, 35–36; and study of American literature, 147–55, 186–87
Incidents in the Life of a Slave Girl (Jacobs), 165–66
Independence Day (movie), 63–64
Indian Nullification of the Unconstitutional Laws of Massachusetts Relative to the Marshpee Tribe (Apess), 85

individual. *See* particular vs. universal
individualism, 76, 106, 115–18, 121, 133, 192–93
The Intermediate Sex (Carpenter), 153
Internet, 47, 64, 145, 170
"In the Land of the Free" (Sui), 195
Inventing America (Wills), 77n
Invisible Man (Ellison), 11, 91–93, 97
Iola Leroy (Harper), 146
Islas, Arturo, 5, 183

Jackson, Jesse, 98
Jacobs, Harriet, 5, 54, 149, 155, 156, 162, 165–66
James, Henry, 149, 154, 171, 190, 196
Jameson, Fredric, 193, 200
JanMohamed, Abdul R., 170
Jay, Gregory S., 15–16, 112–21, 191–97
jazz, 98–99, 186
Jazz (Morrison), 203–4
Jefferson, Thomas, 10, 77, 78, 80, 95, 162; on black inferiority, 82, 162; ironic use of words of, 82–83; on slavery, 85; subversive uses of words of, 82–83, 86, 90, 100, 101. *See also* Declaration of Independence
Jewett, Sarah Orne, 150, 151, 202n
Jews, 19, 63, 150, 155, 194–95
Johnson, Cheryl, 108–9, 126
Johnson, James Weldon, 19
Jordan, June, 115
Joyce, James, 92, 189, 195, 204

Kagan, Donald, 39
Kaplan, Amy, 34, 181n

Mitchell, W. J. T., 32

MLA. *See* Modern Language Association

Moby Dick (Melville), 159–60, 165–66, 189–90

modernism, 138, 166, 188, 189, 195, 203–4

Modern Language Association (MLA), 140, 141, 167

Modern Times (film), 45

Mohr, Nicolosha, 195

Momaday, N. Scott, 199, 212

Moore, Marianne, 203

Moraga, Cherríe, 4, 184

Moral Majority, 44–45

Morrison, Toni, 4, 92, 98, 143, 195, 203–4

Morton, Donald, 132

Mukherjee, Bharati, 195

multiculturalism: anthologies representing, 4, 6, 158–61, 186n, 199; as basis of American culture, 60, 73, 118–21; celebrations of diversity in (pluralism), 14–15, 25–26, 35, 56, 103–4, 119, 122, 124, 132, 158–59, 161, 166–67, 170, 176–78, 181n, 198; commodity aspects of, 37, 115, 121, 122, 174, 197; comparative approaches to, 24, 54–56, 70n, 100–102, 104–6, 156–57, 172–75, 180–206; as contested term, 1, 2; disparate definitions and practices of, 12; and globalization, 32–37; jazz as metaphor for, 98–99; vs. multiracialism, 24; neoconservatives' views of, 2–3; pedagogical ethics of, 9, 11–13, 17, 61, 99–100, 112, 125–27, 130–35, 171, 197, 209, 213; "teaching the conflicts" approach

to, 8, 14–15, 53–55, 64–65, 74, 100–102, 114–15, 118, 125–27, 131–32, 161–62, 171, 191–206, 209; unity-in-diversity view of, 98–99. *See also* cultural identity; identity politics

multinational corporations, 59, 62–64

Murray, Albert, 98

The Myth of Political Correctness (Wilson), 3

Narrative of Alvar Núñez Cabeza de Vaca, 200

Narrative of the Life of Frederick Douglass, 191–93

nation(s), 182–83; collapse of, 61–62; as contested term, 21, 25, 51–52; and globalization, 58–59; many cultures in single, 157, 188; and race, 23, 73–74; vs. state, 77–78; struggles to create a single view of American, 75–76, 98, 176–77, 188–89. *See also* nationalism

National Association of Scholars, 40, 44–45

National Conversation on American Pluralism and Identity, 8

National Council on the Humanities, 40

National Endowment for the Arts, 2

National Endowment for the Humanities (NEH), 2, 8, 45, 47

nationalism, 72–73; global rise of, 51–52, 204; vs. imperialism, 20–21, 34; and literary study, 146–58, 169–71, 177, 182; reevaluating, 176, 183, 186–87. *See also* postnationalism

pluralist multiculturalism. *See*
multiculturalism: celebrations
of diversity in
Poe, Edgar Allan, 149, 162
"political correctness" debate, 1,
31, 44–48, 64–67, 139
politics, 49–51, 65–75; and
aesthetics, 175; and ethics,
132–35; and political parties,
52–53; "whiteness" as category
of, 119–21. *See also* democracy;
power; Republican Party
popular culture: academic study
of, 163; African American
contributions to, 92–93, 98–99;
vs. canon, 46, 138–39; differences
portrayed in, 63–64; possibilities
offered by, 129
Porter, Carolyn, 182, 188
postcolonialism, 2, 62, 63–64, 75,
205
postmodernism, 22, 106–7,
204–5
postnationalism, 182–83
poststructuralism: critiques of
identity in, 74, 106–7; emphasis
on power in, 11, 12, 206–8; and
origins, 206; and pedagogy,
132–34; and representation, 30,
37
Pound, Ezra, 203, 204
power: as focus of oppositional
multiculturalism, 104; as focus of
poststructuralism, 11, 12, 206–8;
unequal distribution of, 60,
65–75, 90–91, 104
Princeton University, 40–41
professors. *See* academia
Proust, Marcel, 204
Provisions (Fetterley), 4
Pryse, Marjorie, 156, 202
Public Access (Bérubé), 3

public sphere, 45–48
Pynchon, Thomas, 204

race, 4, 151; analyses of one's own,
116–17; as contested term, 21,
22–26, 59; as cultural identity
category, 14, 70–71, 111, 119,
207; determinism vs. agency
associated with, 12; and
nation, 23, 73–74; postmodern
approaches to, 106–10; and
uses of "whiteness," 74, 81,
119, 122–23, 178–80. *See also*
antiracist movements; identity
politics; "whiteness"
Race and Curriculum (McCarthy),
105
Race Matters (West), 23
Radhakrishnan, R., 207
Rain God (Islas), 183
Ravitch, Diane, 170, 176–77
Reagan, Ronald, 44, 47, 67, 69,
189
regionalism, 151, 156, 201–3
representation: and Declaration
of Independence, 75–100;
definition of, 29–30; historical
context of, 10, 28–39; by one's
own cultural group, 18–19, 21,
26–27; political vs. cultural,
38–39; vs. recognition, 28–29;
as term, 27–28; universalizing
aspects of, 59. *See also* identity
politics; multiculturalism; texts
Republican Party, 45, 47–48, 67
responsibility. *See* accountability
Rethinking American Studies
(NEH program), 8–9
Revolution and the Word (Davidson),
159
rhetoric, 144, 148, 167, 192–93,
200, 210–11

Stovall, Floyd, 147

Stowe, Harriet Beecher, 146, 162; excluded from canon, 151, 160; included in early canon, 148, 149; reception of works by, 160, 165–66, 190, 201

structuralism, 6, 42. *See also* determinism; poststructuralism

Sui Sin Far, 171, 195

Supreme Court (U.S.), 67, 100

syllabus: "cultural work" type of, 13, 157, 159–67; "equality of representation" type of, 157–59, 164–67; revealing historical construction of, 143–46, 148, 156–58, 164–65, 168, 198. *See also* anthologies; canon; texts

Takaki, Ronald, 24, 70n, 170n, 199

Tan, Amy, 37

Taylor, Charles, 28–29

Teachers for a Democratic Culture, 30, 41

Teaching American Literature (Web site), 145, 198n

Teaching to Transgress (hooks), 4

Tell Me a Riddle (Olsen), 194–95

texts: as agents, 199–200; hybridity of, 195; interpretation of, 144, 187–88; lack of single ideology in, 137, 139, 162, 173, 209; overlooked, 4, 159–60, 166–67; power of, 208–9; roles played by, in canon, 137, 150–64; uses of, 190–93, 210. *See also* anthologies; canon; syllabus

themes (in American literature), 205–6

This Bridge Called My Back (ed. Moraga and Anzaldúa), 3–4

Thoreau, Henry David, 54, 97n, 149, 155, 156, 190

Three American Literatures (ed. Baker), 4

Tise, Larry E., 79n

Tompkins, Jane, 159, 166

Trilling, Lionel, 76, 150, 154–57, 180

Truth, Sojourner, 19

Tubman, Harriet, 19

Twain, Mark, 139, 141, 149, 203

The Twilight of Common Dreams (Gitlin), 3

Uncle Tom's Cabin (Stowe), 146, 160, 165–66, 190

United States: decline of well-paying manufacturing jobs in, 67–69, 123; demographics of, 188; historical amnesia in, 60, 98; imperialism of, 34, 75, 169; origins of, 179, 200; women in manufacturing jobs in, 89–90; writing in, 172–91, 196–98. *See also* American culture; American literature; Constitution; Declaration of Independence; Supreme Court

universal. *See* particular vs. universal

University of Alabama, 112, 113, 191

University of California at Berkeley, 32, 177n

University of Texas, 145

Viaramontes, Helena, 195

Vietnam War, 92, 97

Villanueva, Victor, 178

Virgil, 146

Vonnegut, Kurt, 204

Walden (Thoreau), 190

Walker, Alice, 83n, 98, 191

Walker, David, 82, 90n, 91, 95, 100, 101, 162, 199